Islamic Banking and Finance

The Economics of the Middle East

Series Editor: Dr. Nora Ann Colton

The Middle East has seen much more economic change over the past few decades than sociopolitical change, in spite of the continuous political instability that is often highlighted by the press. Collectively, the region is best known for producing and exporting oil. While the oil industry significantly impacts the region through generating wealth and movement of labor, it also has become the agent of change for endeavors such as development and diversification. With higher rates of growth occurring more in the East than the West, the Middle East sits on the crossroads of this divide, acting as a bridge between these two market places.

This series is dedicated to highlighting the challenges and opportunities that lie within and around this central region of the global economy. It will be divided into four broad areas: resource management (covering such regional topics as oil prices and stock markets, water, labor migration, history of oil, and remittances); international trade and finance (covering topics such as Islamic banking, exchange rate and investments, and the role of foreign direct investment in the region;); growth and development (covering topics such as social inequities, knowledge creation, growth in emerging markets), and lastly, demographic change (covering topics such as population change, women in the labor market, poverty, and militancy).

Dr. Nora Ann Colton is principal lecturer in international business and management as well as a Middle East expert at the Royal Docks Business School, University of East London. Prior to joining the University of East London, Dr. Colton was a professor of economics and business at Drew University as well as the director of Middle East Studies. Dr. Colton has conducted extensive fieldwork in the Middle East and was a Carnegie scholar in 2009 and visiting professor of economics at the American University of Beirut.

Editorial Advisory Board

Sohrab Behdad—Professor and John E. Harris Chair of Economics Denison University

Karen Pfeifer—Professor Emerita of Economics, Smith College

Ghassan Dibeh—Professor of Economics, Lebanese American University; and Editor, *Review of Middle East Economics & Finance*

Roger Owen—A. J. Meyer Professor of Middle East History, Harvard University

Serdar Sayan—Professor of Economics and Director of the Graduate School for Social Science, Tobb University of Economics and Technology, Turkey

Islamic Banking and Finance
By Omar Masood

ISLAMIC BANKING AND FINANCE
DEFINITIVE TEXTS AND CASES

Omar Masood

ISLAMIC BANKING AND FINANCE

First published in 2011 by
PALGRAVE MACMILLAN®
in the United States—a division of St. Martin's Press LLC,
175 Fifth Avenue, New York, NY 10010.

Where this book is distributed in the UK, Europe and the rest of the world,
this is by Palgrave Macmillan, a division of Macmillan Publishers Limited,
registered in England, company number 785998, of Houndmills,
Basingstoke, Hampshire RG21 6XS.

Palgrave Macmillan is the global academic imprint of the above companies
and has companies and representatives throughout the world.

Palgrave® and Macmillan® are registered trademarks in the United States,
the United Kingdom, Europe and other countries.

ISBN: 978–0–230–33839–5

Library of Congress Cataloging-in-Publication Data is available from the
Library of Congress.

A catalogue record of the book is available from the British Library.

Design by Newgen Imaging Systems (P) Ltd., Chennai, India.

First edition: December 2011

10 9 8 7 6 5 4 3 2 1

Printed and bound in Great Britain by
CPI Antony Rowe, Chippenham and Eastbourne

CONTENTS

Contents

An Introduction to Islamic Banking & Finance

Islamic finance is a growing part of the world's financial sector, and it continues to spread wherever there is a sizable Muslim community, *ummah*. Rapid innovations in financial markets and the internationalization of financial flows have changed the face of conventional banking, and particularly after the recent financial crisis.

New information-based activities, like trading in financial markets and creating income through fees, are a major source of a bank's profitability, whether it is a conventional or an Islamic bank. Financial innovations have led to the increased market orientation and entail the use of assets, such as mortgages, automobile loans, and export credits as backing for marketable securities in the securitization process.

Rapid developments in conventional banking have also affected the reshaping of Islamic banks and financial institutions. This general introduction and the first chapter rely heavily on the work by Hennie van Greuning and Zamir Iqbal in "Risk Analysis for Islamic Banks," a World Bank document.

Financial systems are crucial for the efficient allocation of resources in a modern economy. The acquiring and processing of information about economic activities and entities, the packaging and repackaging of financial claims, and financial contracting are common elements that differentiate financial intermediation from other economic activities. Information plays a central role in financial contracts and financial markets. Today, information is considered a valuable commodity.

The main functions of a financial intermediary are asset transformation, conduct of orderly payments, brokerage, and risk transformation. Asset transformation takes place in the form of matching the demand for and supply of financial assets and liabilities (such as deposits, equity, credit, loans, and insurance) and entails transformation of the maturity, scale, and location of the financial assets and liabilities of the ultimate borrowers and lenders.

Shariah provides a set of intermediation contracts that facilitate an efficient and transparent execution and financing of economic activities.

Islamic finance was practiced in the Muslim world throughout the Middle Ages, fostering trade and business activities, with the development of credit. Islamic merchants in Spain, the Mediterranean, and the Baltic States became indispensable middlemen for trading activities. Several techniques and instruments of Islamic finance were later adopted by European financiers.

How This Book Is Organized

Chapter 1 introduces Islamic banking, Islamic finance, financial intermediation, and the role of risk management in Islamic financial institutions.

The Islamic financial system covers capital formation, capital markets, financial intermediation, and risk transfer. The term *Islamic financial system* is relatively new, only introduced in the mid-1980s. Its prohibition of the receipt and payment of an interest rate on the credit side is the nucleus of the system. This is supported by other principles of Islamic doctrine that advocate for the rights and duties of individuals and society in matters of social justice, risk sharing, and property rights.

What distinguishes an Islamic economic system is that it is a rule-based system, formulated by Islamic law, known as shariah. Shariah consists of constitutive (used for formulating new) rules and regulative (drawing on established) rules, according to which Muslims must conduct their affairs. Shariah represents the constitutive and regulative rules based on the Qur'an, the holy book of Islam.

Asset-liability management involves the raising and use of funds. It comprises strategic planning, implementation, and control processes that affect the volume, maturity, profit-rate sensitivity, quality, and liquidity of a bank's assets and liabilities.

A bank engaged in the foreign-currency business is exposed to currency risk, but it is also exposed to liquidity, credit, and repricing risks if it carries open positions or mismatches in its forward book. Operational risks are related to a bank's organization and functioning, including computer-related and other technologies, and compliance with bank policies and procedures.

Chapter 2 deals with the productivity growth in Gulf Cooperation Council (GCC) banking industry for the period 1999–2007. It compares conventional versus Islamic banks. This study examines the impact of financial liberalization on banking-productivity growth in GCC countries during the 1999–2007 period. Employing a non-parametric approach, the Department of Economic Affairs (DEA) in the UK, productivity change has been measured by computing Malmquist's total-factor-productivity index and its components for two groups of banks, conventional and Islamic. The findings indicate that during the period of deregulation, GCC banks have experienced a gain in productivity change of about 1.8 percent, attributed mainly to technical-change progress rather than efficiency-change increase. We also found that conventional banks tend to outperform Islamic banks in most productivity measures. In this chapter, we also investigated the determinants of bank productivity. The results show that bank size has a positive impact on productivity growth for all models, while capitalization is related negatively to efficiency change for the model of Islamic banks only. Finally, the regression findings also demonstrate the strong links of macroeconomic and financial-sector indicators with bank productivity.

Chapter 3 presents an analysis for the growth and rise of smaller Islamic banks in the last decade. It analyzes the factors responsible for this rise and growth in the last decade. Using regression of the Z-score as a function of a number of variables, we test the stability of smaller and lager Islamic banks. We then tested for the regression analysis, using the pooled ordinary-least-squares (OLS) technique. Further, we also assess the robustness of the results with respect to the selected sample on our pooled data set on 30 paramount Islamic banks for the period 1998–2008. We found that smaller Islamic banks were more stable than larger Islamic banks over the last decade. Moreover, we found that smaller Islamic banks correspond to a higher degree of diversification than the larger banks, and the expenditure-to-income ratio values were significantly low for smaller banks than in larger Islamic banks.

Chapter 4 studies the development and scope of Islamic bank bonds, known as *sukuk* (the singular is *sakk*).

Raising finance through investment *sukuk* is becoming more and more popular in the Middle East, Europe, and the Far East. *Sukuk* are a thriving new market in many Islamic economies, especially in GCC countries, Malaysia, and some other countries. This is attracting a lot of interest from European countries, like the United Kingdom and Portugal, and other major countries, like Japan and Singapore.

Investment sukuk are certificates of equal value, representing undivided shares in ownership of tangible, existing (or, well-described and undertaken to be delivered in the future) assets, usufruct, and services for (or, in the ownership of) the assets of particular projects or investment activities.

Given their novelty and unique characteristics and varieties, sukuk can be researched extensively and discussed from various angles. However, under this heading, the focus will be on the definition of sukuk types, what distinguishes each type as well as the nature and salient features of each. Consequently, we offer a critical appraisal of sukuk as Islamic alternatives to conventional bonds or securitization.

Chapter 5 studies the risk-based supervision for Islamic banks. This study includes the design of the risk-based supervisory framework for Islamic banks. Seven policy issues are discussed, which include regulations on Islamic bank activities and banking-commerce links, domestic and foreign Islamic bank entry, capital adequacy, deposit-insurance design; regulations on easing private-sector monitoring of Islamic banks, government ownership of Islamic banks, and supervision.

Findings reveal that supervision by risk approach provides the supervisor and the Islamic banking industry: (a) a high level of consistency in supervision, because it sets and uses minimum core procedures; (b) an allocation of resources based on risk;(c) sufficient flexibility to allow supervisors to tailor the supervisory effort to the risks present; (d) less supervisory intervention in areas of low risk; and (e) help in determining the sufficiency of each Islamic bank's capital and risk-management system.

The other chapters investigate the Islamic banking and Islamic finance experience in several countries.

Chapter 6 develops an understanding of Iran's Islamic banking experience and condisers its future in Islamic finance and banking. The practice of Islamic banking in Iran began in 1984. The transformation from a conventional form of banking to Islamic banking has been a subject of debate among scholars. Analysis of Islamic modes of financing shows that bank authorities and economic policy makers have followed the same path of traditional banking and switch their funds toward more profitable types of contracts. This chapter describes that, due to the heavy concentration of the banking assets on short-term deposits and the private sector's reluctance to commit funds for long-term financing, banks loans were also mainly utilized to finance short-term trade transactions, such as hire-purchase, forward-purchase, and service contracts. Long-term partnerships for project financing and direct investment by the banking system in longterm undertakings, constituted a small percentage of the total operation.

Chapter 7 is devoted to Islamic banking structure and growth in the Sudanese Islamic banking sector. Sudanese Islamic banking history goes back to 1977, when Faisal Islamic Bank of Sudan was established as the first Islamic bank to operate in the country. With the implication of shariah law as the official law in 1984, the entire banking industry converted to Islamic shariah principles. The Sudanese Islamic banking industry has now reached a total of more than thirty banks, and some of them, like Faisal Islamic Bank of Sudan, have twenty-eight branches alone.

This chapter attempts to analyze the financial performance of selected Sudanese Islamic banks and to highlight their growth, using financial-statement analysis (FSA). The procedure involves calculating numerous financial ratios and categorizing them into five key groups in order to examine profitability, earning potential, liquidity, credit risk, and assets activity.

Findings revealed that the Sudanese Islamic banks are doing very well in terms of generating reasonable profits. In addition, we discovered that the liquidity-earning performance and assets-activity performance of the three selected banks was satisfactory. Finally, while analyzing credit risk, we found that Sudanese Islamic banks are taking excessive risks.

Chapter 8 develops Islamic mortgages. The mortgage is considered a major determinant factor, not only to the UK, but in other Western economies as well. Therefore, we thought it fit to conduct an empirical study on Islamic mortgages in the UK. In this chapter, we attempt to critically analyze the Islamic mortgage system in the UK and try find out if it might help create a stable financial environment. The chapter gives a preliminary empirical assessment of role of the shariah board and corporate governance with reference to the UK. The information was gathered through a well-designed questionnaire, assessing banking professionals' point of view on Islamic mortgages. In this study, we also sought answers to two important questions: (a) whether Islamic banking is based on Islamic economic principles, or is it just a replica of conventional banking; and (b) would we still face a financial crisis if the market were regulated by Islamic shariah.

Chapter 9 investigates the role of the Islamic mortgage in the UK. Mortgage is considered a major determinant factor, not only to the UK, but in Western economies as well. Therefore, we thought it fit to conduct an empirical study on the Islamic mortgage in UK. In this paper, we attempt to study and elaborate on the principles behind the overall Islamic banking system, while the main focus will remain on the role of Islamic mortgages in the UK. This paper gives a preliminary empirical assessment of the role of the shariah board and corporate governance with reference to the UK. This study also considers whether Islamic banking is based on Islamic economic principles or on just a replica of conventional banking.

Chapter 10 deals with the Islamic Bank of Britain, in a case-study type of analysis. There is no specific difference between Islamic and conventional banking on the functions basis. Both provide and perform nearly the same functions. The only difference between them is that for Islamic bank to strictly follow the rules and principles of Islam in all their transactions (Henry and Wilson 2004; Iqbal and Mirakhor 2007). Many conventional banks also have begun to open branches, which operate in accordance with the Islamic shariah principles. The Islamic banking system is expected to face strong competition, not only from other Islamic banks, but also from well-established conventional banks that more recently been offering Islamic products and services. In this study, we focus on the Islamic Bank of Britain, the only indigenous bank of its kind in United Kingdom. An attempt is made to assess the degree of customer awareness and satisfaction, as well as other selection criteria. A sample of 200 respondents took part in this study. The responses show a certain degree of satisfaction, and few respondents have expressed their dissatisfaction with some of the Islamic bank's services.

1

ISLAMIC BANKING, FINANCE & FINANCIAL INTERMEDIATION: DEVELOPMENTS & RISK MANAGEMENT

The Islamic financial system covers capital formation, capital markets, financial intermediation, and risk transfer. The Islamic financial system described in these chapters is relatively new, dating from the mid-1980s. At the heart of the system is the prohibition of receiving and paying "interest for credit." This prohibition is supported by other principles of Islamic doctrine, which advocate the rights and duties of individuals and society in regard to social justice, risk sharing, and property rights. The Islamic economic system is rule-based and formulated by Islamic law, known as shariah. Shariah consists of constitutive rules and regulations, based on the Qur'an, according to which Muslims must conduct their affairs.

This chapter is structured into five sections. Section 1 presents the main principals behind Islamic finance. Section 2 explains the developments of Islamic banking and finance since 1950. Section 3 presents the basic financial contracts, statements, and institution. Section 4 investigates financial statements and risk management of Islamic financial institutions and considers operational and other risks, followed by the capital adequacy framework under Basel II of the Basel Accords. And section 5 presents the alternative financial markets. This final section offers suggestions for future developments, which have appeared mainly in Hennie and Zamir's work for the World Bank.

1. ISLAMIC FINANCE: BASIC PRINCIPLES & DEVELOPMENTS

In the religion of Islam, the Qur'an, considered the word of Allah (God), serves as the basic source of law as well as for establishing rules of law for Muslims, the religion's adherents... After the Qur'an, the Prophet Muhammad's sayings and actions are considered the next most important sources for legal findings. The term *sunnah* refers to the prophet's interpretations of the Qur'an, or explanations of Islamic law.

1.1. Islamic Financial Systems: Main Principles

The philosophical foundation of an Islamic financial system goes beyond the interaction of such factors as production and economic behavior. Instead, the conventional financial system focuses primarily on the economic and financial aspects of transactions. The Islamic system places equal emphasis on the ethical, moral, social, and religious dimensions and seeks to enhance equality and fairness for the good of society as a whole.

The Islamic financial system, unlike that commonly found in the Western world, is based on the *absolute prohibition of the payment or receipt of any predetermined, guaranteed rate of return*. This necessarily closes the door on the concept of interest and debt-based instruments.

Given an understanding of the role of institutions, rules, laws, and ideology of Islam, Hennie van Greuning and Zamir Iqbal, in "Risk Analysis for Islamic Banks," a World Bank document, submit the following propositions regarding the Islamic economic system.

- The foremost priority of Islam and its teaching on economics is *justice and equity*.
- The Islamic paradigm incorporates a spiritual and moral framework that values human relations above material possessions. In this way, it establishes a balance between the material and spiritual fulfillment of human beings.
- Self-interest and private gains of the individual are regulated for the betterment of the collective.
- Maximizing an individual's pursuit of profit in enterprise or satisfaction in consumption is not the sole objective of society, and any wasteful consumption is discouraged.
- The recognition and protection of the property rights of all members of society are the foundation of a stakeholder-oriented society, preserving the rights of all.

The shariah consists of a network of ethical and moral rules of behavior that all market participants are expected to internalize and adhere to. Likewise, the basic framework for the Islamic financial system is this set of rules and laws, that in turn govern the economic, social, and cultural aspects of Islamic societies. While shariah originates from the rules dictated by the Qur'an and its practices and explanations, commonly known as sunnah, rendered by the Prophet Muhammad, scholars in Islamic jurisprudence offer further elaboration of these rules within the framework of the Qur'an and sunnah.

Let's summarize a few basic principles of an Islamic financial system, which can vary somewhat from country to country.

- **Riba, or interest**, literally means "excess, addition, and surplus," while the associated verb implies "to increase, multiply, exceed, exact more than was due, or practice usury."

Prohibition of *riba*, "an excess" interpreted as "any unjustifiable increase of capital whether in loans or sales," is the central tenet of the system. More precisely, any positive, fixed, predetermined rate tied to the maturity of the principal amount, guaranteed regardless of the performance of the investment is considered *riba*.

Among Islamic scholars, the general consensus is that *riba* covers not only usury but also the charging of "interest.". This prohibition is based on arguments of social justice, equality, and property rights. Islamic law encourages the earning of profits but forbids the charging of interest because profits, determined ex-post, symbolize successful entrepreneurship and creation of value and wealth. Interest is determined ex-ante and is a cost that is accrued irrespective of the outcome of business operations (and may not create wealth).

Social justice demands that borrowers and lenders share rewards as well as losses in an equitable fashion. It also requires that the process of accumulating wealth in the economy be fair and representative of *true* productivity.

- Money is treated as "potential" capital—that is, it becomes actual capital only when it joins hands with other resources to undertake a productive activity. Islam recognizes the time value of money, but only when it acts as capital, not when it is "potential" capital.
- Suppliers of funds become *investors* instead of *creditors* since interest is prohibited. The provider of financial capital and the entrepreneur share business risks in return for a share of the profits.

Financial transactions need to reflect a **symmetrical risk-return distribution** that each party to the transaction may face. The relationship between the investors and the financial intermediary is based on profit-and-loss-sharing principles. The financial intermediary, then, shares risks with investors.

- An Islamic financial system discourages hoarding. It prohibits transactions featuring extreme uncertainties, gambling, and risks.
- *Qimar is* gambling. They are referred to as *maysur,* or games of chance involving deception, the same as *myisur.*
- Islam upholds contractual obligations and the disclosure of information as a sacred duty. This feature reduces the risk of asymmetric information and moral hazard.
- Business activities that do not violate the rules of shariah qualify for investment. Hence, any investment in business dealing with alcohol, gambling, or casinos is prohibited.
- Any transaction leading to injustice and exploitation is prohibited. A financial transaction should not lead to the exploitation of any party to the transaction. Exploitation entails the absence of information symmetry between parties to a contract.

Beginning with the notion of property as a "sacred trust," as well as prohibitions also present in other monotheistic religions, *shariah* protects property from any exploitation through unjust and unfair dealings.

Prohibition of *riba* (interest), elimination of *gharar* (contractual ambiguity), and restrictions on other forms of exploitation are some implications of this core principle. *Gharar* refers to any uncertainty created by the lack of information or control in a contract or ignorance in regard to an essential element in a transaction.

1.2. Key Concepts in Islamic Finance

An Islamic financial transaction must meet the basic requirements of a valid legal contract: it must not contain certain elements, such as *riba, gharar, qimar* (gambling), and *maysur* (games of chance involving deception). While the prohibition of *riba* is the most critical, one cannot dispute the criticality of *gharar* and other elements.

Historically, jurists or shariah scholars did not interfere unnecessarily in economic activities. They gave economic agents full freedom to contract as long as certain basic requirements—that is, the prohibition of *riba*—were met.[1] The fact that *riba* is not easily translated into any language other than Arabic adds further complexity. There is no single English word that captures the essence of *riba*. This has led to confusion in explaining the concept both to the layperson and to scholars. Muslim scholars have emphasized the lack of a theory to justify the use of interest. Muslim scholars have also rebutted the arguments that interest is a reward for savings—a productivity of capital—and constitutes the difference between the value of capital goods today and their value tomorrow. Regarding interest being a reward for savings, they argue that interest could be justified only if it resulted in reinvestment and subsequent growth in capital and was not a reward solely for forgoing consumption. Regarding interest as productive capital, modern Muslim scholars argue that the interest is paid on the money and required regardless of whether or not capital is used productively and thus is not justified. Regarding interest as an adjustment between the value of capital goods today and their value tomorrow, they argue that this only explains its inevitability and not its correctness. If that is the sole justification for interest, it seems more reasonable to allow next year's economic conditions to determine the extent of the reward.

In financial contracts., contractual ambiguity, or *gharar*, remains the most important element to consider. The term *gharar* refers to any uncertainty created by the lack of information or control in a contract. It can be thought of as ignorance in regard to an essential element in a transaction, such as the exact sale price or the ability of the seller to deliver what is sold. The presence of ambiguity makes a contract null and void. This shows the importance of perfect information in Islamic transactions.

Gharar can also be defined as a situation in which either party to a contract has information regarding some element of the subject of the contract that is withheld from the other party or in which neither party has control over the subject of the contract. Typical examples include transactions where the object of the sale is not in the possession of one of the parties and over which there is uncertainty even about its future possession.

Shariah considers any uncertainty as to the quantity, quality, recoverability, or existence of the subject matter of a contract as evidence of *gharar*. This demonstrates the importance of complete information around transactions. Shariah allows jurists to delimit the extent of *gharar* in a transaction. Therefore, depending on the circumstances, jurists determine whether the contract is valid. By forbidding *gharar*, shariah prohibits many pre-Islamic contracts of exchange, considering them subject to either excessive uncertainty or opaqueness to one or both parties to the contract.

In many cases, *gharar* can be eliminated simply by stating the object of sale and the price. A well-documented contract eliminates ambiguity and highlights the importance of complete disclosure in the transaction process.

Considering *gharar* as excessive uncertainty, we can associate it with the element of "risk." Some argue that prohibiting *gharar* is one way of managing risks in Islam, because a business transaction based on the sharing of profit and loss encourages parties to conduct due diligence before committing to a contract. Prohibition of *gharar*, then, forces parties to avoid contracts with a high degree of informational asymmetry and with extreme payoffs; it also makes parties more responsible and accountable.

When *gharar is considered* as risk, this may preclude the trading of derivative instruments, which are designed to transfer risks from one party to another.

Another area where prohibition of *gharar* has raised concerns in contemporary financial transactions is that of insurance. Writing an insurance (*takaful*) contract on the life of a person falls within the domain of *gharar* and thus invalidates the contract. The issue remains under review and has not been fully resolved.

Here are some terms, translated from the original Arabic, to help you understand the main concepts of Islamic finance.

bay' al-dayn: The sale of debt.

bai' bithaman aji: Sale contract where payment is made in installments after delivery of goods. The sale could be long term. There is no obligation to disclose profit margins.

fatwa: The legal opinion issued by a qualified Muslim scholar on matters of religious beliefs and practice.

fiqh: An Islamic scholar.

halal: Goodness; permissible.

fiqh al-muamalat: Islamic commercial jurisprudence.

hiba: Gifts.

kifalah: Stewardship guarantee or surety.

qard hassan: Goodwill loan, in which the bank receives a loan from depositors and owes the principal amount only.

sadaqah: Voluntary charitable contribution.

salaam: Agriculture-based sales contract.

sarraf: Financier in the early days of Islam.

shiraka: Partnership.

waqf: Charitable trust or endowment (mortmain).

waiah: Safe deposits and guaranteed banking with the principal amount payable on demand.

zakah: An obligatory charitable contribution is one of the five basic pillars of Islam.

2. DEVELOPMENTS OF ISLAMIC BANKING & FINANCE SINCE 1950

Interest in the Islamic mode of banking emerged in Muslim countries during the post-colonial era as part of an effort to revive and strengthen an Islamic identity. But the first commercial banks did not appear until the 1970s. The first commercial bank was established in 1974 in the United Arab Emirates (UAE), followed by creation of the Islamic Development Bank in 1975.

Western analysts initially challenged the feasibility of a financial system operating totally without interest. Of course, countries where some financial institutions operated according to Islamic precepts, and others did not, there was the strong presumption that unless Islamic-based institutions somehow matched interest rates applicable elsewhere, they would never attract funds and thus could not discharge their intermediation function.

Let's begin by first looking at the consequences expected to follow form a full-fledged Islamic banking system.

- Zero interest would mean infinite demand for loanable funds and zero supply.
- Such a system would be incapable of equilibrating demand for and supply of loanable funds.
- Zero interest would mean no savings.
- Zero savings would mean no investment and no growth.
- There could be no monetary policy since instruments for managing liquidity could not exist without a predetermined, fixed rate of interest.
- In countries adopting such a system, there would be one-way capital flight.

Beginning in 1988, research based on modern financial and economic theory was able to establish the following:

- A modern financial system can be designed without the need for an ex-ante positive nominal fixed interest rate. In fact, as Western researchers showed, no satisfactory theory could explain the need for an ex-ante positive nominal interest rate.
- The failure to assume an ex-ante positive nominal fixed interest rate—that is, a no-debt contract—does not necessarily mean that there has to be zero return on capital.
- The return on capital is determined ex post, and the magnitude of the return on capital is determined on the basis of the return to the economic activity in which the funds are employed.
- Expected returns are what determine investment.
- The expected rate of return—and income—is what determines savings. Therefore, there is no justification for assuming that there will be no savings or investment.
- Positive growth is possible in such a system.
- Monetary policy would function as in the conventional system, its efficacy depending on the availability of instruments designed to manage liquidity.
- Finally, in an open-economy macroeconomic model without an ex-ante fixed interest rate, but with returns to investment determined ex post, the assumption of a one-way capital flight is not justified.

Therefore, a system that prohibits an ex-ante fixed interest rate and allows the rate of return on capital to be determined ex post, based on returns to the economic activity in which the funds are employed, is theoretically viable.

By the early 1990s, it was clear that an Islamic financial system not only is theoretically viable, but possessed desirable characteristics. The phenomenal growth of Islamic finance during the 1990s revealed the empirical and practical viability of the system, though again virtually everywhere it was instituted, competing systems offering conventional financial instruments co-existed with Islamic products that are shariah-compliant.

To the best of our knowledge, there is no instance in which Islamic financial institutions operate in an environment where access to competing institutions—national or international—is prohibited. The existence of alternatives thus complicates disentangling the impact of the relative importance of the two phenomena empirically. The more important point, however, is that Islamic banking and finance continues to thrive even where competition exists.

The Development of Islamic Economics & Finance

Pre-1950s

- Barclays Bank opens its Cairo branch to process financial transactions related to construction of the Suez Canal in the 1890s. Islamic scholars challenge the operations of the bank, criticizing it for charging interest. This criticism spreads to other Arab regions and to the Indian subcontinent, where there is a sizable Muslim community. The majority of shariah scholars declare that interest in all its forms amounts to the prohibited element of *riba*.

1950s–1960s

- Initial theoretical work in Islamic economics begins. In 1953, Islamic economists offer the first description of an interest-free bank based on either two-tier *mudarabah* (profit-sharing and loss-sharing contract) or *wakalah* (unrestricted investment account in which the Islamic bank earns a flat fee).
- **Mudarabah** (pl. mudarabat) A contract in which the owner of capital forms a partnership with an entrepreneur or manager who has certain entrepreneurial skills and both agree to share the profits and losses of the venture undertaken. There are two types of funds—multipurpose, having more than one investment purpose or objective (multipurpose, and specific purpose..
- **Wakalah Representation** Entrusting a person or legal entity (*wakil*) to act on one's behalf or as one's representative.
- **Wakalah Account** (pl. *wakalat* accounts) Unrestricted investment account in which the bank earns a flat fee rather than a share of profits.
- The Mitghamr Bank in Egypt and the Pilgrimage Fund in Malaysia begin operations.

1970s

- The first Islamic commercial bank, Dubai Islamic Bank, opens in 1974.
- The Islamic Development Bank (IDB) is established in 1975.
- The accumulation of oil revenues and petrodollars increases the demand for shariah-compliant products.

1980s

- The Islamic Research and Training Institute is established by the IDB in 1981.
- Banking systems are converted to an interest-free banking system in the Islamic Republic of Iran, Pakistan, and Sudan.

- Increased demand attracts Western intermediation and institutions.
- Countries like Bahrain and Malaysia promote Islamic banking parallel to the conventional banking system.

1990s

- Attention is paid to the need for accounting standards and a regulatory framework. A self-regulating agency, the Accounting and Auditing Organization of Islamic Financial Institutions, is established in Bahrain.
- Islamic insurance (*takaful*) is introduced. *Takaful* refers to shariah-compliant mutual insurance; literally, a mutual or joint guarantee.
- Islamic equity funds are established.
- The Dow Jones Islamic Index and the FTSE Index of shariah-compatible stocks are developed.

2000–Present

- The Islamic Financial Services Board is established to deal with regulatory, supervisory, and corporate governance issues of the Islamic financial industry.
- *Sukuks* (Islamic bonds) are launched. *Sukuks* are Islamic asset-backed certificates.
- Islamic mortgages are offered in the United States and United Kingdom.

Source: (Khan 1996; IDB 2005)

3. BASIC FINANCIAL CONTRACTS & INSTRUMENTS

Contracts play a vital role in the Islamic financial system. All financial transactions are based on contractual agreements.

3.1. Financial Instruments

Financial instruments are used to finance obligations arising from the trade and sale of commodities or property. These include instruments generating rental cash flows against exchange of rights to use the assets such as *ijarah* and *istisnah*. Financial instruments are closely linked to a sale contract and, therefore, are collateralized by the product being financed. These instruments are the basis of short-term assets for the Islamic banks.

Murabahah, a cost-plus sales contract, is one of the most popular contracts for purchasing commodities and other products on credit. The concept is that a financier purchases a product—that is, a commodity or raw materials—for an entrepreneur who does not have his or her own capital to do so. The financier and the entrepreneur agree on a **profit margin**, often referred to as **markup**. This margin is added to the cost of the product. The payment is delayed for a specified period of time during which the entrepreneur produces the final product and sells it in the market. To be a valid contract, shariah requires that a *murabahah* contract be the result of an original sale and not a means of financing existing inventory. In addition, the financier must take ownership of the item on sale.

Murabahah was originally a sales transaction in which a trader would purchase a product and then sell it to the end user at a price calculated using an agreed profit margin over the costs incurred by the trader. Today, banks have taken over the trader's role of financier.

Bay' al-muajjal or sale with deferred payment, allows the sale of a product on the basis of a deferred payment in installments or a lump sum. The price of the product is agreed upon by the buyer and the seller at the time of the sale and cannot include any charges for deferring payments.

Bay' al-salaam, or purchase with deferred delivery, is similar to conventional forward contracts in terms of function but is different in terms of the payment arrangements. In the case of *bay' al-salaam*, the buyer pays the seller the full negotiated price of a specific product that the seller promises to deliver at a specified future date.

The main difference between *bay' al-salaam* and a conventional forward contract is that the full negotiated price is payable at the time of the contract, as opposed to the latter, where the full payment is not due in advance. This forward sale benefits both the seller and the buyer. The seller gets cash to invest in the production process, and the buyer eliminates uncertainty in the future price.

Several medium-term financing instruments are available: *ijarah* (a leasing contract) and *istisnah* (a manufacturing contract).

An *ijarah* contract gives something in return for rent. Technically, it is a contract of sale, but it is not the sale of a tangible asset; rather, it is a sale of the *usufruct* (right to use the object) for a specified period of time.

The word *ijarah* conveys the sense of both hiring and lease. It refers to the lease of tangible assets, such as property and merchandise, but it also denotes the hiring of personal services for a fee. Compared with the conventional form of financing, which is generally in the form of a debt, leasing provides financing in relation to a particular asset. In a sense, it combines financing and collateral, because the ownership of the asset serves as collateral and security against any future loss.

A major advantage of *ijarah* is that it resembles the conventional lease agreement. While there are some differences between the two, they function in largely the same way. In *ijarah,* one difference is that the leasing agency must own the leased object for the duration of the lease. Another difference is the absence of compound interest that may be charged under conventional leases in the event of default or delay in the installment payments. Similarities to conventional leasing make this contract attractive to conventional investors and borrowers as well.

An *istisnah* contract facilitates the manufacture or construction of an asset at the request of the buyer. Once the manufacturer undertakes to manufacture the asset or property for the buyer, the transaction of *istisnah* comes into existence. Both parties—namely, the buyer and the manufacturer—agree on a price and on the specification of the asset to be manufactured.

At the time of delivery, if the asset does not conform to the specifications, the party placing the order has the right to retract the contract.

Another important feature of *istisnah* relates to the mode and timing of payment. There is flexibility in regard to the payment, and it is not necessary for the price to be paid in advance. It is also not necessary for it to be paid at the time of delivery. Both parties can agree on a schedule of payment convenient to both, and payments can be made in installments.

Like *ijarah,* *istisnah* has great potential for application in the area of project finance in different sectors and industries. Successful applications include the manufacture of aircraft, locomotives, ships, and heavy-duty machinery. The *istisnah* contract is also suitable for building infrastructure, such as roads, dams, housing, hospitals, and schools.

3.1.1. Investing Instruments

Investing instruments are vehicles for capital investment in the form of a partnership. There are two types of investing instruments: fund management (*mudarabah*) and equity partnerships (*musharakah*).

Mudarabah, which can be short, medium, or long term, is a trust-based financing agreement whereby an investor entrusts capital to an agent to undertake a project. Profits are based on a prearranged, agreed ratio. A *mudarabah* agreement is akin to a Western-style limited partnership in which one party contributes capital, while the other runs the business; profit is distributed based on a negotiated percentage of ownership. The investor bears the loss, but the agent does not share in any financial loss unless there is evidence of misconduct or negligence. *Mudarabah* is used on both the liabilities and the assets side.

Musharakah, which can be either medium or long term, is a hybrid of *shiraka* (partnership) and *mudarabah*, combining the act of investment and management. In the absence of debt security, the shariah encourages this form of financing. The shariah is fairly comprehensive in defining different types of partnerships, in identifying the rights and obligations of the partners, and in stipulating the rules governing the sharing of profits and losses. *Musharakah* is a form of partnership in which two or more persons combine either their capital or their labor, share the profits and losses, and have similar rights and liabilities.

3.2. Structure of Financial Statements: The Balance Sheet

The basic concept is that both the mobilization and the use of funds are based on some form of profit sharing among the depositors, the bank, and the entrepreneurs (users of funds).

A typical Islamic bank performs the functions of financial intermediation by screening profitable projects and monitoring the performance of projects on behalf of the investors who deposit their funds with the bank. This process requires time, resources, and skills and justifies the existence of information costs, often considered as sunk costs in the literature.

Table 1.1 presents a balance sheet of an Islamic bank, showing different activities and financial instruments. Panel A classifies both assets and liabilities using the criteria of the maturity profile of instruments. Some instruments, like *ijarah* and *istisnah*, can be ranked across different maturity groups. The demarcation is based on the most common use of the instruments. Panel B provides an alternative view using the functionality criteria and purpose of the instrument.

amanah: Safekeeping.

bay' al-muajjal: Sale with deferred payment.

bay' al-salaam: Purchase with deferred delivery.

ijarah A leasing contract, technically a contract of sale.

istisnah: A manufacturing contract that facilitates the manufacture or construction of an asset at the request of the buyer.

Table 1.1   Theoretical Islamic Bank Balance Sheet

Panel A. Based on Maturity Profile	
Assets	Liabilities
Short-term trade finance (cash, *murabahah, salaam*)	Demand deposits *(amanah)*
Medium-term investments *(ijarah, istisnah)*	Investment accounts *(mudarabah)*
Long-term partnerships *(musharakah)*	Special investment accounts *(mudarabah, musharakah)*
Fee-based services *(joalah, kifalah,* etc.)	Reserves
Non-banking assets (property)	Equity capital

Panel B. Based on Functionality	
Assets	Liabilities
Cash balances	Demand deposits *(amanah)*
Financing assets *(murabahah, salaam, ijarah, istisnah)*	Investment accounts *(mudarabah)*
Investment assets *(mudarabah, musharakah)*	Special investment accounts *(mudarabah, musharakah)*
Fee-based services *(joalah, kifalah,* etc.)	Reserves
Non-banking assets (property) Equity capital	Equity capital

> *joalah*: Agreement with an expert in a given field to undertake a task for a predetermined fee or commission (as in a consultancy agreement or contract).

Liabilities

The liabilities side of the balance sheet is based on the two-window theoretical model of an Islamic bank. This model divides the "liability," or funding, side of the bank balance sheet into two deposit windows: one for demand deposits and the other for investment or special investment accounts. The investment accounts are not liabilities in a strict sense because investors-depositors in Islamic banks are like partners.

A 100 percent reserve is required for demand deposits, but no reserve requirement is stipulated for the second window. This 100 percent requirement is based on the presumption that the money deposited as demand deposits is placed as *amanah* (demand deposits). They yield no returns and are repayable on demand and at par value.

Money deposited in investment accounts is placed with the depositors' full knowledge that their deposits will be invested in risk-bearing projects; therefore, no guarantee is needed or justified.

Investment account holders are investors or depositors who enter into a *mudarabah* contract with the bank, where investors act as the supplier of funds (*rab al-mal*) to be invested by the bank on their behalf, as the agent (*mudarib*).

Rab al-mal Supplier of funds, the principal.

Mudarib A fund manager or agent.

The investors share in the profits accruing to the bank's investments on the assets side. These profit-sharing investment deposits are not liabilities. Investors' capital is not guaranteed, and they incur losses if the bank does. Islamic banks offer special investment accounts developed on the basis of a special-purpose or restricted *mudarabah* or on profit-and-loss sharing (*musharakah*). These special investment accounts, (similar to close-end mutual funds), are targeted toward high-net-worth individuals (HNWI).

Assets

Islamic banks have several choices of instruments with different maturities and risk-return profiles.

For short-term maturities, trade financing or financial claims resulting from a sales contract—that is, *murabahah*, *salaam*, and so forth—are available.

For medium-term investments, leasing (*ijarah*), manufacturing contracts (*istisnah*), and various partnerships are possible.

For long-term investments, partnerships in the form of *musharakah* can be undertaken.

An Islamic financial intermediary may also engage an external entrepreneur on a *mudarabah* basis in which the bank acts as principal and the entrepreneur (user of the funds) acts as agent. In this capacity, an Islamic bank can form a syndicate with other financial or non-financial institutions to provide entrepreneurs with medium-term to long-term capital. Islamic banks provide customized services, guarantees, and underwriting services for a fee.

3.3. Islamic Financial Institutions: The Practice

The Islamic mode of banking has been mandated and adopted by the governments of the Islamic Republic of Iran, Pakistan, and

Sudan, etc. The supply of shariah-compliant products has been led primarily by the private sector. Private Islamic banks as a group are becoming some of the largest private-sector financial institutions in the Islamic world with growing networks through branches or subsidiaries.

3.3.1. The different types of institutions and models

Islamic financial institutions can be divided into the following broad categories: Islamic banks, Islamic windows, Islamic investment banks and funds, Islamic mortgage companies, Islamic insurance companies, and *mudarabah* companies.

Islamic banks represent the majority of Islamic financial institutions. Islamic banks typically are a hybrid of a conventional commercial bank and an investment bank and resemble a universal bank.

Islamic windows are specialized setups that offer shariah-compliant products. During the 1980s, conventional Western banks acted as intermediaries, deploying funds according to guidelines defined by the Islamic banks.

Islamic investment banks and investment funds emerged during the 1990s, Islamic investment funds are not new but are making a comeback after initial experimentation during which many of them did not survive.

Dow Jones has recognized the significance and potential of Islamic equity funds by setting up an equity benchmark index—the Dow Jones Islamic Market Index (DJIM). DJIM tracks shariah-compliant stocks from the 2,700 stocks in the Dow Jones Global Index.

Targeted at the housing market for Muslim communities in Western countries (Canada, United Kingdom, and United States) with developed conventional mortgage markets, four models of Islamic mortgage are currently in practice.

- *The first model is based on the ijarah (lease)* contract and is the closest to the structure of a conventional mortgage.
- *The second model is based on equity partnership (diminishing musharakah)*, where the mortgagee (lender) and mortgagor (borrower) jointly share ownership, which over a period of time is transferred to the mortgagor, who buys shares of ownership by contributing each month toward buying out the mortgagee's share in the property. Return to the lender is generated out of the fair rental value of the property.

- *The third model is based on murabahah (sales transaction)* and is practiced in the United Kingdom, where the property transfer tax (stamp duty) discriminates against the *ijarah-* or *musharakah-*based mortgage.
- The fourth model is designed along the lines of cooperative societies, where members buy equity (*musharakah*) membership and help each other to purchase property from the pool of the society's funds.

The closest Islamic instrument to the contemporary system of insurance is *takaful*, which literally means mutual or joint guarantee. Typically, *takaful* is carried out in the form of solidarity *mudarabah*, where the participants agree to share their losses by contributing periodic premiums in the form of investments.

The concept of a *mudarabah* company is very similar to that of a close-end fund managed by a specialized professional investment management company. Like a mutual fund, a *mudarabah* company is incorporated as a separate legal entity with a fund management company responsible for its operations.

3.3.2. Corporate governance and key stakeholders

Corporate governance is a collective effort, and the process itself functions optimally only when different stakeholders work collectively.

Effective stakeholder participation is integral to good corporate governance. The stakeholders in the Islamic finance industry include the internal stakeholders, the different interest groups, and the institutions created to regulate, promote, and monitor their activities.

- Shariah boards are a distinct feature of Islamic banks. Operating at the institutional and systemic level, shariah boards have a great responsibility to protect the rights of all stakeholders according to the principles of shariah.
- Shariah boards play a critical role in the introduction of new products and the provision of an oversight function.
- Multilateral institutions have played an important role in the development and growth of Islamic markets and banks. The Islamic Development Bank is dedicated to that purpose. The International Monetary Fund and the World Bank have contributed through research.

- Several key institutions, such as Islamic Financial Services Board and the Accounting and Auditing Organization of Islamic Financial Institutions, were established to strengthen the regulatory framework.
- New stakeholders are emerging to develop financial infrastructure, including institutions dedicated to developing capital markets, rating agencies, and institutions that help to manage liquidity.

Executive management of a bank has to be "fit and proper," meaning

3.3.3. Multilateral Institutions

Multilateral institutions have played an important role in the development and growth of Islamic markets and banks. Multilateral institutions interact with the Islamic banking industry in various capacities, and it is important to understand and evaluate the relationship—past, present, and potential.

Islamic Development Bank (IDB)

Established by the Articles of Agreement in October 1975, the Islamic Development Bank is a multilateral financial institution designed to foster economic development and social progress in the fifty-three member countries of the Organization of Islamic Countries (OIC) and in Muslim communities in non-member countries. IDB provides financial assistance by way of equity and lease financing (*ijarah*), installment sale financing (*murabahah*), and grant (interest-free) loans for projects and assistance in promoting foreign trade among member countries. Projects are financed from ordinary capital resources through interest-free loans, leasing, installment sale, and equity participation. More recently, the IDB has introduced the use of *istisnah* (construction and manufacturing) contracts.

IDB has also established the Islamic Research and Training Institute (IRTI) with the objectives of providing training facilities for professionals engaged in development activities in member countries and undertaking research in the areas of Islamic economics, finance, and banking. IRTI serves as an information center, collecting and disseminating information in related fields. In addition to publication of an academic journal on Islamic economics, IRTI arranges both professional and academic seminars and conferences to promote research on Islamic economics and banking. In 2005, the IDB Board of Governors approved the establishment of the International Islamic

Trade Finance Corporation (IITFC) to finance trade activities of its member countries.

3.3.4. Regulatory Bodies

Market participants' anticipation of the growth of the Islamic finance industry as well as its potential impact has raised public policy issues in the jurisdictions in which it operates.

Accounting and Auditing Organization for Islamic Financial Institutions (AAOIFI)

The objective of the Bahrain-based AAOIFI is to develop a core set of accounting, auditing, governance, and recently, shariah standards for Islamic financial institutions.

Islamic Financial Services Board (IFSB)

The IFSB was established in Kuala Lumpur, Malaysia, in 2002 as a result of the efforts of AAOIFI, Islamic Development Bank, International Monetary Fund, and the central banks of several Islamic countries.

International Islamic Financial Market (IIFM)

The major objectives of the IIFM are (a) to enhance cooperation among regulatory authorities of Islamic banks, (b) to address the liquidity problem by expanding the maturity structure of instruments, and (c) to explore the possibility of sovereign asset-backed securities.

International Islamic Rating Agency (IIRA)

The IIRA aims to assist in the development of regional financial markets by providing an assessment of the risk profile of entities and instruments that can be used for investment decisions.

4. FINANCIAL STATEMENTS & RISK MANAGEMENT

4.1. Balance-Sheet Structure and Balance-Sheet Structural Change

The goal of financial risk management is to maximize the value of a bank, as determined by its level of profitability and risk.

In the context of recession, volatile interest rates, and inflation during the late 1970s and early 1980s and 2010, the management of both assets and liabilities became fundamental in order to maintain satisfactory margin performance.

Assets Composition

The structure of individual balance sheets may vary depending on business orientation, market environment, or economic environment.

Liquid Assets: These are needed to accommodate expected and unexpected fluctuations in the balance sheet.

Cash Balances: These represent the holdings of highly liquid assets, such as bank notes, gold coin, bullion, and deposits with the central bank.

A percentage of deposits is required to be held in order to meet the central bank's reserve requirements and to serve as a tool to reflect monetary policy.

Financing and Investing Assets: These are normally the most important component of an Islamic bank's assets. In conventional banking, these include loans for general working capital (overdrafts), investment lending, asset-backed installment and mortgage loans, financing of debtors (accounts receivable and credit-card accounts), and tradable debt, such as acceptances and commercial paper. Islamic financing and investing assets are extended in domestic and foreign currency and are provided by banks as financing for public or private sector investments.

Trading Portfolios: Trading assets, such as *sukuks* (bonds), show the bank's trading books in securities, foreign currencies, equities, and commodities.

Other Assets: These include comprise a bank's longer-term ownership investments, such as equities held in the bank's long-term investment portfolio.

Fixed Assets: Constitute the bank's infrastructure resources. They include the premises under which the bank operates, other fixed property, computer equipment, vehicles, furniture, and fixtures.

Liabilities Composition

Customer Deposits: *Amanah* (trust), investment accounts, and special investment accounts represent the largest proportion of a bank's total liabilities.

Amounts Due to Banks and Other Financial Institutions: These include all deposits, loans, and advances extended between banks. They are considered as volatile sources of funding.

Other Liabilities: These include trade creditors and other sundry items. In an Islamic bank, the unpaid portion of depositors' share of profits would be an important component. Amounts owed to the central bank are ranked among the bank's liabilities.

Equity: capital provides the buffer available to protect creditors against losses that may be incurred by risks.

Balance-Sheet Structural Change

A successful bank in its market can be expected to grow. An analysis of the balance sheet can be done to determine growth rates and the type of structural changes that occur in a bank. This analysis indicates the general type of business undertaken by a bank and requires an understanding of the structure of its balance sheet and the nature of its assets and liabilities. Even when overall balance-sheet growth is not significant, individual components normally shift in reaction to changes in the market, economic or regulatory environments.

4.2. Income Statement Structure

The income statement is regarded as a key source of information on a bank's profitability. It provides the sources of a bank's earnings, their quantity and quality, as well as the quality of the bank's loan portfolio and the targets of its expenditures.

The income statement structure provides a bank's business orientation. The main source of conventional banking income is interest.

Income Statement Composition

A bank's income statement is a main source of information regarding the sources and structure of its income. Here is an example of an analytical income statement.

Composition of the Income Statement

Income

- Income from Islamic financing and investing assets
- Income from international *murabahah,* short term
- Income from investment properties
- Income from sale of properties under construction, net
- Commissions, fees, and foreign exchange income
- Sundry income
- Total income

Expenses

- General and administrative expenses
- Provisions and reversals of impairment
- Depreciation of investment properties
- Total expenses
- Profit before depositors' share and tax
- Depositors' share of profits
- Profit for the year before tax
- Profit for the year before tax
- Income tax

Financing and Investing Income: For an Islamic financial institution, *Islamic* financing and investing income originates from Islamic products intermediation. A bank calculates income due for each period of time covered by the income statement, regardless of whether or not the income has been received or paid.

Depositors' Share of Profits and Losses: This comprises payments related to investments and partnership income received for customers' current savings and investment deposits.

Trading Income: This comprises income from dealings and brokerage businesses as well as income from trading and from investments in securities, foreign currencies, equities, and commodities.

Investment Income: This comprises income from a bank's longer-term equity-type investments, such as equities and interest-bearing (recapitalization or non-trading) bonds held in the bank's long-term investment portfolio, as well as dividend income from subsidiaries and similar types of investments.

Profit for the Year: This profit is the difference between a banks' asset-related income and expenses.

General and Administrative Expenses: Such expenses include costs related to staff, rent and utilities, auditing and consulting, computer and information technology systems, and general administration. Impairment provisions, included in operating expenses, have the most important impact on the cost of intermediation. They are one of the most controllable items.

Provisions for Losses or Impairment: These expenses are related to the credit risk inherent in granting investing assets and long-term partnerships.

Depreciation: This cost is due to the reduction in value of a bank's fixed assets. It is similar to provisions. Banks typically depreciate buildings over 25 to 50 years, movable assets and office equipment over three to five years, and computers over two to three years.

Profitability Ratios

Profit is the bottom line showing the net effects of bank policies and activities in a financial year.
   Here are some of the main ratios.

- **R** Profit as a percentage of total assets (ROA)
- Expenses as a percentage of total assets
- Gross income as a percentage of total assets
- Basic and diluted earnings per share attributable to shareholders of the parent
- Profit as a percentage of total equity (ROE)
- Expenses as a percentage of gross income
- Provisions and impairments as a percentage of expenses
- Expenses, including amounts owed to depositors, as a percentage of total assets
- Expenses, including amounts owed to depositors, as a percentage of gross income amount
- Expenses, including amounts owed to depositors
- Profitability ratios

4.3. Risk Exposure and Management

The new Basel Accords will heighten the importance of quantitative modeling tools and the bank's capacity to use them, as they will provide a basis for implementing the internal ratings-based (IRB) approach to measuring a bank's capital adequacy.

Analysis of the Overall Banking Sector

The banking sector provides important information regarding the provision of finance to the real sector. Sectoral analysis allows norms to be established for either the sector as a whole or for a peer group within the sector. The performance of individual banking institutions can be evaluated on the basis of these norms.

Financial Analysis

Financial analysis assesses a company's performance and trends in that performance. In essence, analysts convert data into financial metrics

Table 1.2 Contractual Role & Risk in Islamic Banking

Balance Sheet	Contractual Basis	Contractual Role of the Islamic Bank		
		Trustee: Agency, Brokerage	Partnership: Investment Banking	Principal/Agent: Conventional Commercial Banking
Liabilities: Funding Sources				
Demand Deposits	*amanah* (trust)	X		
Investment Accounts	*mudarabah*			X
Special Investment Accounts	*mudarabah*			X
	musharakah (partnership)		X	
Reserves	*amanah* (trust)			
Equity: Shareholders' Funds	*musharakah* (partnership)		X	

Assets: Application of Funds		Contractual Role of the Islamic Bank		
Cash Balances	Cash Balances	Trustee: Agency, Brokerage	Partnership: Investment Banking	Principal/Agent: Conventional Commercial Banking
Financing Assets	*murabahah*			X
	bay' al-salaam			X
	bay' al-muajjal			X
	ijarah, istisnah		X	X
Investment Assets	*mudarabah*			
	musharakah		X	X
Investment in Real Estate	*mudarabah*		X	
	musharakah			
	musharakah			
Property Ownership	ownership		X	
Fee-Based Services	*joalah, kifalah*	X	X	X

that assist in decision making, seeking to answer various questions, like these:

How successfully has the company performed, relative to its own past performance and relative to its competitors?

How is the company likely to perform in the future?

Based on expectations about future performance, what is the value of this company or the securities it issues?

Risk-Based Analysis of Banks

Islamic banks are subject to a similar framework for analyzing their risk and exposures as conventional banks. The principles for measuring and controlling risk are similar, so the analytical framework for assessing risk should be similar as well.

Analysis vs. Computation

Financial analysis is the discipline whereby analytical tools are applied to financial statements and other financial data, in order to interpret trends in a consistent manner. The analyst is in the business of converting data into information, and thereby, enabling the screening and forecasting of information. A primary source of information is the entity's financial statements.

Financial statement analysis comprises a review of financial conditions and specific issues related to risk exposure and risk management.

Analytical Tools

There are many tools to assist with bank analysis, including questionnaires and Excel models. They could be adapted to an Islamic banking environment. These often consist of a series of spreadsheet-based data-input tables that enable an analyst to collect and manipulate data in a systematic manner.

Ratios

A *ratio* is an expression of one quantity relative to another. There are many ratios between financial accounts. Ratios provide a useful way of expressing relationships in the different areas of risk such as these:

- **Activity (operational efficiency)**—the extent to which an entity uses its assets efficiently, as measured by turnover of current assets and liabilities and long-term assets
- **Liquidity**—the entity's ability to repay its short-term liabilities, measured by evaluating components of current assets and current liabilities

- *Profitability*—relation between a company's profit margins and sales, average capital, and average common equity
- *Debt and leverage*—the risk and return characteristics of the company, as measured by the volatility of sales and the extent of the use of borrowed money
- *Solvency*—financial risk resulting from the impact of the use of ratios of debt to equity and cash flow to expense coverage
- *Earnings, share price, and growth*—the rate at which an entity can grow as determined by its earnings, share price, and retention of profits
- *Other ratios*—groupings representing the preferences of individual analysts in addition to ratios required by prudential regulators, such as banking supervisors, insurance regulators, and securities market bodies

4.4. Credit-Risk Management

Credit or counterparty risk is the chance that a debtor (or issuer) of a financial instrument will not repay the principal and other investment-related cash flows according to the terms specified in a credit agreement. It means that payments may be delayed or not made at all, which can affect a bank's liquidity.

Formal Policies to Manage Credit Risk
Supervisors put considerable importance on formal policies laid down by the board of directors and administered by management.

Policies to Reduce Credit Risk
In an effort to reduce credit risk, regulators focus on three issues: exposure to a single customer, related-party financing, and overexposure to a geographic area or economic sector.

Single-Customer Exposure
Modern prudential regulations stipulate that a bank refrain from investing in or extending credit to any individual entity (or related group of entities) in excess of an amount representing a prescribed percentage of the bank's capital and reserves.

Related-Party Financing
Dealing with connected parties is a dangerous form of credit risk exposure. Related parties include a bank's parent, major share-

holders, subsidiaries, affiliate companies, directors, and executive officers.

Overexposure to Geographic Areas or Economic Sectors
Another dimension of risk concentration is the exposure of a bank to a single sector of the economy. This makes a bank vulnerable to weaknesses in a particular industry or region. This issue is relevant for specialized banks or banks in small countries with narrow economic profiles, such as those with predominantly agricultural economies or exporters of a single commodity.

Islamic Banks and Credit Risk
In their study regarding IFSB Standard on Risk Management for Islamic Financial Institutions, Zamir Iqbal and Abbas Mirakhor (2007) show that the specific features of the financial instruments proposed by Islamic financial institutions lead to the following credit risks.

- In *murabahah* transactions, Islamic banks are exposed to credit risks when the bank delivers the asset to the client but does not receive payment from the client in time. In case of a nonbinding *murabahah*, where the client has the right to refuse delivery of the product purchased by the bank, the bank is further exposed to price and market risks.
- In *bay' al-salaam or istisnah* contracts, the bank is exposed to the risk of failure to supply on time or to supply the quality of goods as contractually specified. Such failure could result in a delay in payment, or in delivery of the product, and can expose Islamic banks to financial losses of income as well as capital.
- In the case of *mudarabah* investments, where the Islamic bank enters into the *mudarabah* contract as *rah al-mal* (principal) with an external *mudarib* (agent), in addition to the principal-agent problems, the bank is exposed to credit risk on the amounts advanced to the *mudarib*. The nature of the *mudarabah* contract is such that it does not give the bank appropriate rights to monitor the *mudarib*, which makes it difficult to manage credit risk. The bank is not in a position to decide how the activities of the *mudarib* can be monitored, if losses are claimed. This risk is present in markets where **information asymmetry** is high and transparency in financial disclosure by the *mudarib* is low. The acquisition of information and the costs associated to information are important in this process.

Credit Risk in the Asset Portfolio

The composition of assets provides a good picture of a bank's business profile and priorities as well as the type of intermediation risk that the bank is willing to take.

- Analysis of the aggregate portfolio should include at least the following:a list of government or other guarantees;
- a summary of the major investment and financing assets, including details on the number of customer types, average maturity, and average earnings;
- a review of the distribution of the portfolio, including different perspectives on the number of investment and financing assets and total amounts, (according to currency, short-term and long-term maturities), industrial or other pertinent economic sectors, state-owned and private clients, and corporate and retail lending.

Inter-Bank Deposits

Inter-bank deposits are a significant category of bank assets. They may account for an important percentage of a bank's balance sheet in countries that lack convertibility. Inter-bank deposits are intended to facilitate fund transfers and the settlement of securities transactions or to take advantage of the ability of other banks to perform certain services more economically due to their size or geographic location.

A review of inter-bank (lending) transactions focuses on the these aspects:

- any inter-bank credits for which specific provisions should be made;
- the establishment of counterparty credit limits including a description of the existing credit-limit policy;
- the method and accuracy of reconciliation of *Nostro and Vostro* accounts;
- any inter-bank credits with terms of pricing that are not the market norm;
- the concentration of inter-bank exposure with a listing of banks and amounts outstanding as well as limits.

Inter-bank deposits should be treated like any other credit risk exposure.

Off-Balance-Sheet Commitments

All off-balance-sheet items that incur credit exposure should be reviewed. An assessment should be made of the adequacy of procedures for analyzing credit risk and administration of off-balance-sheet credit instruments, like guarantees.

Nonperforming Assets

Nonperforming assets are assets that are not generating income. Loans are often seen to be nonperforming when the principal or interest on them is due and left unpaid for 90 days or more. The investment cash flow and overall ability to repay amounts owed are significantly more important than whether the payment is overdue or not.

For financial reporting purposes, the principal balance outstanding, rather than delinquent payments, is used to identify a nonperforming portfolio. The nonperforming portfolio indicates the quality of the total portfolio and ultimately of a bank's credit decisions. Another indicator is the bank's collection ratio.

When assessed within the context of nonperforming assets, the aggregate level of provisions indicates the capacity of a bank to accommodate credit risk. The analysis of a nonperforming portfolio covers in general certain points, as follows:

- provision levels, to determine the bank's capacity to withstand defaults;
- classifications, broken down by type of customer and branch of economic activity, to determine overall trends and whether or not all customers are affected equally;
- reasons for the deterioration of the portfolio quality, which allows the identification of possible measures to reverse a trend;
- a list of nonperforming accounts, including all relevant details, assessed on a case-by-case basis, to determine if the situation is reversible, exactly what can be done to improve repayment capacity;
- the impact on profit- and loss-sharing accounts, to determine how the bank will be affected by the deterioration in asset quality.

Asset Classification & Loss Provisioning Policies

Asset classification is a process whereby an asset is assigned a grade for credit risk, which is determined by the likelihood that obligations will be serviced according to the terms of the contract. In general, all assets for which a bank is taking a risk should be classified, including advances, accounts receivable, investment and financing assets, equity participation, and contingent liabilities.

Asset classification is a primary tool for risk management. Assets are classified at the time of origination and then reviewed and reclassified as necessary a few times a year.

The tax treatment of provisions varies considerably, although many economists believe that provisions should be treated as business expenses for tax purposes.

Tax considerations should not, however, influence prudent risk-management policies. In countries where the legal framework for debt recovery is highly developed, such as the United States, approximately 10 percent of substandard assets eventually deteriorate into loss. The percentages for doubtful and loss classifications are approximately 50 and 100 percent, respectively. In developing countries where the legal framework and tradition of collection may be less effective, provisions in the range of 20 to 25 percent for substandard assets may be a more realistic estimate of loss potential.

Table 1.3 presents the level of provisions in countries with less developed legal frameworks.

4.5. Asset–Liability Management, ALM, Liquidity, and Market Risks

Asset-liability management produces a high-quality, large, and growing flow of net interest income by achieving the optimum combination and level of assets, liabilities, and financial risk.

4.5.1. Asset–Liability Management

Asset–liability management risk results from the difference in maturity terms and conditions of a bank's portfolio on its assets and liabilities sides. According to theory, (as shown in the Theoretical Balance Sheet in table 1.2, Islamic banks should be less exposed to asset–liability mismatch and therefore to equity-duration risk, than their conventional counterparts.

Table 1.3 Recommended Provisions

Classification	Recommended Provisions	Qualification
Pass	1–2 percent	(Tier 2) General loss reserve, if disclosed
Watch	5–10 percent	Specific provision
Substandard	10–30 percent	Specific provision
Doubtful	50–75 percent	Specific provision
Loss	100 percent	Specific provision

Trend toward Less Risky Short-Term Assets

On the assets side, Islamic banks have limited themselves to trade financing assets, which tend to be less risky and of shorter maturity.

Low Participation in Profit-Sharing and Loss-Sharing Arrangements

Banks' participation in profit-sharing and loss-sharing arrangements is low. Banks are reluctant to indulge in profit-and loss-sharing instruments for several reasons, such as the inherit riskiness and additional costs of monitoring such investments, low appetite for risk on the part of both banks and their depositors, and lack of transparency in markets.

Lack of Clarity between Shareholders and Investors-Depositors

In theory, the contractual agreement between the bank and the investor's depositors should be based on a pass-through mechanism in which all profits and losses are passed to the depositors-investors. Hence, the problem of an asset–liability mismatch should not exist. This type of financial intermediation contributes to the stability of the financial system. However, in practice, there is no clear differentiation between the shares of investors-depositors and those of equity holders. The means of determining each stakeholder's share is not transparent, as policies for computing profits and losses are poorly defined. In some cases, the practice is not truly a pass-through arrangement, and profits are distributed to investment account holders despite losses on the assets, so that the profits are paid out of equity. This is called "displaced commercial risk."

4.5.2. Liquidity Risk

A bank has adequate liquidity when it gets needed funds (by increasing liabilities, securitizing, or selling assets) promptly and at a reasonable cost. The price of liquidity depends on market conditions and perception of the inherent riskiness of the borrowing institution. Liquidity is necessary to compensate for expected and unexpected balance-sheet fluctuations and to provide funds for growth. It represents a bank's ability to accommodate the redemption of deposits and other liabilities and to cover the demand for funding in the loan and investment portfolio. (Iqbal and Mirakhor 2007)

Liquidity risk is observed when the bank's ability to match the maturity of assets and liabilities is affected. This risk results from the mismatch between maturities on the two sides of the balance sheet, creating either a surplus of cash that must be invested or a shortage of cash that must be funded. Lack of liquidity affects the bank's ability to manage portfolios in a diversified fashion.

For Islamic banks, liquidity risk can be of two types: lack of liquidity in the market and lack of access to funding. When there is a lack of liquidity in the market, illiquid assets make it difficult for the Islamic banks to meet financial obligations. When there is a lack of access to funding, the Islamic banks are unable to borrow or raise funds at a reasonable cost, when needed. Liquidity risk is one of the most significant risks facing Islamic banks for the following reasons:

- Limited availability of a shariah-compatible money market and intra-bank market. Prohibition by shariah law from borrowing on the basis of interest in case of need and the absence of an active inter-bank money market have restricted Islamic banks' liquidity choices.
- Shallow secondary markets are another source of liquidity risk. There are only a few financial instruments traded in the secondary market. The shariah rules impose certain limitations on the trading of financial claims, unless such claims are linked to a **real asset**. Therefore, there is a need to develop asset-backed tradable securities, such as *sukuks*.
- Liquidity management available to conventional banks using the inter-bank market, secondary market for debt instruments, and discount windows from the lender of last resort (central bank) are all considered as based on *riba* (interest). They are not acceptable.
- Islamic banks hold a considerable proportion of funds as demand deposits in current accounts, and these can be withdrawn at any time.

Banks guarantee repayment of the principal deposited, and account holders do not have rights to a share in the profits. Some Islamic banks invest only a small fraction of the current account holders' funds and, in the absence of liquid short-term instruments, maintain a high level of idle cash.

The Islamic financial instruments that are currently being traded in the market on the basis of *bay' al-dayn* (sale of debt) are the green bankers acceptances, Islamic bills, Islamic mortgage bonds, and

Islamic private debt securities. In addition, financial institutions can sell government investment issues to the central bank, as and when required, to meet their liquidity needs. In turn, financial institutions can buy shariah-compliant investment issues from the central bank.

4.5.3. Market Risk

Exposure to market risk may arise as a result of the bank taking deliberately speculative positions or may ensue from the bank's market-making activities.

Market risk results from changes in the prices of equity instruments, commodities, fixed-income securities, and currencies. Each component of risk includes a general aspect of market risk and a specific aspect of risk that originates in the portfolio structure of a bank. Market risk also applies to derivatives instruments.

Markup Risk

Islamic banks are exposed to markup risk, as the markup rate used in *murabahah* and other trade-financing instruments is fixed for the duration of the contract, while the benchmark rate may change. This means that the prevailing markup rate may rise beyond the rate the bank has locked into a contract, making the bank unable to benefit from higher rates.

In the absence of an Islamic index of rate of return, Islamic banks often use the London Inter-Bank Offered Rate (LIBOR) as the benchmark, which aligns their market risk closely with the movement in LIBOR rates.

Price Risk

In case of *bay' al-salaam* (forward sale), Islamic banks are exposed to commodity price volatility during the period between delivery of the commodity and its sale at the prevailing market price. This risk is similar to the market risk of a forward contract if it is not hedged properly. In order to hedge its position, the bank may enter into a parallel (offsetting) *bay' al-salaam* contract.

In this context, the bank is exposed to price risk if there is default on the first contract and is obligated to deliver on the second contract.

Leased-Asset Value Risk

In case of an operating *ijarah*, the bank is exposed to market risk due to a fall in the **residual value** of the leased asset at the expiration of the lease term or, in case of early termination due to default, over the life of the contract.

Currency Risk

Currency risk arises from a mismatch between the value of assets and that of capital and liabilities denominated in foreign currency (or vice versa) or from a mismatch between foreign receivables and foreign payables that are expressed in a domestic currency. Currency risk is of a speculative nature and can therefore result in a gain or a loss.

Securities Price Risk

Islamic banks invest a portion of their assets in marketable securities, like Islamic bonds (*sukuks*). However, the prices of these bonds are exposed to current yields in the market.

Islamic banks holding these bonds are exposed to volatility in yield, unless they hold the security until maturity. Furthermore, the secondary market for such securities may not be very liquid, exposing Islamic banks to distorted prices.

Rate-of-Return Risk

The rate-of-return risk stems from uncertainty in the returns earned by Islamic banks on their assets. This uncertainty can cause a divergence from the expectations that investment account holders have on the liabilities side. The larger the divergence, the bigger is the rate-of-return risk. Consider an Islamic bank that may expect to earn 5 percent on its assets, which is passed on to the investors-depositors. If current market rates rise up to 6 percent, which is higher than what the bank may earn on its investment, the investors-depositors may also expect to earn 6 percent on their deposits.

The rate-of-return risk is different from the interest rate risk in two ways.

First, since Islamic banks have a mix of markup-based and equity-based investments, the uncertainty is higher. Second, the return on deposits in Islamic banks is anticipated, but not agreed in advance. In addition, the return on some investments is not known accurately until the end of the investment period. Islamic banks have to wait for the results of their investment to determine the level of return that investors-depositors will earn. If, during this period, the prevailing yields or expected rates of return change, the investors may expect to receive similar yields from the bank.

Equity Investment Risk

Islamic financial institutions are exposed to equity investment risk in profit-sharing and loss-sharing investments. These include partnership-based *mudarabah* and *musharakah* investments.

Typical examples of equity investments are holdings of shares in the stock market, private equity investments, equity participation in specific projects, and syndication investment. This risk is somewhat unique to Islamic financial institutions, considering that conventional commercial banks do not invest in equity-based assets.

Hedging Risk

Hedging risk is the risk of failure to mitigate and manage different types of risks. This increases the bank's overall risk exposure. The absence of derivative products to hedge risks and shallow secondary markets are sources of the increasing hedging risk of Islamic banks.

Benchmark Risk

Benchmark risk is the possible loss due to a change in the margin between domestic rates of return and the benchmark rates of return.

Business Risk

Business risk is associated with a bank's business environment, including macroeconomic and policy concerns, legal and regulatory factors, and the overall financial sector infrastructure. While Islamic financial institutions are very much exposed to the regular business environment, solvency, and financial sector infrastructure risks, they are exposed to rate-of-return risk.

4.5.4. Market Risk Measurement

The increasing involvement of banks in investment and trading activities and the high volatility of the markets requires the measurement of the exposures on a bank's positions. A simplistic approach to market risk assessment is the value at risk (VaR) concept.

Value at Risk (VaR)

VaR measures a bank's aggregate market risk exposure, given a probability level, by estimating the amount a bank would lose if it were to hold specific assets for a certain period of time. The risks covered by the model include all markup risk, currency, equity, and commodity positions inherent in the bank's portfolio, for both on- and off-balance-sheet positions.

VaR-based models typically combine the potential change in the value of each position that would result from specific movements in underlying risk factors.

The following table provides an example of a practical method of aggregating assets, as reflected on the balance sheet, to arrive at a net open position. Once forward and unsettled transactions have been taken into account, a projected position is determined at book value, translated into market value, and then disclosed in terms of a common denominator representing the equivalent position in the cash markets.

This methodology belongs to the static type of market risk measurement known as standard or table-based tools. Based on the net open position, it is possible to estimate the potential earnings or capital at risk by multiplying the net open position (market-risk-factor sensitivity) by price volatility. This estimate ignores the correlation between positions.

In most Islamic banks, the *rate-of-return risk* is likely to be much more important than market risk. The rate-of-return gap and duration

Table 1.4 Simplistic Calculation of Net-Effective Open Positions

Position	Commodities	Fixed Income	Equities	Currencies
Net-book value of assets per balance sheet				
Forward transactions				
Position at book value				
Position at market value before transactions in derivatives				
Position in derivatives (delta-equivalent position in options)				
Net effective open position after transactions in derivatives				
Possible movements in market prices (price volatility)				
Impact on earnings and capital				

gap applied to the banking book measure the exposure to changes in benchmark rates of return and the impact on bank earnings of present values.

4.5.5. *Market Risk Management*

Market risk requires constant management attention and adequate analysis. Prudent managers should be aware of exactly how a bank's market risk exposure relates to its capital. Market-risk management policies describe the bank's objectives and how to protect capital from the negative impact of unfavorable market-price movements.

Marking to Market refers to the (re)pricing of a bank's portfolios to account for changes in asset prices due to market-price movements. This policy requires that the asset be (re)priced at the market value of the asset in compliance with International Accounting Standard (IAS) 39. The volume and nature of the activities in which a bank engages generally determine the frequency of pricing. The bank (re) price positions are related to its investment portfolio on at least a monthly basis.

4.6. Operational and Islamic Banking Risks

Operational risk is considered high on the list of risk exposures for Islamic banks.

A survey by Khan and Ahmed (2001) shows that the managers of Islamic banks perceive operational risk as the most critical risk after markup risk. The survey finds that operational risk is lower in the fixed-income contracts of *murabahah* and *ijarah* and higher in the deferred sales contracts of *salaam* (agriculture) and *istisnah* (manufacturing). The relatively higher rankings of the instruments indicate that banks find these contracts difficult to implement.

The three methods of measuring operational risk proposed in Basel II could be adapted to apply to Islamic banks.

The use of gross income as the basic indicator approach of operational risk, also referred to as the alpha approach, could be misleading in Islamic banks, insofar as the large volume of transactions in commodities and the use of structured finance raise operational exposures that are not captured by gross income.

In contrast, the standardized approach or beta approach allows for different business lines would be better suited, but it would have to be adapted to the needs of Islamic banks.

In particular, agency services under *mudarabah* and commodity inventory management need to be considered explicitly.

Risks Specific to Islamic Banking

Islamic banks face challenges in the areas of displaced commercial risk, withdrawal risk, governance, fiduciary risk, transparency, shariah risk, and reputation risks.

Displaced commercial risk, the Accounting and Auditing Organization of Islamic Financial Institutions (AAOIFI) has identified as the risk when an Islamic bank is under pressure to pay its investors-depositors a rate of return higher than what should be payable under the "actual" terms of the investment contract. This situation is possible when the bank underperforms during a period and is unable to generate adequate profits for distribution to the account holders.

Business risk, or **"withdrawal risk,"** results mainly from the competitive pressures an Islamic bank faces from other banks. An Islamic bank could be exposed to the risk that depositors will withdraw their funds if they are receiving a lower rate of return than they would receive from another bank.

Fiduciary risk is the risk that arises from an institution's failure to perform in accordance with explicit and implicit standards applicable to its fiduciary responsibilities. Fiduciary risk leads to the risk of facing legal recourse if the bank breaches its fiduciary responsibility toward depositors and shareholders.

Transparency risk is another risk to consider. *Transparency,* according to the Basel Committee on Banking Supervision (1998), is defined as "the public disclosure of reliable and timely information that enables users of that information to make an accurate assessment of a bank's financial condition and performance, business activities, risk profile, and risk-management practices." The lack of transparency leads to the risk of incurring losses due to bad decisions based on incomplete or inaccurate information.

Shariah risk is related to the structure and functioning of shariah boards at the institutional level. This risk could be due to nonstandard practices in respect to different contracts in different jurisdictions. It also results from the failure to comply with shariah rules.

Reputational risk, or **"headline risk,"** is the risk that the irresponsible actions or behavior of management will damage the trust of the bank's clients.

4.7. Capital Adequacy and Basel II

The capital adequacy requirement constitutes Pillar 1 under the Basel II Accord. The capital adequacy standard is based on the principle that the level of a bank's capital should be related to the bank's specific risk profile.

4.7.1. Basel II and Capital Adequacy Requirements

Pillar 1. Capital Adequacy Requirement

Measurement of the capital adequacy requirement is done by three components of risk: credit risk, market risk, and operational risk. Models include some form of standardized approach and an approach based on internal systems. The risk management arrangements of Islamic banks thus bear on their ability to calibrate capital to their business objectives and risk tolerance, to deal with market discipline, and to maintain a dialogue with regulators.

Their characteristic of mobilizing funds in the form of risk-sharing investment accounts in place of conventional deposits, together with the materiality of financing transactions, may alter the overall risk of the balance sheet and, consequently, the assessment of their capital requirements.

Classification of Capital in the Basel Accords

- **Tier 1 (core capital).** Ordinary paid-up share of capital or common stock, disclosed reserves from post-tax retained earnings, noncumulative perpetual preferred stock (goodwill to be deducted)
- **Tier 2 (supplementary capital).** Undisclosed reserves, asset revaluation reserves, general provisions or general loan-loss provisions, hybrid (debt-equity) capital instruments, and subordinated term debts. Eligible Tier 2 capital may not exceed total Tier 1 capital, and long-term subordinated debt may not exceed 50 percent of Tier 1 capital.
- **Tier 3** Unsecured debt: subordinated and fully paid up, to have an original maturity of at least two years and not be repayable before the agreed repayment date unless the supervisory authority agrees. This will be limited to 250 percent of a bank's Tier 1 capital, which is required to support market risks.

International banks in the G-10 countries are required to hold a minimum total capital (Tier 1 and Tier 2) equal to 8 percent of risk-adjusted assets. Tier 1 capital is the same in Islamic banks as in conventional financial institutions.

However, in Islamic banks, the reserves include the shareholders' portion of the profit equalization reserve (PER), which is included in disclosed reserves.

In Tier 2 capital, there are no hybrid capital instruments or sub-ordinated debts, as these would bear interest and contravene shariah principles. However, an issue is the treatment of unrestricted risk-sharing investment accounts, which may be viewed as equity invest-ments on a limited-term basis.

4.7.2. Capital Adequacy Methodology for Islamic Banks

The contractual agreement between Islamic banks and investment account holders is based on the concept of sharing profit and loss, which makes investment account holders a unique class of quasi-liabil-ity holders: they are neither depositors nor equity holders. Although they are not part of the bank's capital, they are expected to absorb all losses on the investments made through their funds, unless there is evidence of negligence or misconduct on the part of the bank.

Determination of Risk Weights

Assigning risk weights to different asset classes reflects the contrac-tual relationship between the bank and the borrower.

For Islamic banks, the assets range from trade financing to equity partnerships.

The calculation of risk weights is different for Islamic banks than for conventional banks:

Sets based on trade are not truly financial assets and carry risks other than credit and market risks.

Nonfinancial assets such as real estate, commodities, and *ijarah* and *istisnah* contracts have special risk characteristics.

Islamic banks carry partnership and profit-and-loss-sharing assets that have a higher risk profile.

Islamic banks do not have well-defined instruments for mitigating and hedging risk, such as derivatives, which raises the overall riski-ness of assets.

In the case of *mudarabah* and *musharakah*, the bank is exposed to both credit and market risks that need to be analyzed in a manner similar to the methodology of the Basel Accords.

When such partnership-based assets are acquired in the form of tangible assets and are held for trading, the only exposure is to mar-ket risk, because credit risk is minimized by direct ownership of the assets. However, there is significant risk of capital impairment when direct investment takes place in partnership-based contracts and the investments will be held to maturity. Treatment of this risk within the Basel framework is not straightforward.

The standard deals with the minimum capital adequacy requirements for both credit and market risks for seven shariah-compliant financing and investment instruments: (a) *murabahah*, (b) *salaam*, (c) *istisnah*, (d) *ijarah*, (e) *musharakah* and diminishing *musharakah*, (f) *mudarabah*, and (g) *sukuk*. The discussion of each contract includes risk weights for credit and market risks. The IFSB standard is defined in two forms: standard and discretionary.

In the standard formula, capital is divided by risk-weighted assets, excluding the assets financed by investment account holders. The size of the risk-weighted assets is determined for the credit risk first and then adjusted to accommodate for the market and operational risks.

To determine the adjustment, the capital requirements for market risk and operational risk are multiplied by 12.5, which is the reciprocal ratio (1/0.08) of the minimum capital-adequacy ratio (CAR) of 8 percent.

The second formula, the supervisory discretion formula, is modified to accommodate the existence of reserves maintained by Islamic banks to minimize displaced commercial, withdrawal, and systemic risks.

In markets where Islamic banks maintain PER and Investment Risk Reserves (IRR), the supervisory authorities are given discretion to adjust the denominator of the CAR formula for them.

Supervisors may adjust the formula according to their judgment of the systemic risk and prevalent practices. In the discretionary formula, the supervisory authority has the discretion to include a specified percentage of assets financed by investment account holders in the denominator of the CAR. The percentage set by the supervisory authority is applied to assets financed by holders of both unrestricted and restricted investment accounts. Further adjustment is made for PER and IRR in such a manner that a certain fraction of the risk-weighted assets funded by the reserves is deducted from the denominator. The rationale given for this adjustment is that these reserves reduce the displaced commercial risk.

IFSB Standard Formula for CAR

Eligible capital/ (Total risk-weighted assets + Operational risk − Total risk-weighted assets funded by profit-sharing investment accounts)
    In this formula, risk weighting includes weights for market and credit risk. Profit-sharing investment account balances include PER and IRR.

IFSB Supervisory Discretion Formula for CAR

Eligible capital/(Total risk-weighted assets + Operational risk − $(1 − a)^*$ Total risk-weighted assets funded by profit-sharing investment accounts and a^* Risk-weighted assets funded by PER and IRR)

In this formula, risk weighting includes weights for market and credit risk. Profit-sharing investment account balances include PER and IRR. The term 'a' refers to the proportion of assets funded by PSIAs, which is to be determined by the supervisory authorities. The value of a normally does not exceed 30 percent.

Pillar 2. Supervisory Review

Supervisory review is the second pillar of Basel II and a critical part of the capital-adequacy framework. The supervisory review assesses whether the banks maintain adequate capital necessary for the risks inherent in their business profile and business environment and to encourage banks to have policies and internal processes for assessing and managing capital adequacy. Banks' management is accountable for ensuring that their bank has adequate capital.

The role of supervisors is to review the bank's internal capital adequacy assessment processes to ensure that the bank's capital targets

Table 1.5 Capital Adequacy Standards for Credit Risk: Basel II vs. IFSB

Criteria	Basel II	IFSB
Risk weight	Calibrated on the basis of external ratings by the Basel committee	Calibrated on the basis of external ratings by the Basel committee; varies according to contract stage and financing mode
Treatment of equity in the banking book	> 150 percent for venture capital and private equity investments	Simple risk-weight method (risk weight 300 or 400 percent) or supervisory slotting method (risk weight 90–270 percent)
Credit-risk mitigation techniques	Includes financial collateral, credit derivatives, guarantees, netting (on- and off-balance sheet)	Includes profit-sharing investment accounts (PSIA), or cash on deposits with Islamic banks, guarantees, financial collateral, and pledged assets

Source: Jabbari (2006)

and capital position are consistent with its overall risk profile and strategy. An important aspect of supervisory reviews is to assess compliance with the minimum standards and disclosure requirements. Supervisors are expected to have an approach for identifying situations where falling capital levels raise questions about the ability of a bank to withstand business shocks.

Pillar 3. Market Discipline

The requirement for market discipline, the third pillar of Basel II, complements the minimum capital requirements and the supervisory review process. Market discipline is based on disclosure requirements. Banks are asked to disclose reliable and timely information that market participants need in order to make well-founded risk assessments, including assessment of the adequacy of capital held as a cushion against losses and of the risk exposures that may give rise to such losses.

5. ALTERNATIVE FINANCIAL MARKETS: ISLAMIC BANKING & FINANCE AS A CASE STUDY

Much of the research into alternative financial arrangements derives from the Marxist perception that markets are a unique manifestation of capitalism: they did not exist before capitalism and will not survive in a post-capitalist (socialist) world. To underscore the point, Marxists note that functioning markets did not exist in classical antiquity or, if they did, they were of only marginal importance (Finley 1985). Production and exchange were typically organized along lines that were influenced either by social conventions and traditions ("reciprocity"), as in the classical world, and thus changed only very slowly, or "redistribution," where a central authority collects and distributes goods, what today would be described as a command economy.

In many instances, this research program was driven by ideological considerations, the desire to have the data conform to the Marxist framework, rather than allow the available data to inform the theory. Recent research demonstrates that when these sources are subject to more careful scrutiny, they appear to undermine the view that markets, whether for goods or financial services, either did not exist or were of only peripheral importance in antiquity. Indeed, some historians now argue that not only did functioning markets exist, but there is also evidence that economic growth outpaced population growth, thus allowing for rising living standards more than a thousand years before the Industrial Revolution (Pollio 2007).

On one point, however, the evidence is unambiguous: systems that organize economic and financial transactions along nonmarket lines, as in the former Soviet Union, have been dismal failures. The collapse of the Soviet Union and the transition of China from a command to a market economy demonstrate clearly the dire consequences that can follow from financial repression.

Other systems that continue to rely upon the market to organize economic activity, however, not only exist but can also flourish. Like capitalist economies, these systems regulate or restrict the types and structure of transactions permitted within financial markets under their control. Unlike capitalist societies, the criteria that inform contract structures in such systems derive from values fundamentally different from those that apply in traditional financial markets.

Islamic banking and finance fall into this category.[2] Market transactions predominate, but the institutions that shape economic activity are to a greater or lesser extent molded by religious precepts as embodied in the shariah (McMilan 2002). Many of the institutions characteristic of traditional financial markets are also found in Islamic finance and exist to serve similar functions. For example, property rights are recognized and respected. Profits are permissible; indeed, Islamic banks are organized as profit-making institutions. Nor is risk-taking anathema, only the way risks and rewards are shared among the participants. Islamic finance thus provides an important instance of whether it is possible to successfully harmonize financial practice with religious principles.

It should be stressed at the outset that our discussion is not meant to establish the superiority of one system over the other, or to determine which is more economically efficient or less susceptible to crisis. Its major aim is to introduce readers to alternative financial arrangements that have become an important, independent source of global capital. Islamic finance has innovated specific instruments that, on the one hand, replace more familiar forms of lending and borrowing, and on the other, complement (or at least are compatible with) traditional financial products. Project financings in the Middle East, for example, increasingly incorporate tranches designed to comply with Islamic financial rules; the Equate project in Kuwait was one of the first and perhaps best known examples of this phenomenon.

Bluntly put, it is our purpose here to adumbrate Islamic finance's unique features and why its products are structured the way they are. Finally, this discussion is *not* concerned with theology per se, although it is impossible to understand Islamic banking and financial institutions without having some understanding of the basic concepts that motivated its development and subsequent growth.

5.1 Basic Data on Islamic Financial Markets

Islamic financial institutions are a modern phenomenon, their origins going back only thirty or so years. Today, Islamic financial institutions can be found in some seventy countries, with all of the major multinational banks now offering Islamic financial products. The aggregate size of the market is currently around $1 trillion, with the lion's share of the total held by Islamic banks; investment banks and *sukuk* "bonds" are also important components of the Islamic financial market.

There is an understandable tendency to regard Islamic banks and financial markets as if they were homogenous entities. The reality, however, is that no single set of rules governs Islamic financial institutions; nor are local accounting and auditing standards, banking codes, or regulatory regimes uniform. This, of course, tends to limit the value of international comparisons but should not affect the general understanding of the broad requirements that have to be met to qualify as an Islamic financial institution. Nor should any of this be at all surprising: banking and financial rules change from time to time and from place to place as shariah law itself is subject to different and changing interpretations.

To illustrate the complexities involved here, we might note that according to some interpretations, investing in the stock market is considered to be a form of gambling and thus barred by the Qur'an; other authorities take the view that the proscription refers specifically to day-to-day trading with the objective of selling the stock so as to realize a quick capital gain.

A second instance is deposit insurance, officially sanctioned measures designed to protect depositors up to a maximum amount (either per account or overall) from losses arising from bank failures. According to shariah law, the nature of the payment received by the depositor cannot take the form of an interest payment; in the more usual case, it is structured as a fee determined in keeping with a contractual profit-and-loss-sharing agreement with an Islamic bank. Thus, if an Islamic bank invests its funds in enterprises that fail, depositors of that bank can lose all their money. This obviously puts depositors in an Islamic bank at a disadvantage vís-à-vis depositors at a conventional commercial bank, and even more so as the risk characteristics of the latter are improved by the existence of deposit insurance.

All this implies that the returns to depositors in Islamic banks should be considerably higher than the interest rates payable at commercial banks. These differential characteristics also shape the nature of competition among the rival institutions. As we shall see shortly, with the exception of the Islamic Republic of Iran, in all other countries both banking systems exist side by side.

Islamic Screening

We noted above that different countries approach *shariah*-compliant activities individually, applying criteria in one place that would be unacceptable elsewhere. This raises practical difficulties for individual institutions or investors given that what may be acceptable in one place may be considered prohibited elsewhere. This in turn can affect the composition of investment portfolios, conferring advantages on those that follow more relaxed rules than those that adhere to more stringent rules.

In other words, the filters applied by issuers or users of Islamic financial products vary both by country and by screening institution. This obviously creates pressures to institute a more uniform set of definitions both to ensure strict compliance with Islamic precepts and to level the playing field in terms of eliminating practices that create competitive advantages or disadvantages.

From a recent study by Masood (2010), we now know much more about the variety of screening approaches employed by the various participants engaged in Islamic financial markets. The major results of this study can be summarized as follows:

1. Shariah-compliant boards around the world apply both qualitative and quantitative screens. Some of these are more specific in their listing of shariah impermissible business and activities, while some are more lenient. The majority of these users practice a two-tier method of screening: qualitative and quantitative. Under a quantitative screen, the range of allowable ratios among impermissible criteria and the measurement formula differ between boards.
2. Some countries, including Malaysia, Russia, and the UAE, have their respective shariah screening boards, and they set different standards depending on the roles and objectives they play in the industry. The concern of a regulator is the development of the industry, and this helps to explain the more relaxed step-by-step

approach in shariah screening as practiced in Malaysia. By contrast, the main concern of the market intelligence providers, namely, the international index providers, is to employ criteria that reflect the market through the selection of high-quality assets for their clients so as to satisfy their investment principles. Private corporations, which include fund managers and shariah service providers, screen assets at the macro level and are motivated by return and fees, and hence, apply a more stringent approach, catering to the bigger Islamic market in the Middle East. Different jurisdictions practiced by the users also play an important role in the differences in standards.

3. Although there are possibilities that other exchanges or countries may provide their own screening method, most fund managers, banks and industry players do not have such screening facilities and thus have to rely on market intelligence providers that screen global assets at the macro level. The most prominent shariah index providers are DJIM, FTSE, MSCI, and S&P, which pre-screen universal stocks to form particular shariah index constituents. Their indices are licensed for use by institutional investors around the world for portfolio management and benchmarking purposes. They also serve as the basis of structured products and other index-linked investment vehicles, including ETFs.

4. Based on the findings of qualitative screening, only minor differences exist in the types of businesses considered to be shariah noncompliant, albeit some are more specific than others. Wider dispersion is found on the threshold limit toward businesses that are considered impermissible. Consequently, there are some stringent users who immediately label companies as shariah noncompliant, according to any involvement in impermissible activities in the qualitative screen; some more flexible users still accept such companies as permissible until the next process of excessive ratios in their quantitative screen.

To summarize, DJIM and Azzad can be categorized as very stringent shariah-compliant users because they reject companies that in one way or another are involved in shariah-noncompliant businesses in the first round of the qualitative screen. It is also obvious from our comparison that SC is the only user that does not apply the debt and liquidity screen. Alfa Bank also does not apply a liquidity screen, while Al-Meezan as well as Azzad do not apply interest screens. A degree of consensus applies among FTSE, MSCI, S&P, and DIB to apply all four quantitative screens.

Different references of shariah jurisdictions may have also contributed to the dispersion between the different screening methods. The Middle East jurisdiction, which can be represented by NCB and DIB are very much concerned with the prohibition of *riba* and apply stringent screens for interest received and paid. Securities Commission, Malaysia's (SC's) shariah board is concerned mainly with providing a wider range of investment instruments and concentrates on lawful and pure returns of businesses, regardless of how capital is generated; this can seen from the absence of a debt and liquidity screen.

The bulk of Islamic bank assets are concentrated in countries that have large Muslim populations, though in virtually all of these, traditional commercial banks also exist. To begin with, the number of Islamic banking institutions in selected countries, the market breaks down into three broad categories, the first tier comprising Bahrain, Iran, United Arab Emirates, and Malaysia, in that order. The second tier also consists mainly of Middle Eastern countries, the principal exception being Pakistan, which along with Kuwait and Sudan are at the top this grouping. The lowest tier includes a disparate group of countries having a much wider geographic distribution.

Shifting from the number of institutions to the volume of credit generated by the alternative banking systems, several significant differences emerge. For the reasons just stated, Iran remains at the top. Islamic banks in Bahrain and other Gulf Cooperative Countries, which included a large percentage of the total number of local banks, actually account for a significantly smaller share of credit outstanding, with none accounting for more than one-fifth of the banking sector's total. However, the data upon which these conclusions are based, period averages, may no longer provide an accurate representation of the relative importance of the different banking systems;. Later data on credit shares may more closely approximate the importance indicated by banking numbers, though on balance we would still expect Islamic banks to be less visible than their commercial-bank counterparts.[3]

All this suggests that the bulk of Islamic banks are comparatively small, generating a relatively modest share of total credit expansion. The question naturally arises in this context whether size matters; that is, are smaller banks riskier than their larger counterparts? Cihak and Hesse (2008) have shown that the truth may be the other way around, with smaller Islamic banks (assets of less than $1 billion) exhibiting less risk than their larger counterparts. The authors suggest these differences could be due to the greater difficulty larger Islamic banks experience adjusting their credit-risk-management systems as they become bigger.

Their findings further indicate that small Islamic banks tend to be more stable (less likely to fail) than traditional commercial banks, though the opposite conclusion applies in respect to large Islamic banks. On the whole, Islamic banks exhibit greater stability than commercial banks, though the conclusion may be sensitive to the way the effect is measured.[4] A few other points emerge from the Cihak and Hesse study that are worth noting. For one thing, large Islamic banks have, on average, higher loan-to-asset ratios than commercial banks, a finding that does not apply to smaller Islamic banks. The former conclusion reflects the fact that Islamic banks are barred from investing in treasury bills or bonds, implying that a larger fraction of their assets would take the form of loans, though there is no obvious reason that the same does apply to smaller Islamic banks. Also, Islamic banks tend to have higher cost-to-income ratios than commercial banks, though the effect is significant again only for large Islamic banks. Given the nature of their lending activities, where returns depend upon the success of the venture financed, we would expect greater due diligence and the attendant higher costs such effort entails.

The bulk of Islamic bank assets are concentrated among institutions located in the Muslim heartland. In the Gulf region, for example, Islamic banks hold on average a quarter of the banking system's assets. For Saudi Arabia, Kuwait, and Bahrain, the percentage tends to be above the regional average, while in the UAE and Qatar, the figure is well below the regional average, at around 10 percent of the total. Outside this region, Islamic banks control roughly 20 percent of Malaysian bank assets; Turkish banks, by contrast, account for the smallest percentage among the leading Islamic countries, the asset share amounting to only around 3.5 percent of total assets (Imam and Kpodar 2010).These percentages tend to obscure the fact that Islamic bank assets have been growing considerably more rapidly in recent years than commercial banks generally, with the fastest rate of increase, not surprisingly, accounted for by countries having the lowest asset shares. More to the point, in the UAE and Qatar, asset growth rates of between 60 to 66 percent have outpaced total bank asset growth over the past six or seven years by a factor of 1.6 and 1.7, respectively. Even in Turkey, with the lowest percentage for all of the countries surveyed, Islamic banking assets rose by twice the rate indicated for total bank assets. In more mature Islamic banking markets, asset growth rates have also remained high and well above those indicated for total asset growth.

Finally, Islamic assets account for a negligible share of the countries' gross domestic product (GDP). The data further indicate the relatively undeveloped nature of the financial sector in most of the countries having a significant Islamic banking sector. Given the well-known relationship between financial depth and economic growth, we can almost correlate the the GDP ratio and per capita income. Among the countries, Malaysia stands out, with a bank-asset-to-GDP ratio well above the sample average, but even here, where the Islamic financial sector is perhaps the most developed of any of the countries sampled, the Islamic percentage is negligible.

One of the more important issues raised by the preceding discussion is how to account for the rapid growth and diffusion of Islamic banking over the past three decades. Though dwarfed by the commercial banking sector, at least as measured in relation to GDP, Islamic banking has grown at rates well above those for the financial services sector. While a relatively large list of factors could be adduced to explain the sector's historic growth, only recently have analysts attempted to quantify the more critical influences. Table 1.6 summarizes the results of a recent econometric study by Imam and Kpodar (2010). The table entries indicate the variables used in their study, their expected relationship to Islamic bank growth, and their levels of statistical significance.

The results are not all that different from what might have been expected. The percentage of the total population that is Muslim, the level of per capita income, and the impact of developments in the oil market, positively influence the size of the Islamic banking sector, whether measured in terms of the number of Islamic banks or their share of assets in the banking sector total. Interest rates, too, are important, in that they constitute the opportunity cost of depositing funds in Islamic institutions. There is, however, a threshold effect; that is, their impact becomes relevant only after real interest rates have risen above some critical level, 3.5 percent in the Imam and Kpodar study. Since both during and after their period of estimation, real interest rates have been either low or negative, they clearly have played a major role in supporting the growth of Islamic banking; on the other hand, once real rates begin to recover, they could portend a reversal of recent trends.

Macroeconomic stability, too, benefits the growth of Islamic banking, whether the effect is measured in terms of inflation or the budget balance. The evidence for integration with the Middle East region is

Table 1.6 Factors Affecting the Rate of Growth of Islamic Banking

Variable	Explanation	Hypothesized Relationship	Statistical Significance
Islamic population	The higher the percentage of the national population that is Muslim, the greater will be the rate of diffusion.	Positive	Yes/Yes
Real Interest Rates	Given the existence of a commercial banking sector, the higher the posted interest rates, the higher is the opportunity cost of depositing funds with Islamic banks.	Negative	Yes/Yes
Per Capita Income	Rising per capita incomes stimulate the demand for financial services, including Islamic financial services.	Positive	Yes/Yes
11 September 2001	Reduced the attractiveness for Muslim investors to invest capital in Western financial markets, owing to an apparent increase in seizure risk.	Positive	No[c]
Oil-Producing Countries	Directly affects the level of local income; increases the remittances of Muslims working in oil-exporting countries.	Positive	Yes/Yes
Economic Integration in the Middle East	Countries with close ties to the Middle East are likely to develop their own Islamic banking systems back home.	Positive	No/Yes
Distance from Major Islamic Financial Sectors (Bahrain and Malaysia)	The greater the proximity to either of these centers, the higher is the likelihood of an indigenous Islamic banking sector developing.	Positive	Yes/Yes[b]

Continued

Table 1.6 Continued

Variable	Explanation	Hypothesized Relationship	Statistical Significance
Financial Sector Development	One possible channel is that more sophisticated financial systems substitute for Islamic banks. Another is that sophistication implies the existence of a developed infrastructure capable of supporting the development of local Islamic banks.	?	Yes/No
Macroeconomic Stability	Declining stability, measured by inflation and the budget balance, should discourage disintermediation and add an additional element of risk to risk-sharing financial contracts.	Positive	Yes/No
Institutions	Factors such as rule of law, shareholder rights, regulatory policy, and legal origin, provide a sounder foundation upon which to build an Islamic financial sector.	Positive	Yes[a]/Yes[a]

Source: Imam and Kpodar (2010)

Notes: Two measures of diffusion were used: the number of Islamic banks and the share of Islamic bank assets in total bank assets. Under the "Statistical Significance" column, the first response refers to the results using the number of banks and the second, the asset proportion.

[a] Only legal origin matters: countries with a common law are more likely to encourage the growth of Islamic banking however it is measured.

[b] Distance from Bahrain remains statistically significant.

[c] Relevant only in the second specification.

ambiguous as is the level of financial development, affecting growth when the dependent variable is the number of Islamic banks, but statistically insignificant when measured in terms of the asset share. Legal origin also seems to matter, but only for countries belonging to the common law tradition. Finally, the 9/11 attacks on U.S. soil do not appear to have had any significant impact on the growth of Islamic banking, although the effect may have been obscured by the concurrent rise in oil prices, which, in any event, appears to have had the larger direct impact.

The fact that the principles governing Islamic finance are fundamentally different from those applying to conventional commercial banks would have a direct and significant bearing on the structure of their lending and investment policies, confirmed by the above discussion. In keeping with these broad considerations, we might reasonably ask whether Islamic banks are less prone to the sorts of financial dislocations that recently affected commercial banks and, by extension, global financial markets. In particular, analysts have noted that Islamic banks, being barred from investing or trading in fixed-income instruments, such as mortgage-backed securities, a major cause of the banking crisis that triggered the recent (beginning in 2007) financial turmoil, were unlikely to have suffered to the same extent as their conventional commercial bank counterparts.

Of course, the broader question is whether the principles that underpin Islamic banking were instrumental in averting the difficulties faced by other commercial banks; whether such principles directly or indirectly encouraged more effective risk management, which, combined with lending restrictions, contributed to their greater relative stability; or, finally, whether Islamic banks simply followed the example of banks in other emerging market economies, acting more prudently than their Western counterparts. These broad considerations suggest a number of testable hypotheses. The first is whether Islamic banks did escape recent financial difficulties? Second, did they exhibit greater stability than their conventional counterparts in the same countries in which they operate? And third, was their performance significantly different than that of financial institutions in emerging market economies generally?

As to the first two hypotheses, the available evidence is mixed. Imam and Dridi (2010) conclude that Islamic banks (IB) fared differently than did commercial banks (CB) during the global financial crisis. Factors related to Islamic banks' business model helped contain the adverse impact on profitability in 2008, while weaknesses in risk management practices in some Islamic banks led to a larger decline in profitability compared to commercial banks in 2009. In particular, adherence to shariah principles precluded Islamic banks from financing or investing in the kinds of instruments that have adversely affected their conventional competitors and triggered the global financial crisis. The weak performance in some countries was associated with sectoral/ name concentration and, in some cases, was facilitated by exemptions from concentration limits, highlighting the importance of a neutral regulatory framework for Islamic banks and commercial banks and strengthening risk management in some banks. Despite higher profitability during the period before the global crisis (2005–2007), Islamic banks' average profitability for 2008–2009 was similar to that of commercial banks, indicating better cumulative (pre-crisis and post-crisis) profitability and suggesting that higher pre-crisis profitability was not driven by a strategy of greater risk-taking. Large Islamic banks have fared better than small ones. Better diversification, economies of scale, and stronger reputation(s) might have contributed to this better performance.

A recent S&P (2010) survey reaches a similar conclusion, noting that while specific Islamic rules helped to avert losses experienced by conventional banks, in general such institutions are neither immune to economic recession—the assets of the five largest GCC Islamic banks rose by only 1.3 percent in the first half of 2009 as against 21.5 percent in 2008—nor to asset-quality deterioration. The weighted average ratio of nonperforming financing facilities (mainly *murabaha* and *ijara* transactions) to total financing facilities increased to 5.1 percent at year-end 2008, from 3.1 percent a year before, for the five largest Islamic banks in the GCC region. In fact, S&P concludes that there are no compelling reasons to differentiate the lending policies of Islamic and conventional banks, a rather startling finding considering that the nature of risk-sharing arrangements that underpin lending, and by extension bank profits, would seem to favor more thorough due diligence than among conventional banks. It may just be that commercial banks, regardless of their orientation, are not very good at evaluating and quantifying equity risks. If such is indeed the case, this implies that Islamic bank asset portfolios, proportionately larger and less diversified than those of their conventional counterparts, are exposed to greater risks.

As to the second point, recent studies have shown that emerging market economies in general fared considerably better than did the Organisation for Economic Cooperation and Development (OECD) economies, raising the possibility that either factors unique to the largest multinational banks were key to their financial difficulties, or that existing supervisory arrangements were inadequate to detect emerging problems, or that regulation accommodated the sorts of practices that contributed directly to the financial crisis. Indeed, it is very likely these effects operated concurrently. The fact that emerging market economies, above all, those in the Asian region, escaped the worst of the financial crisis, and have since shown the strongest economic rebound, may have more to do with their objective circumstances than to superior foresight or risk management. It is, important, however, to differentiate Asian emerging market economies (EMEs) from those in Europe. The key difference between the two regions is that credit booms among the latter were financed with imported capital rather than, as among Asian economies, by domestic savings. Moreover, shifts in the nature of capital flows to emerging market economies have contributed to a further reduction in their vulnerability to abrupt declines in capital inflows, in particular, away from (mainly short-term bank) debt, and toward more stable portfolio and foreign direct-investment inflows (Kose and Prasad 2010). Thus, it is not easy, conceptually or empirically, to distinguish the various strands that contributed to the greater stability of many emerging market economic regions compared with the severe dislocations experienced in Western economies. It is axiomatic that anything, including Islamic banking and finance, that contributes to more responsible policies is consistent with greater overall economic and financial stability.

6. DEVELOPMENTS & FUTURE CHALLENGES

Illiquidity

Islamic banks are operating with a limited set of short-term traditional instruments, and there is a shortage of products for medium-term to long-term maturities. One reason for these shortcomings is the lack of markets in which to sell, trade, and negotiate the financial assets of the bank. There are no venues for securitizing dormant assets and taking them off the balance sheet. In other words, the secondary markets lack depth and breadth. An effective portfolio-management strategy cannot be implemented in the absence of liquid markets, as opportunities for diversification become limited.

Limited Scope

In the absence of debt markets, underdevelopment of equities markets, and lack of derivatives markets, financial intermediaries play a critical role in the provision of Islamic financial services. Financial intermediaries not only are the main source of capital and risk mitigation but also are expected to undertake activities with wider scope.

Concentrated Banking

Islamic banks tend to have a concentrated base of deposits or assets. They often concentrate on a few select sectors and avoid direct competition. For example, one Islamic bank may specialize in financing the agricultural sector, while another might do the same in the construction sector, and neither attempts to diversify to other sectors. This practice makes Islamic banks vulnerable to cyclical shocks in a particular sector.

Dependence on a small number of sectors—lack of diversification—increases their exposure to new entrants, especially foreign conventional banks that are better equipped to meet these challenges.

Weak Risk-Management and Governance Framework

Several studies have identified weaknesses and vulnerabilities among Islamic banks in the areas of risk management and governance. Operational risk, which arises due to the failure of systems, processes, and procedures, is one area of concern. Weak internal-control processes may present operational risks and expose an Islamic bank to potential losses.

Governance issues are equally important for Islamic banks, investors, regulators, and other stakeholders.

Steps Forward: Some Recommendations

Improvement can be made in several areas to promote and enhance the functioning of Islamic banks and other institutions providing Islamic financial services. However, certain areas deserve immediate attention, which I'll discuss here.

Financial engineering and financial innovations are driving the global financial system toward greater economic efficiency by expanding the opportunities for sharing risk, lowering transaction costs, and reducing asymmetrical information and agency costs. Financial engineering involves the design, development, and implementation of innovative financial instruments and processes as well as the formulation of creative solutions. Financial engineering may lead to a new consumer type of financial instrument, a new security, or a new process or creative solution to corporate finance problems, such as the need to lower funding costs, manage risk better, or increase the return on investments. For Islamic financial institutions, a financial engineering challenge is to introduce new shariah-compatible products that enhance liquidity, risk management, and portfolio diversification.

Generally, attempts to apply financial-engineering techniques to Islamic banking will require committing a great deal of resources to understand the risk-return characteristics of each building block of the system and offering new products with different risk-return profiles that meet the demand of investors, financial intermediaries, and entrepreneurs for liquidity and safety. Securitization is a prime candidate for financial engineering. New financial innovations are also needed to satisfy the demand for instruments at both ends of the maturity structure: extremely short-term deposits and long-term investments. Money markets that are shariah-compatible do not exist at present, and there is no equivalent of an Islamic inter-bank market where banks could place, say, overnight funds or could borrow to satisfy a need for temporary liquidity. Although securitization of a pool of lease portfolios could help to develop the inter-bank market, the volume of transactions offered by securitization may not be sufficient to meet the demand (Iqbal 1999).

Related to the challenge of financial engineering is another operational challenge for Islamic banks: the need to standardize the process for introducing new products in the market. Currently, each Islamic bank has its own religious board that examines and evaluates each new product without coordinating the effort with other banks. Each religious board adheres to a particular school of thought. This process should be streamlined and standardized to minimize time, effort, and confusion.

Islamic financial institutions are, in general, of small size and cannot afford to invest substantial funds in research and development. They are unable to reap the benefits of economies of scale. Considering the importance of financial engineering, Islamic financial institutions should seriously consider making joint efforts to develop the basic infrastructure for introducing new products. Conducting basic research and development collectively may save some of the costs required to build this infrastructure individually.

Risk Management and Diversification

Financial markets are becoming more integrated and interdependent, thus increasing the probability of expeditious contagion effects and leaving little room for swift measures against unexpected risk. Insufficient understanding of the new environment can create a sense of greater risk even if the objective level of risk in the system remains unchanged or is even lower. The current wave of capital-market liberalization and globalization is prompting the need for enhanced risk-management measures, especially for the developing economies and emerging markets. Whereas risk management is practiced widely in conventional financial markets, it is underdeveloped in Islamic financial markets.

Challenges for Risk Management

Implementation of a risk-management framework requires close collaboration among the management of Islamic financial institutions, regulators, and supervisors. Implementation of risk management at the institutional level is the responsibility of management, which should identify clear objectives and strategies for the institution and establish internal systems for identifying, measuring, monitoring, and managing various risk exposures.

Although the general principles of risk management are the same for conventional and Islamic financial institutions, there are specific challenges in the management of risk in Islamic financial institutions:

- *The need to establish supporting institutions.* Such institutions include a lender of last resort, a deposit-insurance system, a liquidity-management system, secondary markets, a legal infrastructure favorable to Islamic instruments, and an efficient system for resolving disputes.
- *The need to achieve uniformity in and harmonization of shariah standards across markets and borders.* The current practice of maintaining separate shariah boards for each institution is inefficient and should be replaced by a centralized shariah board for a jurisdiction.
- *The cost of developing risk-management systems.* Many Islamic financial institutions are too small to afford the costs. Efforts should be made to collaborate with other institutions to develop systems that are customized to the needs of Islamic financial institutions and that address the need for instrument-specific modeling.
- *The challenges of integrating Islamic financial institutions with global financial markets.* Efforts should be made to enhance transparency in financial reporting and develop accounting and reporting standards across markets.

- *The scarcity of highly skilled human resources.* Efforts should be made to develop customized research and training programs on risk management. Such training programs should certify participants after successful completion of the program.

Non-Bank Financial Services

For further growth, the role of intermediation should be extended beyond its traditional setup. In particular, there is a need to broaden the scope and range of financial services offered, similar to the concept of a "financial products supermarket." Such a supermarket would act like an all-in-one-bank covering all sorts of financial services.

Performance Benchmarks

The practice of measuring performance of an asset by comparing its return and risk relative to a well-defined benchmark is well established in a market-centered financial system. Markets are good at offering an efficient, measurable, and consistent benchmark for different asset classes and securities. The absence of benchmarks makes it difficult to evaluate the performance of Islamic financial institutions.

The dearth of transparent benchmarks that can be used to compare risk-adjusted returns complicates the task of evaluating the efficiency of financial institutions. Such benchmarks are valuable tools for measuring the relative performance of different asset classes and, ultimately, the performance of the financial intermediary. The current practice of using interest-based benchmarks, such as the London Inter-Bank Offered Rate (LIBOR), has been accepted on an ad-hoc basis in the absence of better benchmarks, but several researchers have raised the need to develop benchmarks based on the rate of return, reflecting Islamic modes of financing.

Universal Banking

The nature of financial intermediation and the style of financial products and services offered make Islamic banks a hybrid between commercial and investment banking, similar to a universal bank. Universal banking benefits from economies of scope due to its close relationship, established client base, and access to private information gained through the relationship.

Combining different product lines (such as banking and insurance products) or commercial and investment banking lines may increase the relationship value of banking at a much lower average cost of marketing. Islamic financial institutions could realize the benefits of universal banking by strengthening this aspect.

Regulation, Governance, and Transparency

Corporate governance in Islamic finance entails implementation of a rule-based incentive system that preserves social justice and order among all members of society (Iqbal and Mirakhor 2001). Islamic banks emphasize service to multiple stakeholders. Governance processes and structures inside and outside the firm are needed to protect the ethical and pecuniary interests of shareholders and stakeholders.

Having a shariah board for every institution is not efficient; only one set of shariah-compliant rules is needed for appropriate corporate governance. A shariah board for the system as a whole, consisting of scholars from different disciplines including shariah, economics, finance, and commercial law, is needed to ensure that rules are defined and enforced so that economic agents comply fully with their contractual obligations to all stakeholders (Iqbal and Mirakhor 2003).

Complementing existing arrangements, a harmonized system-wide shariah board could be guided by standardized contracts and practices, set by an international standard-setting self-regulatory association. Such an approach would ensure consistency of interpretation and enhance the enforceability of contracts before civil courts.

Development of Capital Markets

Responding to the current wave of oil revenues and growing demand for shariah-compliant products, Islamic capital markets are expanding at a quickening pace, and stakeholders are starting to realize their potential. Development of institutional infrastructure, such as accounting standards and regulatory bodies, is a step in the right direction. However, the market needs host governments to undertake strong leadership and constructive policy actions.

Replacing Interest Rates by "Information Costs"

It is fundamental in Islamic finance to replace interest-rate benchmarks like LIBOR, EURIBOR, SIBOR, etc. by a rate reflecting all the costs incurred by a financial institution. Information costs reflect somehow the "cost of funds" since it accounts for all expenses needed in order to obtain and transmit information, to develop analysis, to test and elaborate models, and for all other expenses needed for the business.

The information cost expressed in percentage as a rate must be the benchmark for the financial institution rather than interest rates. For more details regarding the substitution of interest rates by information cost theory, refer to Bellalah (1998, 2008, 2009) and the references therein.

2

PRODUCTIVITY GROWTH IN THE GCC
BANKING INDUSTRY, 1999–2007:
CONVENTIONAL VS. ISLAMIC BANKS

1. INTRODUCTION

Market conditions in the banking sector have undergone profound and extensive changes over the last two decades.[1] The liberalization of financial markets, the increasing use of new and advanced technology, the financial innovations, the change in customer preferences, and the information revolution have put competitive pressure on banking institutions and modified the technology of bank production (Carvallo and Kasman 2005; Al-Jarrah and Molyneux 2007). In response to these changes and to rapid globalization, Arab countries, following developed economies, have introduced since the 1980s a series of financial reforms in their banking sector. The economic growth in this region depends on the banking industry, which constitutes the main financial intermediary to manage funds and to channel savings and investment (Iimi 2004). Indeed, in emerging markets, banks remain the principal suppliers of credit to private and public investment projects, besides financing government deficits.

The Gulf Cooperation Council (GCC), which includes six Arab countries, namely Bahrain, Kuwait, Oman, Qatar, Saudi Arabia, and the United Arab Emirates, is a region where the processes of financial liberalization and deregulation have been accelerated recently as part of the GCC countries' overall strategies to free their economies. During the last decade, the financial and monetary authorities in GCC countries have undertaken several changes with the intentions of promoting financial market development and increasing the competitiveness of their banking sector. According to Al-Obaidan (2008) and Srairi

(2009b), these measures included liberalizing trade; encouraging foreign direct investment (FDI); liberalizing interest rates; allowing entry of new private banks, both domestic and foreign;[2] strengthening the central bank's supervisory capacity; and implementing regulations that helped in progressively moving the Gulf States toward market-based economies. We estimate that these economic and financial reforms encouraged competition in the GCC banking sector, which will improve the quality of services offered, diversify products and reduce costs, and in turn increase the efficiency and productivity of banks. To test this hypothesis, we assess the impact of financial-sector reforms on the productivity growth of the GCC banking industry over the period of 1999 to 2007. By employing a non-parametric method, data envelopment analysis (DEA), developed by Fare, et al. (1985), we measure the productivity change of commercial banks operating in six Gulf countries, using the Malmquist productivity index (MPI). In addition, the sampled banks are categorized into two sub-groups: conventional banks and Islamic banks. This enables us to examine the effect of environmental changes on productivity by organizational type. To our knowledge, this is the first study to apply this approach in the comparison of productivity change between conventional and Islamic banks in GCC countries.

Established in 1981, the GCC countries as a regional economic bloc share many common features, notably the similarities in their political, economic, social, demographic, and cultural structures (Peterson 1988). These traits, especially the role of oil in their economies, are important factors in facilitating economic and financial development and growth (Saab 2007). Despite many efforts to diversify their economies, the energy sector continues to dominate the GCC countries' revenues. On average, oil represents more than 80 percent of export receipts and budget revenues, respectively. The non-oil sector is dominated by trade and financial and business services.

Early in their economic development, the GCC countries (through the unified economic agreement in 1981) liberalized their trade and exchange rates regimes, which are pegged to the U.S. dollar (with the exception of Kuwait, which had opted in 2007 for a basket of currencies), opened their capital markets and imported foreign labor. During the last decade, there have increasingly been attempts to reform and liberalize the financial and capital market in this region. In order to integrate their banking systems, the resolution of the 18th summit of GCC countries, held in Kuwait in December 1997, allowed each member state to open branches of its national banks in the other GCC countries. The economic agreement signed in 2001 added other areas of economic cooperation. It allowed GCC citizens and businesses to own and trade shares of joint companies in other GCC countries, and to establish companies as well. According to this economic agreement, the six Gulf countries adopted a common customs tariff in 2003 (reducing it to 5 percent of all imported goods) and created the Gulf customs union, where trade barriers, taxes, and related procedures are reduced or eliminated among them. In addition, a common market was launched in 2008, and GCC states decided to establish a monetary union and to have a single currency before 2010. However, some technical problems may have delayed the realization of this union on the target date. Moreover, since 2005, all GCC countries became members of the World Trade Organization (WTO), and in consequence, are also members of General Agreement on Trade in Services (GATS). On the other hand, the degree of openness of banking systems in GCC states varies from one country to another. In Bahrain, Oman, Qatar, and the UAE, several international banks have been operating for many years without any restrictions. However, Saudi Arabia and Kuwait only started receiving branches of foreign banks in 2004.

The GCC region has been an important financial center for decades. The GCC banking sector is well developed and banks continue to play a major role in economic development. In recent years, GCC banks have witnessed a growth in both size and sophistication as a result of the very favorable economic environment. Since 2002, the GCC economies have been in a relatively strong position and continue to benefit from the sustained rally in oil prices as well as from the healthy performance of the non-oil sector (8 percent growth between 2002 and 2005 in real terms). Nominal GDP, which was $349 billion in 2002, has more than doubled and has risen to $828 billion in 2007. (All figures in this chapter are in U.S. dollars unless otherwise specified.) In real terms, economic growth averaged a solid 7 percent a year during the period 2002–2008. The total assets of banks, which amounted to $310 billion to 2001, have also more than doubled to reach over $854 billion in 2007. Gulf banks are still small compared to the big international banks, but they are financially strong, well capitalized, and have adopted modern banking services (Srairi 2009a). Their operations can be characterized by satisfactory asset quality, adequate liquidity, and high levels of profitability (Islam 2003). Local banks follow International Account Standards (IAS), and the central monetary authorities of Gulf countries have strengthened the prudential norms in line with

Basel I and II requirements. They have also amended their banking regulations to include internal corporate governance, such as establishing transparency and disclosure in financial statements, establishing board-level audit, nomination and compensation committees, and improving risk management (Saidi and Kumar2007). In addition, the participation of foreign banks through joint ventures with local banks and the development of the financial sector in this region[3] have enhanced the performance and the competitiveness of the GCC banking sector. Moreover, international institutions, such as the International Monetary Fund (IMF), World Bank, and Bank for International Settlements (BIS) have played a role in providing technical assistance and building knowledge and capacity to the GCC financial market. According to international ratings agencies, most of GCC banks are expected to continue with robust financial performance in the medium term.

GCC countries have also succeeded in implementing a dual banking system. Indeed, an important number of Islamic banks are operating side by side with traditional banks. In 2007, the financial sector represented about 18 percent of the region's financial system and captured about 36 percent ($178 billion) of the global Islamic financial assets. Islamic institutions are focused on financing and leasing operations. They also manage a wide-ranging portfolio of equities in companies and businesses whose activities are compatible with Islamic rules (Elton 2003). In addition, many conventional banks, especially in Saudi Arabia, Bahrain, UAE, and Kuwait, have added Islamic banking services to their regular banking operations either through a separate Islamic window or through a subsidiary.

The GCC banking sector is expected to become more liberalized, opened, transparent, and better governed. However, with globalization, consumerism, economic diversification, increased Islamic banking activities, deregulation, and the explosion of technology, GCC banks are under greater pressure to be more productive and efficient and to respond quickly to more sophisticated customer needs (Srairi 2009b).

Based on this background, we attempt in this study to examine empirically whether financial liberalization has improved the productivity growth of the GCC banking sector and contributed to the debate about the link between productivity and deregulation. The literature review related to this question has presented mixed results. Empirical studies suggest decrease (see, for example, Elyasiani and Mehdian 1995 for U.S. banks; Grieffell-Tatjé and Lovell 1996 for Spanish banking; Avkiran 2000 and Sathye 2002 for Australian banks), or increase (see, for example, Casu, et al. 2004 for Italian and Spanish banks; Rezitis 2006 for the Greek banking industry; Park and Weber 2006 for Korean banks; Tortosa-Ausina, et al. 2008 for Spanish savings banks) of bank productivity growth in a deregulated period.

By using a sample of 71 commercial banks (48 conventional and 23 Islamic banks), our empirical analysis of productivity change is done in three steps. In the first step, we estimate the total productivity change of GCC banks over the eight-year period, using the output-oriented Malmquist index based on a comparison of adjacent years. To analyze the sources of productivity, this index is decomposed into technical change, efficiency change, scale change, and pure technical change. According to Maniadakis and Thanassoulis (2004, 396), "such decompositions promote the understanding of the determinants of better performance and provide valuable information for managers and planners in both the private and the public sector." Moreover, we compare these Malmquist indices between the two subperiods 1999–2003 and 2003–2007, since 2003, with the economic agreement and the Gulf customs union, the process of liberalization in GCC countries has increased and been reinforced. As a second stage in this chapter, we compare the five Malmquist indexes between the two types of banks and across countries. The first comparison allows us to answer the question if conventional banks are more productive than Islamic banks during the deregulation period in this region. Also, we contrast the Malmquist indexes and its decompositions between the six Gulf States to explore the effect of economic and financial reforms on banks' productivity growth in each country. Finally, in order to investigate the determinants of banking-sector productivity, we regress total productivity change, technical and efficiency change on a number of variables including bank-specific, macroeconomic and financial industry indicators, and using the fixed-effect model. In addition, we complement this analysis by identifying factors that explicate revealed differences in productivity changes across conventional and Islamic banks.

The present chapter is organized as follows. In section 2, we briefly review the relevant literature on productivity changes in financial institutions. We present methodology related to the Malmquist index in section 3, and describe data and variables used in the study in section 4. Section 5 discusses the empirical findings by comparing productivity indices across the country and between conventional and Islamic banks. Section 6 provides conclusions and recommendations.

2. REVIEW OF THE LITERATURE

The empirical literature related to the analysis of productivity growth in financial institutions has been developed tremendously over the last two decades, using both parametric and non-parametric approaches (see Goddard, et al. 2007). Most of these studies were focused especially on developed countries. Notable and recent among them are Daniels, et al. (2005) for U.S. banks; Asmild, et al. (2004) for Canadians banks; Fukuyama and Weber (2002) for Japanese banks; Avkiran (2000) for Australian banks; Tortosa-Ausina, et al. (2008) for Spanish banks; Casu and Girardone (2004) for Italian banks; and Drake (2001) for United Kingdom banks. More recently, there have been a number of research studies that examined banks' productivity in other regions, mainly in Asia and European countries. [See, for instance, Dogan and Fausten 2003 for Malaysia; for Taiwan, Chiou (2009); for India, Rezvanian, et al. (2008); for China, Sufian (2009a); for Turkey, Isik (2008); for Greece, Rezitis (2006); for Portugal, Rebelo and Mendes (2000)].

Another strand of the productivity research has concerned a panel of countries. For instance, Pastor, et al. (1997), using the Department of Economic Affairs (DEA) in the UK technique and Malmquist index with value-added approach, compared the productivity, efficiency and differences in technology of several banking systems in different countries for the year 1992 (United States Spain, Germany, Italia, Australia, United Kingdom, France, and Belgium). They found that banks in France have the highest efficiency level followed by banks in Spain, while the selected banks in the UK were found to be the least efficient in the sample. Casu, et al. (2004) employed parametric and non-parametric approaches to estimate the productivity change in five principal European banking sectors (France, Germany, Italy, Spain, UK) between 1999 and 2000. Overall, the findings suggested an increase of productivity growth for all countries, especially in the Italian (9 percent) and Spanish (9.5 percent) banks. The decomposition of total-factor productivity index showed only an improvement in technological change. In general, the two approaches used in this study yield the same results related to the main components of productivity growth. Jaffry, et al. (2007) examined changes in productivity and technical efficiency levels in the banking sectors of India, Pakistan, and Bangladesh over the period 1993–2001. The results indicate that technical efficiency has generally increased across countries (especially in Indian and Bangladeshi banks) in response to reform. Using Tobit regression, the study has also revealed that the main internal variable, which has a positive impact on efficiency, was the type of business with which each bank is engaged. The sizes and ages of banks were not found to have any effect. Finally, the authors also found a slight upward trend in the total factor productivity (TFP) index. Bangladesh presented the highest levels of Malmquist index, while India registered low levels of TFP. Recently, Delis, et al. (2009) analyzed the relationship between the regulatory and supervisory framework and the productivity growth of 533 banks operating in 22 transition countries over the period 1999–2006. They found that regulations related to the market discipline (Third pillars of Basel II) and restrictions on banks' activities have a positive impact on productivity.

Coming to the Arab Gulf countries, despite considerable development in their banking sector during the last decade, only a few papers have explored the productivity growth of banks in this region. For example, Ariss, et al. (2007) employed the DEA approach to calculate Malmquist productivity index of 45 banks operating in GCC countries. The results show that between 1999 and 2004, these banks on average have experienced a decline in the productivity of their banking system, although in different degrees. The decline in productivity of banking in Kuwait, Oman, and Qatar was due to both technological regress and decline in overall technological efficiency. However, for Bahrain, Saudi Arabia, and UAE, the decline in MPI was the net result of technological regress and improvement in overall technical efficiency. Ramanathan (2007) examines nearly the same sample (over nine banks), the same period (2000–2004), and uses the same approach (MPI and DEA) as that adopted by Ariss, et al. (2007). He finds that all GCC countries have registered reductions in productivity in terms of technology change (a similar result was reached by Ariss, et al. 2007). However, banks in four of the six GCC countries (Bahrain, Kuwait, Saudi Arabia, and the UAE) registered progress in terms of MPI during 2000–2004. The highest improvement in MPI (1 percent) is registered by the selected banks in Bahrain, while the selected banks in Qatar have presented the highest reductions (4 percent) in productivity during the same period. Using data from 52 banks over ten years (1993–2002), Al-Muharrami (2007) employed the same technique as the other two studies. Findings show an overall decrease in total-factor productivity of 5 percent attributed simultaneously to a decline in technical efficiency (3 percent) and technological regress (3 percent). However, in 2002 banks in this region exhibited the highest productivity growth of 6 percent, due mainly to an increase in technological change rather than to that of efficiency.

To fill the gap in the literature related to productivity in GCC banking, the present study complements these three studies cited above and differs from them in several ways. First, we update the period of analysis from 1999–2004 to 1999–2007. Second, we include in our sample Islamic banks which are omitted in the above papers. Third, we undertake a comparison of productivity growth between conventional and Islamic banks. Fourth, we examine the sources of efficiency change by decomposing this index into two other indices: pure technical-efficiency change and scale-efficiency change. Fifth, our specification of inputs and outputs differs completely from these studies by using a profit-oriented approach of Drake, et al. (2006). Finally, in the second stage of our analysis, we attempt to explore the effect of a number of variables on productivity change for the two groups of banks: conventional and Islamic.

3. METHODOLOGY

In order to investigate productivity change in the banking industry of the GCC countries during the period 1999–2007, we use a two-stage procedure. In the first stage of analysis, we employ a non-parametric frontier approach[4] to calculate the Malmquist productivity index (MPI) and its components. In the second stage, we examine the determinants influencing the conventional and Islamic banks' productivity changes.

In the banking literature, the Malmquist index, introduced firstly by Caves, et al. (1982), was frequently used to evaluate productivity change. According to Grifell-Tatjé and Lovell (1997), the Malmquist index, as a measure of change in total-factor productivity (TFP) from year to year, presents several advantages relative to the other index numbers (Fisher 1922; Tornqvist 1936). First, it does not make any assumptions on the economic behavior of production unity, such as cost minimization or profit maximization. Second, it does not require information about prices of input and outputs. MPI uses only quantity information. Finally, the Malmquist index provides further information about the sources of productivity change. Hence, if panel data is available, it can be decomposed into several components: technical change (shifts in the frontier), efficiency change (catch-up to the frontier), pure technical-efficiency change (improvements in management practices) and scale-efficiency change (improvements toward optimal size).

In this section, we briefly describe the theoretical details[5] to calculate the output-oriented[6] Malmquist productivity indexes. Let

(x^t, y^t) represent the observed input and output vectors of a bank at time period t = 1,2,.....T. Following Fare, et al. (1994), the Malmquist index (M) based on ratios of output-distance functions[7] between periods t (the reference technology period) and t+1 (the base technology period) can be defined as:

$$M^t = \frac{D^t(x^{t+1}, y^{t+1})}{D^t(x^t, y^t)}$$ Equation 1

Where Dt (x^{t+1}, y^{t+1}) represents the distance from the period t+1 observation to the period t technology. This distance measures the maximum proportional change in outputs required to make (x^{t+1}, y^{t+1}) feasible in relation to the technology at t (Casu, et al. 2004).

In the case that t+1 is the reference technology period, equation (1) becomes:

$$M^{t+1} = \frac{D^{t+1}(x^{t+1}, y^{t+1})}{D^{t+1}(x^t, y^t)}$$ Equation 2

To avoid the choice of arbitrary benchmark, the Malmquist TFP index can be calculated as the geometric mean of M^t and M^{t+1}:

$$M = \left[\frac{D^t(x^{t+1}, y^{t+1})}{D^t(x^t, y^t)} x \frac{D^{t+1}(x^{t+1}, y^{t+1})}{D^{t+1}(x^t, y^t)} \right]^{1/2}$$ Equation 3

Alternatively, in the assumption of constant return to scale (CRS), the equation (3) can be written as:

$$M = \frac{D^{t+1}(x^{t+1}, y^{t+1})}{D^t(x^t, y^t)} \left[\frac{D^t(x^{t+1}, y^{t+1})}{D^{t+1}(x^{t+1}, y^{t+1})} x \frac{D^t(x^t, y^t)}{D^{t+1}(x^t, y^t)} \right]^{1/2}$$ Equation 4

The first term in equation 4 represents the efficiency change or the catching-up effect (EFFCH) and shows how much closer a bank gets to the efficient frontier (Isik and Hassan 2003). The index inside the brackets (geometric mean of the shift in technology between two periods) denotes the technical-change effect or the frontier-shift effect (TECCH), and indicates whether the best practice relative to the evaluated bank compared is improving, stagnating, or deteriorating (Tortosa-Ausina, et al. 2008). These shifts in the production frontier could be due to the change of market structure (bank-merged, increased competition), the change of government policy (financial liberalization or deregulation), and the innovations in management (customer-relationship management systems) or in production processes (Angelidis and Lyroudi 2006; Chiou 2009). Thus, the total-factor productivity change (TFPCH) can be defined as the product of technical efficiency change and technical change:

$$TFPCH = EFFCH \times TECCH \qquad \text{Equation 5}$$

A TFP index value greater than one implies increases in productivity, while a value less than one indicates productivity deterioration; value concentrated around one indicates no productivity change. The same interpretation applies to other Malmquist indices.

In the assumption of variable return to scale (VRS), Fare, et al. (1994) showed that there are two additional sources of productivity growth. Thus, the efficiency change (EFFCH) calculated under CRS can be further decomposed into two components[8]: the pure technical- efficiency change (PEFFCH) and the scale-efficiency change (SECH). These two indexes can be formulated as:

$$PEFFCH(VRS) = \frac{D^{t+1}(x^{t+1}, y^{t+1} / VRS)}{D^{t}(x^{t}, y^{t} / VRS)} \qquad \text{Equation 6}$$

$$SECH(VRS) = \left[\frac{D^{t}(x^{t}, y^{t} / VRS)}{D^{t}(x^{t}, y^{t} / CRS)} x \frac{D^{t+1}(x^{t+1}, y^{t+1} / CRS)}{D^{t+1}(x^{t+1}, y^{t+1} / VRS)} \right]^{1/2} \qquad \text{Equation 7}$$

Hence, we have: $EFFCH = PEFFCH \times SECH$ Equation 8

The PEFFCH measures the changes in proximity of banks to the frontier. According to Chiou (2009), this index represents the manner that managers in banks manage input resources more efficiently between two periods. The SECH indicate improvements towards the optimal scale in terms of cost control (Isik and Hassan 2003).

Finally, the complete decomposition of the Malmquist TFP index becomes:

$$TFPCH = TECCH \times PEFFCH \times SECH \qquad \text{Equation 9}$$

The above five Malmquist indexes (TFPCH, TECHH, EFFCH, PEFFCH, SECH) are defined with a set of distance functions, which can be estimated using the DEA approach (see, for instance, Charnes, et al. 1994). More specifically, to calculate these indices, a total of six different linear programming problems have to be solved (see Coelli, et al. 1998 for details) corresponding to six output-distance functions: $D^t(x^t, y^t)$, $D^{t+1}(x^{t+1}, y^{t+1})$, $D^t(x^{t+1}, y^{t+1})$, $D^{t+1}(x^t, y^t)$, $D^{t+1}(x^{t+1}, y^{t+1}/$ VRS), $D^t(x^t, y^t/VRS)$. Each of these distance measures presented in equations 4, 6, and 7 are computed for each bank in each adjacent pair of time periods $((t, t+1), \ldots\ldots\ldots, (T-1, T))$.

Once the Malmquist productivity indices are calculated,[9] we run regressions in order to explain the variations in the TFP, efficiency, and technical change. In particular, by using the fixed-effect model,[10] we examine the effect of bank-specific characteristics and economic and financial environmental factors on the productivity changes of conventional and Islamic banks.

The general form of this model is:

$$M = \alpha R + \text{\ss} E + \varepsilon \qquad\qquad\qquad \text{Equation 10}$$

Where M is the Malmquist productivity index (TFPCH, EFFCH, TECCH), R represents the vector bank specific, B is the set of external factors, α and ß are the vectors of parameters to be estimated, and the error term ε.

4. Data & Variables

Data

To construct the productivity frontiers, we use annual data from the balance-sheet accounts and income statements of 71 commercial banks (48 conventional and 23 Islamic) operating in six Gulf Arab countries (14 banks in Bahrain, 11 banks in Kuwait, 5 banks in Oman, 8 banks in Qatar, 11 banks in Saudi Arabia, and 22 banks in the United Arab Emirates). The number of banks during the sample period varies between 60 and 71 banks. This is due mainly to the new entry in the sector. We have collected data of banks from Bankscope Database of Bureau Van Dijk's Company. The macroeconomic variables and financial-industry indicators required to analyze the determinants of banks' productivity changes are sourced from annual reports published by central banks in each GCC country and from the International Financial Statistics (IFS).

Since all countries have different currencies, all the annual financial values are converted in U.S. dollars, using appropriate average exchange rates for each year. Also, to ensure comparability of data across countries, all values are deflated to the year 1999, using each country's consumer price index (CPI).

Specification of Inputs and Outputs

As indicated in several research studies, there has been a lack of agreement over what banks produce and over what resources banks consume in the process of production (Berger and Humphrey 1992). Two alternative approaches, namely the intermediation approach and the production approach, are adopted extensively in the most efficiency banking studies to define the inputs and outputs of a financial institution. The intermediation approach, which treats a bank as intermediaries between savers and borrowers, defines loans and other earning assets as outputs, while various funding sources (deposits and other liabilities), labor, and physical capital are treated as inputs. On the other hand, in the production approach, the bank utilizes capital and labor as inputs to produce loans and deposit accounts as outputs. This approach measures outputs in terms of the number of account services;whereas, in the intermediation approach, outputs are measured in value terms [see Berger and Humphrey (1997) and Mester (1987) for a comprehensive discussion of these two approaches]. In the last few years, Berger and Mester (2003) and Drake, et al. (2006) have proposed a new, profit-oriented approach, which treats revenue components as outputs and cost components as inputs. According to Berger and Mester (2003, 80), this approach takes into account unmeasured changes in the quality of banking service by including higher revenues paid for the improved quality, and it helps to capture the profit-maximization goal by including both the costs and revenues. Furthermore, the profit-oriented approach has the advantage to better understand the strategies banks use to respond to the changes in environment (Pasiouras 2008).

Following Drake, et al. (2006), Pasiouras (2008a), and Sturm and Williams (2004), among others, we adopt in this study the profit-oriented approach to define inputs and outputs. Accordingly, three inputs and two outputs are selected to estimate Malmquist indexes. Hence, the vector of inputs comprises: employee expenses ($\times 1$), other operating expenses ($\times 2$) and loan-loss provisions ($\times 3$). The third input is chosen to capture the cost of risk-taking in lending (Leightner and Lovell 1998). Since Gulf commercial banks have been more engaged in non-traditional activities in recent years, we include the variable non-interest income in our model to proxy these business activities.[11] Rogers (1998) argue that models which ignore off-balance sheet activities understate bank efficiency. Thus, the two outputs concern: net interest income ($y1$ = interest income – interest expense) and other operating income ($y2$ = fee and commission).

Determinants of Productivity

In addition to computing Malmquist indexes, we conduct regression analysis in this stage of the study to examine the effect of a number of variables on the bank–productivity growth. The vector of explanatory variables comprises: five bank-specific characteristics, three macroeconomic indicators, and three financial-industry determinants.

Following several studies that examine productivity change in the banking sector (see for example, Chiou 2009; Sufian 2009b; Isik and Hassan; 2003, and Jaffry, et al. 2007), we select in our model of regression (equation 10) the following variables related to internal factors of bank: size, capitalization, diversification, quality of management, and loan intensity.

We use the logarithm bank asset as a proxy for bank size. Empirical studies presented mixed results. Mukherjee, et al. (2001); Isik and Hassan (2003); and Sufian (2009b) found that larger banks have more productivity growth. However, other researches report no significant (Sathye 2002; Chiou 2009) or negative (Dogan and Fausten 2003) relationship between size and productivity scores. Capital adequacy is measured as equity divided by total assets. The results of many studies (see, for instance, Mukherjee, et al. 2001; Sufian and Haron 2008) show that higher capitalization associates with lower productivity growth. In contrast, some research (see, for example, Esho 2001; Kaparakis, et al. 1994) found that capital adequacy is positively related to productivity change. According to Chiou (2009), bank with capital strength has more capacity to prevent insolvency and to control managers to improve performance; in consequence, the productivity of banks can be increased. To capture the effect of diversification on productivity, we follow Wu (2005) and include in our model the ratio non-interest income to total income as a measure of diversification of business.[12] In the literature, the effect of this variable is ambiguous. Dogan and Fausten (2003) in the case of Malaysian banks found that specialization has a negative effect on productivity change, while several studies (see, for example, Mukherjee, et al. (2001) and Fung (2006), concerning the U.S. banking industry; Chan and Liu (2006) and Chiou for Taiwanese banks) reveal that more specialized banks are associated with higher productivity growth. A fourth variable, other operating expenses in total assets, is included as a measure of bank-management quality and is expected to be negatively related to productivity. The last measure of banks concerns the proxy of loan intensity, which is calculated as loans to total assets. According to Mukherjee, et al. (2001, 933), "loans are the most risky and least liquid of assets." In consequence, this ratio also measures some of this risk. Generally, since loans are the principal source of a bank's income, hence higher lending could be transformed into higher efficiency and productivity.

To isolate the effect of bank-specific on productivity change, we also control in this study for cross-country differences in the microeconomic conditions and structure of the financial industry. Three macroeconomic variables are chosen: per capita GDP, degree of monetization, and inflation rate. Per capita GDP is used as an index of country economic development. Many studies (see, for instance, Jaffry, et al. 2007; Fries and Taci 2005) suggested that higher growth in macroeconomic conditions is translated into higher demand for credit and higher efficiency and productivity. The degree of monetization is the ratio of money supply (M2) to the gross domestic product (GDP). This economic indicator is also expected to have a positive impact on the bank productivity. The rate of inflation is proxied by the growth of CPI. Banks obtain higher profits in higher inflationary countries and should be more efficient and productive (Jaffry, et al. 2007).

As in Srairi (2009a) and Pasiouras (2008b), among others, we also examine the impact of the development of the financial sector in each country on productivity by using three indicators: banking-sector development, financial-market development, and banking concentration. The credit to the private sector divided by GDP represents the proxy of banking development. This variable is also used to measure the importance of bank financing in the economy. Financial-market development is calculated as a stock-market capitalization to GDP. It indicates the importance of the stock market in financing the economy. Bank productivity may also be affected by the concentration ratio, which is computed as the assets of the three largest banks divided by the total assets of the sector. All these indicators are expected to be positively related to productivity growth. Table 2.1 gives the summary statistics of these variables in each country. First, we can observe that there are large differences in all macroeconomic measures across GCC countries. Second, the banking-development ratio is still far below the comparable levels which exceed 100 percent in developed countries. Thus, the banking sector in Gulf countries has ample room for growth. A third feature of the data is the variation in financial-market development between countries. This index ranges from 38 percent in Oman to 115 percent in Kuwait. Finally, the ratio of concentration is relatively high and differs widely across countries (UAE, 42 percent; Bahrain, 87 percent).

Table 2.1   Descriptive Statistics of Country-Specific Variables (average values)

Variables/ Country	UAE	Saudi Arabia	Bahrain	Kuwait	Qatar	Oman
Per capita GDP (U.S.)	2,4041	11,193	15,009	20,229	34,908	10,074
Degree of monetization	64.59	41.11	74.62	70.68	43.83	33.91
Inflation rate	5.05	0.57	1.04	2.26	5.18	1.00
Banking-sector development	43.18	30.81	27.29	55.72	31.14	37.39
Financial-market development	100.14	87.01	104.56	115.42	99.18	38.08
Concentration ratio	42.52	50.41	87.21	60.88	78.08	80.73

Note: All variables are in percentages, except where indicated.

5. Empirical Results & Analysis

First, we estimate the productivity changes for 71 commercial banks operating in GCC countries using the output-oriented Malmquist index. Then, we divide our sample into two groups—conventional banks and Islamic banks—to analyze the relationship between productivity growth and type of bank and to explore the sources of productivity change in each group. We also compare Malmquist indexes between different countries in the Arab Gulf region to examine the impact of liberalization and deregulation on productivity. Finally, we attempt to identify internal and external factors that explicate differences in productivity changes between conventional and Islamic banks.

Estimation of Malmquist Productivity Indices in the GCC Banking Sector

Table 2.2 summarizes the annual geometric means of five types of Malmquist indices (TFPCH, TECCH, EFFCH, PEFFCH, and SECH) for the entire sample (Panel A), for conventional banks (Panel B), and for Islamic banks (Panel C). It also reports the Malmquist indexes for both pairs of consecutive years and the two sub-periods 1999–2003 and 2003–2007 and the whole sample period 1999–2007. All indices are calculated for adjacent periods instead of the fixed-based periods.[13] A value of one for the Malmquist index and its components indicates stagnation in productivity growth; a value >1 indicates productivity gain, and a value <1 indicates productivity decline.

Table 2.2 Malmquist Productivity Indexes in GCC Banks in Consecutive Years and by Type of Bank during the 1999–2007 Period

Bank Type/Years	Total Factor Productivity Change (TFPCH)	Technical Change (TECCH)	Technical Efficiency Change (EFFCH)	Pure Technical Change (PEFFCH)	Scale Efficiency Change (SECH)
Panel A: All Banks					
1999–2000	0.944	0.976	0.968	0.962	1.007
2000–2001	0.967	0.960	1.007	0.990	1.018
2001–2002	0.979	0.949	1.032	1.101	0.946
2002–2003	1.009	1.079	0.962	1.013	0.951
2003–2004	1.074	1.029	1.049	1.001	1.049
2004–2005	1.044	1.036	1.008	1.024	0.983
2005–2006	1.082	1.072	1.009	0.996	1.013
2006–2007	1.055	1.060	0.995	1.002	0.993
1999–2003	0.975	0.983	0.992	1.015	0.980
2003–2007	1.064	1.049	1.015	1.006	1.009
Geometric Average	1.018	1.015	1.003	1.010	0.994
Panel B: Conventional Banks					
1999–2000	0.930	0.975	0.953	0.938	1.016
2000–2001	0.934	0.943	0.990	1.041	0.952
2001–2002	0.941	0.923	1.020	1.115	0.951
2002–2003	1.044	1.105	0.944	1.031	0.915
2003–2004	1.087	1.036	1.052	0.988	1.072
2004–2005	1.065	1.057	1.007	1.015	0.992
2005–2006	1.102	1.106	0.996	0.988	1.008
2006–2007	1.097	1.086	1.010	1.020	0.990
1999–2003	0.961	0.984	0.976	1.029	0.958
2003–2007	1.088	1.071	1.016	1.003	1.015
Geometric Average	1.022	1.027	0.996	1.016	0.986
Panel C: Islamic Banks					
1999–2000	1.001	0.977	1.023	1.057	0.968
2000–2001	1.013	0.997	1.017	1.032	0.985
2001–2002	0.948	0.971	0.976	1.052	0.927
2002–2003	1.019	0.999	1.019	0.954	1.068
2003–2004	1.017	0.993	1.025	1.032	0.993
2004–2005	1.007	0.998	1.010	1.048	0.963
2005–2006	1.035	0.993	1.041	1.014	1.026
2006–2007	1.004	1.010	0.995	0.995	0.999
1999–2003	0.995	0.986	1.009	1.023	0.986
2003–2007	1.016	0.998	1.018	1.027	0.995
Geometric Average	1.005	0.992	1.013	1.022	0.990

Notes: All indexes are geometric averages. TFPCH = TECCH × EFFCH. EFFCH = PEFFCH × SECH.

Over the sample period, the results in table 2.2 (panel A) indicate that, on average, the annual productivity growth rate of banks in GCC countries grew by 1.8 percent as a result of improvement in technical change (1.5 percent) and a smaller increase in efficiency change (0.3 percent). The latter, in turn, is due to the improvement in pure technical efficiency (1 percent) rather than in sale efficiency (–0.06 percent), implying perhaps the improvement in management practices of the GCC banking sector during the period 1999–2007. Looking at changes through the years, it is also apparent from panel A of table 2.2 that commercial banks in GCC countries have experienced a productivity loss between 1999 and 2002. However, since 2003 the total-factor productivity has exhibited a progress that ranges between about 4 percent and 8 percent. Hence, in the second subperiod (2003–2007), the average annual productivity increased by 6.4 percent, while productivity decreased by 2.5 percent in the first subperiod (1999–2003). The deterioration of productivity in this period is dominated by the decline in technical change (1.7 percent) and a small decrease of efficiency change (0.8 percent). These findings are in line with those of Ariss, et al. (2007) and Al-Muharrami (2007) who found an overall decrease in TFP of Arab Gulf banks during the period 1999–2004. However, the main source of productivity gains in the second sub-period was technical change (4.9 percent) rather than efficiency change (1.5 percent). Indeed, this period witnessed heavy investment to introduce advanced technologies in the GCC banking sector, such as automated-teller machines (ATMs), credit and debit cards, points-of-sale networks (POS), home banking, and telephone and online banking.[14] In addition, the high growth of productivity in the second period of study (after 2003) can be explained by the increase of competition between banks due to the accelerated liberalization and deregulation of the banking system in GCC countries and by the very favorable economic environment in this region as a result of the considerable increase in oil prices. During the last six years, commercial banks in GCC countries have been forced to operate more efficiently and utilize new technologies in order to compete with foreign banks and other financial companies whose numbers have increased considerably in this period.

Productivity Growth of Conventional vis-à-vis Islamic Banks

We now turn to an analysis of productivity change relative to conventional and Islamic banks in GCC countries. A comparison of panels

B and C of table 2.2 reveals some important differences between the two groups of banks. Under the sample period, for both conventional and Islamic banks, the average annual total-productivity change is constantly positive except in the first years of study (2000, 2001, and 2002). However, the productivity growth rate in conventional banks (2.2 percent) was significantly higher than in Islamic banks (0.5 percent). It appears that conventional banks are more exposed to competition in the period of liberalization than Islamic banks. The source of productivity gains for conventional banks was mainly technical progress (2.7 percent). On the contrary, the productivity growth of Islamic banks is attributed to enhancement in efficiency change (1.3 percent) rather than improvement in technological efficiency (regress of 0.8 percent). These findings suggest that the major differences between conventional and Islamic banks are related to technical change. It is apparent that Islamic banks have experienced some difficulties to improve their production technologies in the period of study. Furthermore, the decomposition of efficiency change into two components (PEFFCH and SECH) shows that both conventional and Islamic banks enjoyed improvement in pure technical efficiency (1.6 percent vs. 2.2 percent) and decline in scale efficiency (1.4 percent vs. 1 percent). According to Sufian (2009a, 123), this result implies that these banks are relatively efficient in managing their operating costs but have been operating at a non-optimal scale of operations.

While substantial changes and reforms are taken in the GCC banking industry essentially after 2003, it is interesting to compare the productivity change and its components of the two groups of banks in the two sub-periods 1999–2003 and 2003–2007. As can be seen from table 2.2 (panels B and C), in both cases of conventional and Islamic banks, the productivity growth rate is higher in the second sub-period than in the first one. For conventional banks, the TFPCH increases by around 8.8 percent in the second period as a result of an increase in both efficiency change (1.6 percent) and technical change (7.1 percent). The enhancement in efficiency change seems to be due to a slight improvement of pure efficiency (0.3 percent) and higher scale efficiency increase of 1.5 percent. In the case of Islamic banks, the rate of productivity change (0.5 percent), as well as the technical change (1.4 percent), are also negative in the first sub-period, like in conventional banks (TFPCH $=-3.9$ percent TECCH $=-1.6$ percent), indicating their difficulties to better exploit new technologies. However, in the second sub-period, the TFPCH for Islamic banks has improved (1.6 percent) as liberalization and deregulation have proceeded. The source of this improvement is attributed to an increase in technical efficiency (1.8 percent) and a lower deterioration in technical change (0.2 percent). Most of the efficiency gains in Islamic banks throughout the second sub-period result mainly from the improvement in pure technical efficiency (2.7 percent).

In order to determine whether differences in the Malmquist indexes between conventional and Islamic banks have statistical significance, we use the non-parametric Mann-Whitney U test. The results show that there were significant differences between the two groups of banks at 5 percent level in TFPCH ($Z = 4.631$, prb>Z = 0.001), EFFCH ($Z = -2.687$, prb>Z = 0.028) and TECCH ($Z = 2.641$, prb>Z = 0.021). In contrast, the other Malmquist indices PEFFCH ($Z = 1.213$, prb>Z = 0.276) and SECH ($Z = 0.057$, prb> $Z = 0.198$) are not statistically significant. In consequence, we can conclude that conventional banks in GCC countries outperformed Islamic banks in terms of total productivity change. While the productivity gain is mainly driven by technical change in conventional banks, it is dominated by efficiency change in Islamic banks.

Analysis of Productivity Growth Measures by Country

The mean annual values of Malmquist productivity index and its components of each country in the Gulf region are provided in table 2.3 for the whole period (1999–2007) and for the two sub-periods 1999–2003 and 2003–2007.

Overall, as can be seen in table 2.3, on average all GCC countries, with the exception of sultanate Oman, have exhibited high TFP change during the sample period 1999–2007. In particular, the United Arab Emirates (3.7 percent), Bahrain (3 percent), and Saudi Arabia (2.1 percent), have the highest TFP growth rate while Qatar (1.7 percent) and Kuwait (0.7 percent) presented much lower TFPCH. The results indicate that selected banks in UAE, Bahrain, and Saudi Arabia have reacted more quickly than other banks in response to the liberalization and deregulation of their financial system. It appears that reforms undertaken lastly in these countries have affected positively the productivity growth of banks. Indeed, with a rapid growth of the economic situation in these countries during the last seven years, commercial banks have made heavy investments in technology to develop their communication networks and information systems. The improvement of TFPCH in banks of these countries is mainly attributed to technical progress which ranges between 2.9 percent (UAE) and 3.8 percent (Bahrain) and is less due to efficiency change. However, Kuwait and Oman suffered from negative technical change

Table 2.3 Malmquist Productivity Indexes in GCC Banks (1999–2007)

Country/ Year	Total Factor Productivity Change (TFPCH)	Technical Change (TECCH)	Technical Efficiency Change (EFFCH)	Pure Technical Change (PEFFCH)	Scale Efficiency Change (SECH)
Bahrain					
1999–2007	1.030	1.038	0.992	0.995	0.996
1999–2003	0.990	1.010	0.980	0.994	0.985
2003–2007	1.069	1.063	1.005	0.998	1.007
Kuwait					
All period	1.007	0.998	1.009	1.012	0.997
1999–2003	1.006	0.993	1.013	1.008	1.004
2003–2007	1.007	1.003	1.004	1.014	0.990
Qatar					
1999–2007	1.015	1.015	1.000	1.007	0.993
1999–2003	1.017	1.012	1.004	1.016	0.990
2003–2007	1.013	1.018	0.995	0.998	0.996
Oman					
1999–2007	0.995	0.982	1.013	1.022	0.991
1999–2003	0.986	0.962	1.025	1.024	1.001
2003–2007	1.003	1.002	1.000	1.019	0.981
Saudi Arabia					
1999–2007	1.021	1.031	0.990	1.010	0.980
1999–2003	0.981	1.014	0.967	1.002	0.964
2003–2007	1.058	1.044	1.013	1.017	0.996
UAE					
1999–2007	1.037	1.029	1.007	1.013	0.994
1999–2003	0.992	0.993	1.001	1.004	0.998
2003–2007	1.077	1.065	1.011	1.021	0.990
All Countries	1.018	1.015	1.003	1.010	0.994

Note: All indexes are geometric averages, TFPCH = TECCH × EFFCH, EFFCH = PEFFCH × SECH.

and exhibited on average a positive EFFCH of 1 percent, owing to increase in pure technical efficiency (1.2 percent and 2.2 percent respectively for Kuwait and Oman). Furthermore, as observed in table 2.3, the dominant source of efficiency change increases in most GCC countries was related to improvements in managerial practices (PEFFCH) rather than scale-related change (SECH).

Regarding the Malmquist productivity indexes in the two sub-periods 1999–2003 and 2003–2007, we note first of all that the TFP growth of most GCC countries in the second sub-period is positive and quite larger than in the first period. Only in Kuwait and Qatar the differences between TFPCH are slightly large. The growth in this second period is mainly due to the implementation of new technologies

(TECCH ranges between 0.2 percent and 6.5 percent) and less due to the improvement in efficiency change (EFFCH ranges between −0.5 percent and 1.3 percent). On the contrary, during the first sub-period, we observe a decrease in TFPCH in countries such as Bahrain (−10 percent), Oman (−14 percent), Saudi Arabia (−19 percent) and UAE (−8 percent), whereas banks in Kuwait (0.6 percent) and Qatar (1.7 percent) experienced a smaller increase in TFPCH. The major source of a productivity loss in UAE, Kuwait, and Oman was technical regress while it was an efficiency decrease for Saudi and Bahraini banks. Overall, the pattern of productivity growth in this first period is characterized by a decline in productivity and in technical change. Our findings related to this period are generally in conformity with those found by Ariss, et al. (2007) and Al-Muharrami (2007).

Determinants of GCC Banks' Productivity Growth

In the second stage of this analysis, we regress three Malmquist indexes, TFPCH, EFFCH, and TECCH, on a number of variables including bankcharacteristic, macroeconomic-indicator, and financial-structure measures by employing the fixed-effect model. The regression results concerning the determinants of banks' productivity change for the full sample and for conventional and Islamic banks are reported in table 2.4.

Regarding bank-specific variables, the results indicate that the coefficient of size has a positive and statistically significant effect on productivity (TFPCH at 5 percent level) and technical change (TECCH at 1percent level) for all banks and conventional-bank models. This finding, which is supported by several studies (Worthington 1999 for Australian credit unions; Mukherjee, et al. 2001 for U.S. commercial banks; and Sufian and Haron 2008 for the Malaysian Islamic banking sector), implies that productivity improvements are higher for large banks than for smaller ones. The positive relationship between size and productivity growth can be explained by the fact that large banks have the capacity to invest and utilize better new technologies, to hire a qualified team, and to have more diversified products and services (Kyj and Isik 2008; Sufian 2009b). Furthermore, the results suggest that conventional banks have benefited from a higher productivity growth due to their size (conventional banks are three times bigger than Islamic banks) and to the improvement in technical change compared to Islamic banks.

The proxy of capital adequacy (equity/total assets) for Islamic banks model reveals a significant negative relation to efficiency

Table 2.4 Regression Results on the Determinants of Bank Productivity Change

Type of Bank/Explanatory Variables	All Banks			Conventional Banks			Islamic Banks		
	EFFCH	TECCH	TFPCH	EFFCH	TECCH	TFPCH	EFFCH	TECCH	TFPCH
Bank Characteristics									
Size	0.036	0.127*	0.131**	0.039	0.661**	0.117**	0.063	0.106	0.077
	(0.46)	(3.01)	(2.03)	(0.43)	(2.98)	(2.18)	(0.50)	(1.09)	(0.43)
Capitalization	0.230	0.135	0.119	1.005	0.054	1.191	−2.491**	0.117**	−1.000
	(0.24)	(1.04)	(1.20)	(0.43)	(0.99)	(0.94)	(−2.95)	(2.18)	(−1.42)
Diversification	−0.629	−1.734**	−1.582*	−0.348	−3.270*	−1.864*	−1.240**	−0.094	−1.634**
	(−1.79)	(−2.33)	(−3.73)	(−0.65)	(−2.72)	(−3.05)	(−2.27)	(−0.20)	(−2.65)
Quality of management	−0.741**	0.436	−0.039	−0.733**	0.785	−0.910	−0.948**	−0.061	−0.033
	(−2.59)	(1.06)	(−0.96)	(−2.47)	(1.84)	(−1.21)	(−2.39)	(−0.97)	(−0.37)
Credit risk	−0.544	−1.959**	−0.327	−0.780	−2.290**	−0.380	0.533	0.075	0.454
	(−1.52)	(−2.73)	(−1.13)	(−1.76)	(−2.25)	(−0.73)	(1.23)	(0.25)	(0.67)
Financial and Economic Variables									
Per capita GDP	0.119	0.032	0.847***	0.138	0.171	0.699***	0.367	0.042	0.033
	(1.30)	(0.47)	(1.97)	(1.29)	(0.85)	(2.13)	(0.50)	(0.82)	(0.26)
Degree of monetization	0.035	0.253	0.462***	0.074	0.412	0.562	0.253	0.084	0.049
	(0.50)	(0.22)	(2.15)	(0.95)	(1.46)	(2.31)	(0.22)	(1.13)	(0.22)
Inflation rate	0.041	0.134	0.069	0.092	0.254	0.057	0.613	0.015	0.073
	(0.78)	(0.91)	(1.27)	(0.81)	(0.36)	(0.48)	(0.85)	(0.23)	(1.20)
Banking sector development	0.167*	0.674	0.158	0.387*	0.668	0.064	0.956**	0.072	0.042
	(2.59)	(0.75)	(1.47)	(2.66)	(0.99)	(0.26)	(2.42)	(1.72)	(1.25)
Financial market development	0.103	0.022	0.033	0.090	0.014	0.028	0.615	0.077	0.330
	(0.62)	(0.05)	(0.20)	(0.47)	(0.15)	(0.94)	(1.02)	(0.37)	(1.15)
Concentration ratio	−0.093	−0.861	−0.025	−0.423***	−0.148	−0.033	−0.023	−0.067	−0.036
	(−0.95)	(−1.48)	(−1.53)	(−1.98)	(−1.02)	(−0.25)	(−0.02)	(−0.59)	(−0.39)
Adjusted R2	0.215	0.272	0.311	0.246	0.271	0.258	0.337	0.148	0.122
Nb. of observation	523	523	523	381	381	381	142	142	142

*Note: t- statistics are between parentheses. *, ** and *** indicate statistical significance at 1%, 5% and 10%, respectively. TECCH: technical change, EFFCH: technical efficiency change, TFPCH: total factor productivity change.*

change (EFFCH) and significant positive relation to technical change (TECCH), a finding consistent with the studies of Sufian and Haron (2008) and Chiou (2009). While Islamic banks in GCC countries are better capitalized than conventional banks, our results mean that banks which held a higher level of equity, have a difficulty in generating scale economy (Islamic banks experienced a SECH decline of 1 percent during the period 1999–2007) and, in consequence, have a negative technical efficiency (Chiou 2009). In addition, banks with higher equity tend to exhibit technical progress. The regression models results for all banks and conventional banks show an insignificant positive relationship between capital adequacy and productivity measures.

The ratio of diversification is statistically significant and negatively related to the most Malmquist indexes (especially TFPCH and TECCH) in all models. It seems that specialized banks are more productive than diversified banks. Although the higher level diversification of banks decreases the risk, it causes banks to be less professional and increases information asymmetry, so that the productivity of banks can be decreased (Chan and Liu 2006; Chiou 2009).

As expected, the indicator of management quality is associated negatively with technical efficiency change (EFFCH) in all models. Similar results are reported by Das and Ghosh (2006) and Sufian (2009b). They argued that a decline of technical efficiency is caused essentially by poor senior management practices, which concern the use of inputs, daily operations, and loan-portfolio management. Their explanation is based on the bad-management hypothesis of Berger and De Young (1997).

Finally, as shown in table 2.4, the loan-to-asset ratio exhibits a negative relationship with all Malmquist levels for all banks and conventional banks models, even though this is not statistically significant (only for TECCH). Dogan and Fausten (2003) and Sufian and Haron (2008), in the case of Malaysian banks, have also found a negative association between productivity growth and loan intensity. Our results support the view that banks with a higher level of loans undertake additional costs and contain more non-performing loans. In contrast, Wu (2005) reports regarding the Australian banking sector that banks with a large share of loans have experienced greater TFP change and technological progress. It is interesting to note that in the regression results of Islamic banks, the ratio of loan intensity is insignificant but related positively to productivity change. This result can be explained by the nature of Islamic products, which present less bad loans and in consequence need less reserve for these loans compared to conventional banks.

Turning to the macroeconomic indicators, two of these variables display the expected signs. Per capita GDP and degree of monetization have a significant positive impact on TFPCH in all banks and in the conventional banks model. This finding provides additional support to the strong association between economic growth and the performance of banks. Indeed, in countries with higher income, the demand for financial products and services increases substantially and generates more revenues for banks (Grigorian and Manole 2005; Sufian 2009b). Since the inflation rate was largely moderate in GCC countries during the period 1999–2007, this variable had an insignificant effect on Malmquist indices.

Regarding the financial-structure variables, table 2.4 suggests that banking-sector development (credit to private sector/GDP) entered the EFFCH all regression models positively and is statistically significant at 5 percent level. This implies that banking development increases the productivity growth of a bank, a result which is supported by several studies (see, for instance, Jaffry, et al. 2007; Pasiouras 2008b). On the other hand, the financial market development variable (stock-market capitalization/GDP) is positively related to all productivity measures, but not statistically significant. On the contrary, some studies (see, for example, Grigorian and Manole 2005) indicate that the development of the stock market can reduce the efficiency and productivity of banks, which is mainly attributed to the decrease of the demand of loans by the best borrowers on the market. Finally, we find a negative and significant relationship between the concentration indicator and efficiency change only for conventional banks. According to Maudos, et al. (2002), banks that operate in a concentrated market can charge higher prices and have less pressure to control their costs. Accordingly, high concentration decreases the productivity growth of banks, a finding that is in contradiction with the market-power hypothesis.

6. CONCLUSION

During the last decade, the process of liberalization and deregulation of the GCC financial system has been realized at an accelerated pace. Indeed, to support economic growth in Gulf countries and to transform their economies into international financial and trade centers, decisions makers and monetary authorities have implemented several important reforms in their banking sectors. These measures included liberalizing interest rates, according new licenses to domestic and foreign banks, implementing progressive legal and regulatory reforms, and reducing the direct government control (Srairi 2009b). In this chapter, we have investigated the effects of these reforms on the productivity growth of the GCC banking sector by comparing conventional and Islamic banks. Our sample consisted of a panel data of 71 commercial banks from six Gulf States. By employing a DEA-based Malmquist productivity index, we have computed total-factor productivity change and its components for each GCC bank in adjacent years during the period 1999–2000 and 2006–2007. Additionally these Malmquist indices are contrasted between two subperiods (1999–2003 and 2003–2007), two groups of banks (conventional and Islamic banks) and countries. Finally, we have examined the factors influencing bank productivity change for all banks and for each type of bank.

Overall, empirical results suggest that GCC banks during the period 1999–2007 have on average experienced productivity progress of about 1.8 percent per year driven essentially by improvement in technical change (1.5 percent) more than by an increase in efficiency change (0.3 percent). This smaller catching-up with best practice was only due to the improvement in management practices (PEFFCH = 1 percent, SECH = –0.06 percent). It is interesting to note that the productivity growth was much lower or negative in the first years of deregulation (TFPCH = –2.1 percent and 0.09 percent in 2001 and 2002, respectively), but with the acceleration of financial and economic reforms, productivity change of GCC banks has rapidly improved (8 percent and 6 percent in 2006 and 2007, respectively). Indeed, a comparison of Malmquist indices between the two subperiods revealed that all GCC banks in the second sub-period had higher TFP change (6 percent), while this index decreased by 2.5 percent in the first sub period (1999–2003) The increase of the productivity change in the second sub-period is also attributed solely to the technological progress (4.9 percent) rather than to efficiency increase (1.5 percent). The results clearly indicate that the productivity of banks has improved significantly in a period of financial liberalization of the GCC banking sector, especially after 2003. We estimate that this fact can be explained by the increase in competition between GCC banks in this period and also by the very favorable economic conditions in these countries. Our findings are in accordance with other recent studies conducted in emerging countries (see, for example, Leightner and Lovell 1998 for Thai banks; Isik and Hassan 2003 for Turkish banks; Koutsomanoli-Filippaki, et al. 2009 for the banking industry in 10 countries of Central and Eastern Europe), which found that deregulation increased the productivity growth of the banking sector.

Furthermore, the empirical findings also show an improvement in productivity of the two types of banks, with conventional banks exhibiting higher productivity change (2.2 percent) than Islamic banks (0.5 percent). The most important sources in determining the level of productivity appear to be technical progress (2.7 percent) for conventional banks, whereas it is due to enhancement of efficiency change (1.3 percent) in the case of Islamic banks. This indicates that conventional banks have benefited from expanding their productivity through capital investment in technology while Islamic banks did not make sufficient investment to take advantage of the new technologies. Moreover, the decomposition of efficiency change into two components indicates that the increase in efficiency change of both conventional and Islamic banks were attributed to the improvement in pure technical efficiency (1.6 percent vs. 2.2 percent) rather than scale efficiency, which declined by 1.4 percent and 1 percent, respectively. This means that all GCC banks are more efficient in managing their input resources than in operating at optimal scale operations.

Concerning the comparative analysis of Malmquist indices in different GCC banking sectors, the results during the sample period suggest clear high productivity change in the Emirati (3.7 percent), Bahraini (3 percent) and Saudi banks (2.1 percent), whereas Qatari (1.7 percent) and Kuwaiti (0.7 percent) banks presented lower productivity and a decline in productivity growth for Omani banks (−0.3 percent). The productivity gains are higher if we consider only the second sub-period (7.7 percent, 6.9 percent and 5.8 percent for the UAE, Bahrain, and Saudi Arabia, respectively). Moreover, productivity increases in the UAE, Bahrain, Saudi Arabia, and Qatar were due to technical-change progress, while Kuwait and Oman suffered from negative technical change and exhibited a small improvement in efficiency change owing to the increase in pure technical efficiency. In view of these results, it appears that the selected banks in UAE, Bahrain, Saudi Arabia, and, to lesser extent, Qatar, have reacted more quicker to the new competitive environment in the Gulf region resulting from financial reforms than other banks in Kuwait and Oman. Indeed, The UAE, Bahrain, and Qatar have the most open financial sectors, as their total banking assets exceed the size of their GDP (167 percent, 114 percent, and 113 percent in 2007, respectively for these countries).

As a side analysis, we have also investigated the effect of a set of bank-specific, macroeconomic and financial variables on GCC banks' productivity growth. The results suggest that bank size has a positive impact on total-productivity change and technical change for all banks and for conventional-banks model. This implies that large banks are more productive that the smaller ones because they have more capacity to invest and utilize new technologies (Kyj and Isik 2008). Our findings are in line with the recent study on the cost efficiency in GCC banks of Srairi (2009b), which also concluded that the larger the size of the bank, the higher the efficiency. We also find that the ratio of equity to total assets is related positively to technical change and negatively to efficiency change for only the Islamic-banks model. This finding could be explained by the fact that banks that hold a higher level of equity have difficulty in generating scale economy while they tend to experience technical progress (Sufian and Haron 2008; Chiou 2009). The ratio of diversification has a negative effect on the most Malmquist indices for all models. This result is in agreement with the opinion that specialization increases the risk but stimulates the productivity growth of banks (Mukherjee, et al. 2001; Chan and Liu 2006). According to Chiou (2009), in a liberalization and competitive environment, specialization is a better strategy for a bank manager who cannot operate too many operational-revenue items. Consistent with our expectations, the proxy of management quality and the ratio of loan intensity are associated negatively to efficiency and technical change in most models. These findings, which are in accordance with several studies (Dogan and Fausten 2003; Das and Ghosh 2006; Sufian and Haron 2008), mean that banks with poor management practices and a large share of loans generate additional costs and, in consequence, are less productive. In contrast, the regression result of Islamic banks reports a positive relationship between Malmquist indices and the ratio of loan to asset. Indeed, Islamic banks provide financing on a partnership, and, in turn, their products contain less bad loans compared to traditional banks. Thus, the higher level of loan intensity may increase the productivity change of the type of bank.

Regarding the macroeconomic and financial indicators, our findings suggest that the degree of monetization, the per capita GDP, and the variable of banking-sector development are significantly and positively related to some Malmquist indexes (especially TFPCH and EFFCH) while the inflation rate and the financial-market-development measure do not have any impact on productivity change in all models. Finally, the empirical results show that the concentration indicator has a significant and negative effect on conventional banks' efficiency change. As the banking sector becomes more concentrated, competition becomes low, intermediation margins are relatively wide, there is less pressure on costs, and banks are likely to experience low productivity growth rates. Overall, these results confirm the strong association between the performance of banks and the characteristics of the environment and the sector in which they are active.

In conclusion, many policy implications and recommendations may follow from the findings of this research. First, since there is an improvement in productivity growth across most of the GCC banking sector over the period of deregulation and liberalization, legislators and regulators in the Gulf region should increase economic integration between their countries, contemplate further liberalization of their financial market, and improve participation of the private sector. Second, the results indicate that large banks are more productive than smaller banks and provide a justification for further mergers among GCC banks. In addition, with the rapid expansion of the GCC economies and the entry of foreign banks, and, due to the limited size of the GCC markets, commercial banks in this region should gradually move toward national, regional, and international consolidation in order to be more competitive and efficient. Such a strategy allows banks to expand their services, improve the quality of their assets, increase their scale of operation and facilitate transfers of new skills and technology. Finally, according to several international ratings agencies (e.g., Standard & Poor's), it is expected that in 10 years Islamic banks will account for 40 to 50 percent of the total savings for the Muslim population, and the potential market for Islamic products is estimated to be $4,000 billion. Thus, Islamic banks have to improve their efficiency and productivity to satisfy the large needs of the market and to compete with conventional banks. Accordingly, while the study shows that Islamic banks have experienced a lower level of productivity growth, both in technical change and technical efficiency, compared to conventional banks, it is necessary for this group of banks to increase the size of investment in information technology and to utilize specialized and automated systems to measure, monitor, and control market credit and operational risk as indicated in Basle II. Furthermore, to improve their technical efficiency, Islamic banks have also to extend their size via mergers and acquisitions with other Islamic financial institutions, create and design new Islamic products and services, and rationalize their operating costs.

3

ANALYSIS OF THE GROWTH & RISE
OF SMALLER ISLAMIC BANKS
IN THE LAST DECADE

INTRODUCTION

What are the reasons behind the recent growth in Islamic finance? Why is Islamic finance developing at a remarkable pace? What are the determinants of the profitability of the Islamic banking sector over the last decade? There are many reasons that can be attributed for the rise in Islamic banking; the first is the strong demand from a large number of immigrant and nonimmigrant Muslims for shariah-compliant financial services and transactions. Second, growing oil wealth has brought a demand for suitable investments, which have been soaring in the Gulf region. Third, the competitiveness of many products have attracted Muslim and non-Muslim investors, and finally, Islamic banking has so far been spared from a serious financial crisis, with the exception of a few minor cases, such as the Dubai Islamic Bank in 1998 and Ihlas Finans in Turkey in 2001.

Since its inception three decades ago, the number of Islamic financial institutions worldwide has risen from one in 1975 to over 300 today in more than 75 countries. They are concentrated in the Middle East and Southeast Asia (with Bahrain and Malaysia the biggest hubs), but they are also appearing in Europe and the United States. Total assets worldwide are estimated to exceed $250 billion, and, although cross-border data remain scarce, they appear to be growing at an estimated 15 percent a year.

Due to the lack of literature, very few articles are written on governance structures in Islamic banking, despite the rapid growth of Islamic banks since the mid 1970s and their increasing presence on world financial markets. There are now over 180 financial institutions worldwide, which adhere to Islamic banking and financing principles. These banks operate in 45 countries encompassing most of the Muslim world, along with Europe, North America, and various offshore locations.

How have conditions in Islamic banking changed overall banking and regulations in the last decade? Within the scope of this chapter, we answer this question by using econometric techniques to provide a cross-country empirical analysis of the rise of smaller Islamic banks.

Islamic banking represents a radical departure from conventional banking, and from the viewpoint of corporate governance, it embodies a number of interesting features, since equity participation, risk, and profit-and-loss sharing arrangements from the basis of Islamic financing. Because of the ban on interest (*riba*), an Islamic bank cannot charge any fixed return in advance, but rather participates in the yield resulting from the use of funds. Depositors also share in the profits, according to a predetermined ratio, and are rewarded with profit returns for assuming risk. Unlike a conventional bank, which is basically a borrower and lender of funds, an Islamic bank is essentially a partner with its depositors, on the one side, and a partner with entrepreneurs, on the other side, when employing depositors' funds in productive direct investment.

The motivation behind our research is limited literature tackling the market structure of the Islamic banking sector. This study contributes to the literature on market structure in Islamic banking systems by using a larger sample of banks over a significant amount of time. We collected our data set collected from 30 paramount banks in the Islamic banking sector for the period 1998–2008. The aim of this research is to analyze the reason and the factors for the rise and growth of smaller Islamic banks and Islamic finance over the last decade. Previous studies of the Islamic banking sector mainly concentrate on the rise of Islamic banking as a whole. Very little literature has focused on the significance and impact of smaller banks Islamic banks on Islamic finance, e.g., Yudistira (2004).

The chapter is divided into five sections. Section 1 provides a review of the literature and section 2 gives a brief overview of Islamic banking. Section 3 demonstrates the methodology used in the chapter. Section 4 offers our empirical findings, and section 5 provides a short summary in conclusion.

1. LITERATURE REVIEW

Choong and Liu (2006) argue that Islamic banking, practiced in Malaysia, deviates from the profit-and-loss-sharing (PLS) paradigm, and in practice, it is not very different from conventional banking. The authors therefore suggest that, for purposes of financial-sector analysis, Islamic banks should be treated in a similar was as their commercial counterparts. A large part of the literature contains comparisons of the instruments used in Islamic and commercial banking and discusses the regulatory and supervisory challenges related to Islamic banking (e.g., Sundararajan and Errico 2002; World Bank and IMF 2005; Ainley, et al. 2007; Sole 2007; Jobst 2007).

A lot of literature that interrogates risks in Islamic financial institutions has been developed, but it does so in theoretical terms instead of thorough analysis of data, while empirical papers on Islamic banks focus on issues related to efficiency (e.g., Yudistira 2004; Moktar, Abdullah, and Al-Habshi 2006).

Hasan, et al. (2003) investigated the relative efficiency of the banking industry of Bahrain by applying a panel data of 31 banks for the years from 1999 to 2000. They employed non-parametric data analysis to estimate efficiency measures. They found that the dominant source of inefficiency of Bahrain banks is due to technical efficiency rather than to allocative efficiency. Hasan, et al. also examined for differences in efficiency measures in Bahrain between domestic and foreign banks. They found that both of the category of banks differ only in scale efficiency. Recent studies by Ozkan-Gunay (1996, 1998), Mahmud and Zaim (1998), Yildirim (1999), and Mercan and Yolalan (2000) concluded that liberalization increased the efficiency of the banking sector. Mahmud and Zaim (1998) focused on private commercial banks, while Cingi and Tarim (2000) studied the efficiencies of 21 commercial banks (some state-owned and some private) with a deposit share of more than 1 percent in the banking sector.

Favero and Papi (1995) found that their results were not sensitive to re-specifying deposits as an output rather than as an input. However Heffernan (2005) indicates that deposits may be treated either as inputs or as outputs. Brown and Skully (2004) believe the use of deposits has been used more as output than input in most bank-efficiency studies that apply DEA technique. Berger, et al. (1993) argued that the chosen approach has an impact on the levels of efficiency scores but that does not imply strong modifications in their rankings.

A research of Islamic financial institutions in 28 countries by Khan and Ahmed (2001) find that credit risk is found highest in *musharakah* (3.69 from a score of 5) followed by *mudarabah* (3.25). Their findings highlight the idea that the bankers perceive profit-and-loss-sharing modes to have higher credit risk. Markup risk is found highest in product-deferred contracts of Istina (3.57). Sundararajan and Errico (2002) opine that, while PLS modes may shift the direct credit risk of Islamic banks to their investment depositors, they may also increase the overall degree of risk of the asset side of the banks' balance sheet since the assets under this mode are not backed by collateral. Their deductive intuition is that, in principle, the ratio of riskier assets to total assets should typically be higher in an Islamic bank than in a conventional bank.

Samad and Hasan's (1999) study on Malaysian Islamic banking reveals that Bank Islam Maylasia Berhad (Bank Islam) performance of risk from 1984 to 1997 in risky business measured by debt-equity ratio (DER), debt to total assets (DTAR) and earning multiplier (EM) increased over the years. DER and EM are significantly related to profitability. In comparison with two conventional banks, Agro Bank (formerly known as Bank Pertanian Maylasia Berhad) and Affin Bank (formerly known as Perwira Habib Bank), Bank Islam risk indicators are lower. The reason for low risk of the Islamic bank is that its investment in government securities is much larger than that for conventional banks.

Berger and Mester (1997) argue that profit efficiency is superior to cost efficiency, since profit efficiency accounts for the errors on the output side, i.e., revenues as well as the input side, i.e., cost. Berger and Mester (1997) further argue that the bank may be more successful in minimizing cost than another firm, but it still makes less profit than other firms because it does not make good choices in its output mix.

Hasan and Marton (2001) proposed that non-U.S. studies found that foreign banks, such as Hungarian banks, are more efficient than domestic banks. Similar results were found by Zaim (1995)and Isik and Hassan (2002) for Turkish banks. Whereas Sathye (2001) reveals that there is no comparative advantage in accruing to foreign banks. Al-Jarrah and Molyneux (2003) in their study include banks in Bahrain, Egypt, Sudan, and Saudi Arabia and found that the Islamic banks are the most efficient banks in their sample. They observed that it was due to the fact that the cost of funds for Islamic banks is relatively cheaper than cost of funds of other financial institutions. Hussein, et al. (2004) found that Islamic banks outperform their conventional counterparts; whereby, in best-practice earnings, Islamic banks can gain 75 percent for their profit while conventional banks would earn 66 percent of their profit. They also proposed that the difference between the profit efficiency of Islamic and conventional banks is due to the difference in performance of commercial rather then investment banks.

Islam has high regard for efficiency, but very few studies have focused on the aspect of Islamic banking efficiency. The bulk of production-efficiency studies of banks have concentrated on conventional banks.

2. ISLAMIC BANKING: AN OVERVIEW

Islamic banking must obey a different set of rules—those of the Holy Qur'an—and meet the expectations of the Muslim community by providing Islamic-acceptable financing modes. These profit-and-loss-sharing methods, in turn, imply different relationships than those under interest-based borrowing and lending. Islamic organizations must serve Allah (God). They must develop a distinctive corporate culture, the main purpose of which is to create a collective morality and spirituality, which, when combined with the production of goods and services, sustains the growth and advancement of the Islamic way of life Janachi (1995). The interest-free banking is based on the Islamic legal concepts of *shirakah* (partnership) and *mudarabah* (profit-sharing). An Islamic bank is conceived as a financial intermediary mobilizing savings from the public on a *mudarabah* basis and advancing capital to entrepreneurs on the same basis.

More than two-thirds of the Islamic finance business originated in the Middle East. The Gulf Cooperation Council (GCC) countries, with the exception of Oman, are all major markets for Islamic finance. Bahrain is regarded as the hub for Islamic finance. Other major non-GCC markets for Islamic finance include Egypt, Malaysia, Turkey, Indonesia, and Pakistan. Malaysia operates a dual banking system promoted by the government. This allows conventional financial institutions, investment banks, commercial banks, and finance companies to launch separate Islamic banking divisions, competing alongside two Islamic banks, Bank Islam Malaysia and Bank Muamalat Malaysia. Bank Negara Malaysia (also known as Central Bank of Malaysia) has its own shariah advisory board, which sets the rules for the entire Islamic banking sector, ensuring the uniformity of products and services.

Over 150 Islamic financial institutions now operate in over 40 countries around the world, from commercial banks, investment banks, and investment companies to leasing and insurance companies.

The Islamic financial system employs the concept of participation in the enterprise, utilizing the funds at risk on a profit-and-loss-sharing basis. This by no means implies that investments with financial institutions are necessarily speculative. This can be excluded by a careful investment policy, diversification of risk, and prudent management by Islamic financial institutions. It is possible that investment in Islamic financial institutions can provide potential profit in proportion to the risk assumed to satisfy the differing demands of participants in the contemporary environment and within the guidelines of the shariah.

Islamic banks around the world have devised many financial products based on the risk-sharing and profit-sharing principles of Islamic banking. For day-to-day banking activities, a number of financial instruments have been developed that satisfy the Islamic doctrine and provide acceptable financial returns for investors. Broadly speaking, the areas in which Islamic banks are most active are in trade and commodity finance, property, and leasing. Almost every Islamic bank has a committee of religious advisers whose opinions are sought on the acceptability of new instruments and services and who have to provide a religious opinion of the bank's activities for year-end accounts.

Central to the framework of corporate governance for Islamic bank is the shariah supervisory board (SSB). The SSB is vital for two reasons. First, those who deal with an Islamic bank require assurance that it is transacting according to Islamic law. Should the SSB report that the management of the bank has violated the shariah, it would quickly lose the confidence of the majority of its investors and clients. Second, some Islamic scholars argue that strict adherence to Islamic religious principles will act as a counter to the incentive problems outlined above. The argument is that the Islamic moral code will prevent Muslims from behaving in ways which are ethically unsound, so minimizing the transaction costs arising from incentive issues. In effect, Islamic religious ideology acts as its own incentive mechanism to reduce the inefficiency that arises from asymmetric information and moral hazard

An investment account operates under the *mudarabah al-mutlaqa* principle, in which the *mudarib* (active partner) must have absolute freedom in the management of the investment of the subscribed capital. The conditions of this account differ from those of the savings accounts by virtue of: (a) a higher fixed minimum amount, (b) a longer duration of deposits, and (c) most importantly, the depositor may lose some of or all his funds in the event of the bank making losses.

Special investment accounts also operate under the *mudarabah* principle and usually are directed toward larger investors and institutions. The difference between these accounts and the investment account is that the special investment account is related to a specified project, and the investor has the choice to invest directly in a preferred project carried out by the bank.

If the paying and receiving of interest is prohibited, how do Islamic banks operate? It is necessary to distinguish between the expressions "rate of interest" and "rate of return." Whereas, Islam clearly forbids the former, it not only permits, but rather encourages, trade. In the interest-free system sought by adherents to Muslim principles, people are able to earn a return on their money only by subjecting themselves to the risk involved in profit sharing. As the use of interest rates in financial transactions is prevented, Islamic banks are expected to undertake operations only on the basis of profit-and-loss-sharing (PLS) arrangements or other acceptable modes of financing. *Mudarabah* and *musharakah* are the two profit-sharing arrangements preferred under Islamic law.

A *mudarabah* is a contract between at least two parties whereby one party, the financier *(sahib al-mal)*, entrusts funds to another party, the entrepreneur *(mudarib)*, to undertake an activity or venture. This type of contract is in contrast with *musharakah*. In arrangements based on *musharakah*, there is also profit-sharing, but all parties have the right to participate in managerial decisions. In *mudarabah*, the financier is not allowed a role in management of the enterprise. Consequently, *mudarabah* represents a PLS contract where the return to lenders is a specified share in the profit/loss outcome of the project in which they have a stake, but no voice.

Under *musharakah*, the entrepreneur adds some of his own to that supplied by the investors, so exposing them to the risk of capital loss. Profits and losses are shared according to pre-fixed proportions, but these proportions need not coincide with the ratio of financing input. The bank sometimes participates in the execution of the projects in which it has subscribed, perhaps by providing managerial expertise.

3. METHODOLOGY

Estimation of Bank Stability

In this chapter we use the Z-score as the measure of bank risk. The Z-score has become a popular measure of bank robustness lately. However, very few studies have used this methodology to measure bank risks, e.g., Boyd and Runkle (1993), Maechler, Mitra, and Worrell (2005) and Martin Čihák and Heiko Hesse (2008). The Z-score can be summarized as $z \equiv (k+\mu)/\sigma$, where k is equity capital and reserves as the percent of assets, μ is average return as percent of assets, and σ is standard deviation of return on assets as a proxy for return volatility The Z-score measures the number of standard deviations in which a return realization has to fall in order to deplete equity, under the assumption of normality of the banks' returns. A higher Z-score corresponds to a lower upper bound of insolvency risk—a higher Z-score therefore implies a lower probability of insolvency risk.

The Z-score applies equally to banks that use a high-risk/high-return strategy and those that use a low-risk/low-return strategy, provided that those strategies lead to the same risk-adjusted returns. If an institution "chooses" to have lower risk-adjusted returns, it can still have the same or higher Z-score if it has a higher capitalization. In this sense, the Z-score provides an objective measure of soundness.

A large portion of Islamic banks' financial liabilities consists of investment accounts that can be viewed as a form of equity investment (generally based on the principle of *mudarabah*). Investment accounts are offered in different forms, often linked to a preagreed period of maturity. The profits and returns are distributed between the depositors and the bank, according to a predetermined ratio, e.g., 80 percent to the depositors and 20 percent to the bank (Iqbal and Mirakhor 2007).

Regression Analysis

Using regression of Z-score as a function of a number of variables, we test the stability of smaller and lager Islamic banks. We estimate the general class of panel models of the form:

$$Z_{i,j,t} = \alpha + \beta B_{i,j,t-1} + \gamma I_{j,t-1} + \Sigma \, \delta_s \, T_s + \Sigma \, \phi_s \, T_s \, I_{j,t-1} +$$
$$\Sigma \, \phi_s \, B_{i,j,t-1} \, T_S + \omega M_{j,t-1} + \Sigma \, \lambda_j \, C_j + \Sigma \, \pi_t \, D_{t+} \, \epsilon_{i,j,i} \quad \text{Formula 3.1}$$

where the dependent variable is the Z-score $z_{i,j,t}$ for bank i in country j at time t $B_{i,j,t-1}$ is a vector of bank-specific variables $I_{j,t-1}$ contains time-varying industry-specific variables; $T_s \, I_{j,t-1}$ are the type of banks and the interaction between the type and some of the industry-specific variables; $M_{j,t}$, C_j and tD_t are vectors of macroeconomic variables, country and yearly dummy variables, respectively; and finally, $\epsilon_{i,j,t}$ is the residual.

A negative sign for the interaction of the Islamic banks' market share and the Islamic bank dummy would indicate that a higher share of Islamic banks reduces their soundness (reduces their Z-scores). We want to examine the Islamic banks' impact on other banks and the hypothesis that the presence of Islamic banks lowers systemic stability; hence, we calculated the market share of Islamic banks by assets for each year and interacted it with Islamic banking dummies.

The regression includes a number of other control variables which levels for bank-level differences in size, asset composition, and cost efficiency, we include the bank's asset size in U.S. dollars(by the billion), loans over assets, and the cost-income ratio. Also, to control for differences in the structure of the bank's income, we calculate a measure of income diversity. This enables us to determine the degree to which banks diversify from traditional lending activities from other activities. For Islamic banks, the net interest income is generally defined as the sum of the positive and negative income flows associated with the PLS arrangements. We also measure differences of Islamic banks in their business orientation; we interact the income diversity variable with the Islamic bank dummy. Controlling for these variables is important because there are differences in these variables between various Islamic banks.

To account for cross-country variation in financial stability caused by differences in market concentration, we include the Herfindahl index, defined as the sum of squared market shares (in terms of total assets) of all major Islamic banks. The index can have values from 0 to 10,000. The macroeconomic and bank specific variables, the Herfindahl index, and the Islamic banks' market share and its interaction with the Islamic and commercial bank dummies are lagged to capture the possible past effects of these variables on the banks' individual risk. We also test for the robustness of the lagged effects by restricting the explanatory variables to contemporaneous effects.

We test for the regression analysis by the pooled ordinary-least-squares (OLS) technique. To test the sensitivity of the results with respect to the estimation method, we also estimate fixed effects and median least squares regressions. We also assess the robustness of the results with respect to the selected sample. Specifically, we estimate the regressions separately for sub-samples of large Islamic banks. We categorize the large Islamic banks as the ones having total assets worth more the $2 billion and all others as small Islamic banks.

The complete list of all the variables used for the regression analysis is as follows:

Z-score. Defined as $z \equiv (k+\mu)/\sigma$, where k is equity capital as percent of assets, μ is average return as percent of assets, and σ is standard deviation of return on assets as a proxy for return volatility. Measures the number of standard deviations a return realization has to fall in order to deplete equity, under the assumption of normality of banks' returns.

Total Assets. The total assets of the bank in USD.

Loans Assets. Ratio of loans to assets (percent).

Exp inc. Ratio of total expenditure to total income.

Income Diversity. 1–| (Net operating income – other operating income).

Total Operating Income.

Islamic Bank Dummy. Equals 1 for large Islamic banks; 0 otherwise.

Market Share. The share of the bank among various paramount Islamic banks in the data set.

Herfindahl Index: Sum of squared market shares of banks in the data set.

Source: Čihák and Hesse 2008.

Data

The data used in this chapter was collected from 30 paramount Islamic banks functioning in different countries of the world for the period 1998–2008. The Islamic banks whose data were collected are ABC Islamic Bank (E.C.), Abu Dhabi Islamic Bank, Al-Baraka Bank (South Africa), Al-Baraka Islamic Bank B.S.C. (E.C.), Al-Rajhi Bank, Al-Baraka Turk Participation Bank, Arcapita Bank B.S.C., Bahrain Islamic Bank B.S.C., Bank Al-Jazira, Bank Asya, Bank Islam Malaysia Berhad, Bank Muamalat, Boubyan Bank, CIMB Islamic Bank Berhad, Faisal Islamic Bank of Egypt, Faysal Bank (Pakistan), Hong Leong Islamic Bank, International Islamic, Islamic Bank Bangladesh Limited, Islamic Bank of Britain, Islamic International Arab Bank, Jordan Islamic Bank for Finance and Investment, Kuwait Finance House, Kuwait Turk Participation Bank, Meezan Bank, Qatar Islamic Bank, RHB Islamic Bank, Sharjah Islamic Bank, Tadhamon International Islamic Bank, and Turkish Finance Participation Bank.

The pooled data was made by combining the data sets from all the banks. The regression analysis was performed on this pooled data to obtain the results, which are mentioned in the next section. The mean square and double accounting techniques were also used on the data set, wherever required.

4. EMPIRICAL ANALYSIS

The summary statistics and regression analysis on the data sample for Islamic banks over the period 1998–2008 are shown in table 3.1. The 1st percentile of the distribution of the income-diversity variable is excluded. The Z-score without the outliers excludes the 1st and 99 th percentile of its distribution

Table 3.1 Summary Statistics of the Data Sample & Regression Results

	Large Islamic banks	Small Islamic banks
Z-score	10.68**	29.21**
Z-score excluding outliers	09.53	15.52
Loans/assets	0.79*	0.66*
Income diversity	0.41	0.39

A. Regression Results: Ordinary Least Squares (dependent variable—Z-score)

Variable	All Banks	Large Banks	Small Banks
Islamic dummy	−1.563 (0.151)	−13.771 (0.011)	5.929 (0.007)
Loan/assets	−2.503 (0.284)**	2.003 (0.332)**	−3.475 (0.023)**
Expenditures/ income	−0.029 (0.007)**	−1.153 (0.636)**	−2.969 (0.449)
Assets	0.192 (0.001)	0.281 (0.003)	−2.112 (0.011)
Income diversity	3.487 (0.474)**	17.734 (0.001)*	−4.873 (0.295)**
Market share		−0.575 (0.064)	0.011 (0.717)
Herfindahl index	−0.001 (0.006)*	−0.005 (0.001)*	−0.001 (0.013)*
R-square	0.177	0.295	0.198
Constant	64.872	88.981	29.326

B. Regression Results: Robust estimation (dependent variable – Z-score)

Variable	All Banks	Large Banks	Small Banks
Islamic dummy	0.22 (0.431)	−6.256 (0.048)	1.235 (0.019)
Loan/assets	−5.727 (0.004)**	−12.026 (0.002)**	−3.292 (0.051)**
Exp_inc	−0.039 (0.009)**	−0.112 (0.001)**	−0.229 (0.009)
Assets	0.082 (0.239)	0.155 (0.047)	−4.571 (0.020)
Income diversity	−1.635 (0.128)**	−2.946 (0.038)*	0.321 (0.295)**
Market share		−0.368 (0.027)	0.019 (0.545)
Herfindahl index	−0.001 (0.104)*	−0.003 (0.153)*	−0.001 (0.262)*
R-square	0.272	0.259	0.181
Constant	55.783	45.357	16.399

Note: p-values are in parenthesis ** and * denotes significance at 1% and 5%, respectively

The basic data analysis suggests that smaller Islamic banks are found to be more stable then larger Islamic banks, as higher Z-scores indicates higher stability. A paired comparison of means suggests that in both cases the difference is significant at the 1 percent level. Table 3.1 also illustrates that the treatment of outliers is important. Furthermore, even with the outliners, we found that the smaller Islamic banks have higher a Z score. The large Islamic banks have, on average, higher loan-to-asset ratios than smaller Islamic banks, reflecting the fact that Islamic banking prohibits investment in non-lending operations, such as regular bonds or T-bills.

We then turn to regression analysis; the results of our tests are shown in table 3.1, parts A and B. Table 3.1, part A will give the results for the OLS estimation, whereas, table 3.1, part B shows results of a robust estimation technique, which assigns lower weights to observations with large residuals, thereby, making the estimation less sensitive to outliers.

The regression results show that smaller Islamic banks are more stable then larger Islamic banks. We observe that for larger Islamic banks, the Islamic dummy is negative while it is positive for smaller banks. We also observe that banks with higher Z scores tend to have low Z scores. Moreover, we found that Z scores tend to increase with bank size for large Islamic banks, but decrease with size for the small Islamic banks.

Our results show that the larger banks have greater income diversity then the smaller banks. This suggests that they do not rely much on income-bearing assets. Similarly, higher expenditure-to-income ratios have a consistently negative link to the Z-scores; the sign is consistently significant, except for regressions for small banks.

We found that the Herfindahl index had a negative impact on Islamic banks. Hence, our findings are in accordance with previous literature; Schaeck, Čihák, and Wolfe (2006) and Čihák and Hesse (2008), who also found higher concentration to be associated with lower stability.

The robust regression results confirms our earlier findings that smaller Islamic banks are more stable than larger banks, as the Islamic dummy is again negative while it is positive for smaller banks.

The difference in the results of income diversity of larger and small banks is important because there are significant differences in these variables between Islamic banks. We observe that the smaller Islamic banks correspond to a higher degree of diversification than the larger banks.

Moreover, we observe that the expenditure-to-income ratio is smaller for smaller Islamic banks than larger Islamic banks in both the OLS regression results and the robust regression results. This can be used to explain the major factor for the rise and growth of smaller Islamic banks and Islamic finance in the last decade, even after the prohibition of investment in non-lending operations, such as regular bonds or T-bills in Islamic banking.

The robust regression results for the Herfindahl index show similar results as the OLS regression, as it is still negative and significant for both the smaller and the larger Islamic banks. We conducted several additional checks to test the robustness of our results; we have also tested for the robustness of the lagged effects by restricting the explanatory variables to contemporaneous effects, finding again no substantive change in the main results.

5. CONCLUSION

This chapter investigates the factors responsible for the rise and growth of smaller Islamic banks in the last decade. Using regression of Z-score as a function of a number of variables, we tested the stability of smaller and lager Islamic banks. We then tested for the regression analysis using the pooled ordinary-least-squares (OLS) technique. Further, we also assessed the robustness of the results with respect to the selected sample on our pooled data set for the period 1998–2008.

Our results show higher Z-scores for smaller Islamic banks; hence, we conclude that smaller Islamic banks are found to be more stable than larger Islamic banks over the last decade, as having higher Z-scores implies higher stability. We found that, even with the outliners, the smaller Islamic banks have a higher Z-score. The large Islamic banks have, on average, higher loan-to-asset ratios than smaller Islamic banks, reflecting the fact that Islamic banking prohibits investment in non-lending operations, such as regular bonds or T-bills. We also observed that Z-scores tend to increase with bank size for large Islamic banks, but decrease with size for the small Islamic banks.

The OLS regression results obtained confirms our previous finding, that smaller Islamic banks are more stable then larger Islamic banks. Our findings suggest that larger banks have greater income diversity than the smaller banks. We also found that expenditure-to-income ratios were negative and significant for larger Islamic banks. Furthermore, the Herfindahl index was found to have a negative impact on Islamic banks.

Our robust regression results prove that the smaller Islamic banks correspond to a higher degree of diversification than the larger banks, which is also responsible for the growth of these smaller Islamic banks. We found significantly low expenditure-to-income ratio values for smaller banks than in larger banks, which can be regarded as one of the paramount factors responsible for the growth and rise of smaller Islamic banks.

4

THE DEVELOPMENT & SCOPE OF
ISLAMIC BANK BONDS (*SUKUK*)

INTRODUCTION

According to Khan and Bhatti (2008), "Sukuks constitute about 85 percent of the Middle Eastern capital market—U.S. $13 billion of them have been issued there with an average growth rate of over 45 percent during 2002–2007 (Islamic Finance News 2006b). The Middle East and Asian regions will primarily rely on sukuks to meet their U.S. $1.5 trillion infrastructure needs over the next five years (Khaleej Times 2007)." (All dollar amounts are expressed in USD.)

Therefore, the interest in sukuk (*sukuk* is plural; the singular is *sakk*) is definitely growing as demand for Islamic products is rising and continuing to enjoy a period of sustained growth. Islamic finance is developing at a remarkable pace. Since its inception three decades ago, the number of Islamic financial institutions worldwide has risen from one in 1975 to over 300 today in more than 75 countries. They are concentrated in the Middle East and Southeast Asia, with Bahrain and Malaysia the biggest hubs, but they are also appearing in Europe and the United States. Total assets worldwide are estimated to exceed $250 billion, and are growing at an estimated 15 percent a year (although cross-border data remain scarce).

Islamic financial products are aimed at investors who want to comply with the Islamic laws (shariah) that govern a Muslim's daily life. These laws forbid giving or receiving interest (because earning profit from an exchange of money for money is considered immoral); mandate that all financial transactions be based on real economic activity; and prohibit investment in sectors such as tobacco, alcohol, gambling, and armaments. Islamic financial institutions are providing an increasingly broad range of many financial services, such as fund mobilization, asset allocation, payment and exchange settlement services, and risk transformation and mitigation. But these specialized financial intermediaries perform transactions using financial instruments compliant with shariah principles.

What are the reasons behind the recent growth in Islamic finance? One is the strong demand from a large number of immigrant and non-immigrant Muslims for shariah-compliant financial services and transactions. A second is growing oil wealth, with demand for suitable investments soaring in the Gulf region. And a third is the competitiveness of many of the products, attracting Muslim and non-Muslim investors. Yet despite this rapid growth, Islamic banking remains quite limited in most countries and is tiny compared with the global financial system. For it to take off and play a bigger role, especially in the Middle East, policymakers must tackle enormous hurdles, notably on the regulatory front. Islamic banking has so far been spared from a serious financial crisis, with the exception of a few minor cases, such as the Dubai Islamic Bank in 1998 and Ihlas Finans in Turkey in 2001. Nevertheless, building confidence in a new industry is fundamental for the development of Islamic finance.

Despite the increasing popularity of Islamic banking, Corporate governance in banking has been analyzed almost exclusively in the context of conventional banking markets, and this is mainly attributable to many countries not being Muslim, and, therefore, not really interesting in adopting an Islamic banking system. For example, there has recently been some discussion of the role "market discipline" exerted by bank shareholders and depositors in constraining the risk-taking behavior of bank management. At the same time, there is growing interest in, and analysis of, banks as stockholders in companies themselves playing a central role in corporate governance, especially in Germany and other countries with universal banking structures of the traditional type.

By contrast, little is written on governance structures in Islamic banking, despite the rapid growth of Islamic banks since the mid-1970s and their increasing presence on world financial markets. There are now over 180 financial institutions worldwide, which adhere to Islamic banking and financing principles. These banks operate in 45 countries encompassing most of the Muslim world, along with Europe, North America, and various offshore locations. Islamic financing increasingly is a market segment of interest to Western banks, and the latest addition to the list of Islamic banks in October 1996 in the

Citi Islamic Investment Bank, Bahrain, a wholly owned subsidiary of Citicorp.

Islamic banking represents a radical departure from conventional banking, and from the viewpoint of corporate governance, it embodies a number of interesting features since equity participation, risk and profit-and-loss-sharing arrangements form the basis of Islamic financing. Because of the ban on interest (*riba*), an Islamic bank cannot charge any fixed return in advance, but rather participates in the yield resulting from the use of funds. The depositors also share in the profits according to predetermined ratio, and are rewarded with profit returns for assuming risk. Unlike a conventional bank, which is basically a borrower and lender of funds, an Islamic bank is essentially a partner with its depositors, on the one side, and also a partner with entrepreneurs, on the other side, when employing depositors' funds in productive direct investment.

These financial arrangements imply quite different stockholder relationships, and by corollary governance structures, from the conventional model since depositors have a direct financial stake in the bank's investment and equity participations. In addition, the Islamic bank is subject to an additional layer of governance, since the suitability of its investment and financing must be in strict conformity with Islamic law and the expectations of the Muslim community. For this purpose, Islamic banks employ an individual shariah advisor and/or board.

My examination of corporate governance in Islamic banking begins with the comparison of governance structures in the Islamic bank and will continue with the principles of Islamic banking. This study compares the Islamic banking, financial model and its implications for governance structures, with the intention of discovering whether Islamic bonds are viable options to replace conventional bonds. Therefore, this research is concerned with investment sukuk (*sukuk* is plural; the singular is *sakk*) in the banking industry, whether retail or investment banks. Hence, it does not include sukuk issued directly by financing companies, since these are yet in their early beginnings. It takes into consideration those bonds and sukuk that have been practiced/issued in the last few years up until now, not taking into consideration historical forms of both. This research will deal with sukuk that have been issued in or through Middle East banks, especially UAE. Bonds, however, are handled more extensively in Western countries, such as in the European Union and the United States. Thus, samples most useful to the comparison will be taken, whether from Western countries or the Middle East.

1. AIMS & OBJECTIVES

This researcher has noted a distinct lack of existing literature on the topic of Islamic sukuk, and while there are a multitude of existing studies, academic papers, and books on conventional banking instruments, including bonds. There is a distinct lack of information on Islamic banking.

Almost all banking systems abide by the conventional banking system. Islamic banking, by contrast, is a new equity-based financial system, that has only been implemented, in its modern shape and continued to serve present-day market needs for the last 25 years. Investment sukuk (i.e., Islamic bonds) are a fairly new addition to Islamic banking. The literature available on it is based on the classical reference materials on Islamic *fiqh*. Furthermore, there has not been enough educational material in comparison with conventional banking material.

Therefore, there is an obvious gap in comparing conventional bonds to investment sukuk with the objective of assessing the potentiality of sukuk as substitutes to conventional bonds, at least in the Muslim world. This research seeks to address this gap and to look at whether sukuk are a viable option to the banking customer.

The primary hypothesis here is that investment sukuk are a better economic, commercial, and legal substitute to conventional bonds, and this will be tested by an analysis comparing conventional bonds and investment sukuk. It seeks to identify similarities, dissimilarities, and important economic and financial issues, both in principle and actual practice.

2. LITERATURE REVIEW

This chapter will seek to provide a solid background of information on Islamic banking and its underlying principles, and to fully identify the characteristics and qualities of Islamic sukuk, as well as outlining the nature of a conventional bond.

The Islamic Bank

Governance structures are quite different from these under Islamic banking because the institution must obey a different set of rules—those of the Qur'an—and meet the expectations of the Muslim community by providing Islamic-acceptable financing modes. These profit-and-loss-sharing methods, in turn, imply different relationships than under interest-based borrowing and lending.

In an Islamic bank there are two major differences from the conventional framework. First and foremost, an Islamic organization must serve Allah (God). It must develop a distinctive corporate culture, the main purpose of which is to create a collective morality and spirituality, which, when combined with the production of goods and services, sustains the growth and advancement of the Islamic way of life. To quote:[1]

"Islamic banks have a major responsibility to shoulder....all the staff of such banks and customers dealing with them must be reformed Islamically and act within the framework of an Islamic formula, so that any person approaching an Islamic bank should be given the impression that he is entering a sacred place to perform a religious ritual, that is the use and employment of capital for what is acceptable and satisfactory to God."

There are equivalent obligations upon employees:

"The staff in an Islamic bank should, throughout their lives, be conducting in the Islamic way, whether at work or at leisure."[2]

Further, obligations also extend to the Islamic community:

"Muslims who truly believe in their religion have a duty to prove, through their efforts in backing and supporting Islamic banks and financial institutions, that the Islamic economic system is an integral part of Islam and is indeed for all times...through making legitimate and *Halal profits.*"[3]

Second, interest-free banking is based on the Islamic legal concepts of *shirkah* (partnership) and *mudarabah* (profit-sharing). An Islamic bank is conceived as a financial intermediary mobilizing savings from the public on a *mudarabah* basis and advancing capital to entrepreneurs on the same basis. A two-tiered profit-and-loss-sharing arrangement operates under the following rules:

The bank receives funds from the public on the basis of unrestricted *mudarabah*. There are no restrictions imposed on the bank concerning the kind of activity, duration, and location of the enterprise, but the funds cannot be applied to activities that are forbidden by Islam.

The bank has the right to aggregate and pool the profit from different investments and to share the net profit (after deducting administrative costs, capital depreciation, and Islamic tax) with depositors, according to a specified formula. In the event of losses, the depositors lose a proportional share or the entire amount of their funds. The return to the financier has to be strictly maintained as a share of profits.

The bank applies the restricted form of *mudarabah* when funds are provided to entrepreneurs. The bank has the right to determine the kind of activities, the duration, and location of the projects and to monitor the investments. However, these restrictions may not be formulated in a way that harms the performance of the entrepreneur, and the bank cannot interfere with the management of the investment. Loan covenants and other such constraints usual in conventional commercial-bank lending are allowed.

The bank cannot require any guarantee, such as security and collateral from the entrepreneur, in order to insure its capital against the possibility of an eventual loss.

The liability of the financier is limited to the capital provided. On the other hand, the liability of the entrepreneur is also restricted, but in this case solely to labor and effort employed. Nevertheless, if negligence or mismanagement can be proven, the entrepreneur may be liable for the financial loss and be obliged to remunerate the financier, accordingly.

The entrepreneur shares the profit with the bank according to a previously agreed division. Until the investment yields a profit, the bank is able to pay a salary to the entrepreneur based on the ruling market salary.

Many of the same restrictions apply to *musharakah* financing, except that in this instance the losses are borne proportionately to the capital amounts contributed. Thus, under these two Islamic modes of financing, the project is managed by the client and not by the bank, even though the bank shares the risk. Certain major decisions, such as changes in the existing lines of business and the disposition of profits, may be subject to the bank's consent. The bank, as a partner, has the right to full access to the books and records, and can exercise monitoring and follow-up supervision. Nevertheless, the directors and management of the company retain independence in conducing the affairs of the company.

These conditions give the finance many of the characteristics of non-voting equity capital. From the viewpoint of the entrepreneur, there are no fixed annual payments needed to service the debt as under interest financing, while the financing does not increase the firm's risk in the way that other borrowings do through increased leverage. Conversely, from the bank's viewpoint, the returns come from profits—much like dividends—and the bank cannot take action to foreclose on the debt should profits not eventuate.

The Markets and the Players

More than two-thirds of current Islamic finance business originated in the Middle East. The GCC countries, with the exception of Oman, are all major markets for Islamic finance. Bahrain is regarded as the hub for Islamic finance. Other major non-GCC markets for Islamic finance include Egypt, Malaysia, Turkey, Indonesia, and Pakistan.

Malaysia operates a dual banking system promoted by the government. This allows conventional financial institutions, investment banks, commercial banks and finance companies to launch separate Islamic banking divisions, competing alongside two Islamic banks, Bank Islam Malaysia Berhad and Bank Muamalat Malaysia. Bank Negara Malaysia (also called Central Bank of Malaysia, or BNM) has its own shariah advisory board, which sets the rules for the entire Islamic banking sector, ensuring the uniformity of products and services.

Over 150 Islamic financial institutions now operate in over 40 countries around the world, from commercial banks, investment banks, and investment companies, to leasing and insurance companies.

Principles of Islamic Banking

An Islamic bank is based on the Islamic faith and must stay within the limits of Islamic law or the shariah in all of its actions and deeds. The original meaning of the Arabic word *shariah* was "the way to the source of life," and it is now used to refer to the legal system in keeping with the code of behavior called for by the Qur'an.

Islam not only prohibits dealing in interest but also in liquor, pork, gambling, pornography, and anything else, which the shariah (Islamic law) deems *haram* (unlawful). Islamic banking is an instrument for the development of an Islamic economic order. Some of the salient features of this order may be summed up as:

While permitting the individual the right to seek his economic well-being, Islam makes a clear distinction between what is *halal* (lawful) and what is *haram* (forbidden) in pursuit of such economic activity. In broad terms, Islam forbids all forms of economic activity, which are morally or socially injurious.

While acknowledging the individual's right to ownership of wealth legitimately acquired, Islam makes it obligatory on the individual to spend his wealth judiciously and not to hoard it, keep it idle, or squander it.

While allowing an individual to retain any surplus wealth, Islam seeks to reduce the margin of the surplus for the well-being of the community as a whole, in particular the destitute and deprived sections of society, by participation in the process of *zakat* ("that which purifies" or "aims," one of the five pillars of Islam).

While making allowance for the ways of human nature and yet not yielding to the consequences of its worst propensities, Islam seeks to prevent the accumulation of wealth in a few hands to the detriment of society as a whole, by its laws of inheritance.

Viewed as a whole, the economic system envisaged by Islam aims at social justice without inhibiting individual enterprise beyond the point where it becomes not only collectively injurious but also individually self-destructive.

The Islamic financial system employs the concept of participation in the enterprise, utilizing the funds at risk on a profit-and-loss-sharing basis. This by no means implies that investments with financial institutions are necessarily speculative. This can be excluded by a careful investment policy, diversification of risk, and prudent management by Islamic financial institutions.

It is possible that investment in Islamic financial institutions can provide potential profit in proportion to the risk assumed to satisfy the differing demands of participants in the contemporary environment and within the guidelines of the shariah.

The concept of profit-and-loss sharing as a basis of financial transactions is a progressive one because it distinguishes good performance from the bad and the mediocre. This concept, therefore, encourages better resource management.

Islamic banks are structured to retain a clearly differentiated status between shareholders' capital and clients' deposits in order to ensure correct profit-sharing according to Islamic law.

Four rules govern investment behavior: (1) the absence of interest-based *(riba)* transactions; (2) the avoidance of economic activities involving speculation *(ghirar)*; (3) the introduction of an Islamic tax, *zakat*; and (4) the discouragement of the production of goods and services, which contradict the value pattern of Islam *(haram)*.

In what follows, I explain these four elements that give Islamic banking its distinctive religious identity.

Riba

Perhaps the most far-reaching of these is the prohibition of interest *(riba)*. The payment of *riba* and the taking of it, as occurs in a conventional banking system, are explicitly prohibited by the Qur'an, and thus, investors must be compensated by other means. Technically, *riba* refers to the addition in the amount of the principal of a loan according to the time for which it is loaned and the amount of the loan. While earlier there was a debate as to whether *riba* relates to interest or usury, there now appears to be a consensus of opinion among Islamic scholars that the term extends to all forms of interest.

In banning *riba*, Islam seeks to establish a society based upon fairness and justice (Qur'an 2: 239). A loan provides the lender with a fixed return irrespective of the outcome of the borrower's venture. It is much fairer to have a sharing of the profits and losses. Fairness in this context has two dimensions: the supplier of capital possesses a right to reward, but this reward should be commensurate with the risk and effort involved, and thus, be governed by the return on the individual project for which funds are supplied.

Hence, what is forbidden in Islam is a predetermined return. The sharing of profit is legitimate and that practice has provided the foundation for Islamic banking.

Ghirar

Another feature condemned by Islam are economic transactions involving elements of speculation, *ghirar*. Buying goods or shares at low and selling them for a higher price in the future is considered to be illicit. Similarly, an immediate sale in order to a void a loss in the future is condemned. The reason for this is that speculators generate their private gains at the expense of society at large.

Zakat

A mechanism for the redistribution of income and wealth is inherent is Islam, so that every Muslim is guaranteed a fair standard of living, *nisab*. An Islamic tax, *zakat* (a term derived from the Arabic *zaka*, meaning "pure") is the most important instrument for the redistribution of wealth. This tax is a compulsory levy, one of the five basic tenets of Islam, and the generally accepted amount of the *zakat* is one-fortieth (2.5 percent) of a Muslim's annual income in cash or kind from all forms of assessed wealth exceeding *nisab*.

Every Islamic bank has to establish a *zakat* fund for collecting the tax and distributing it exclusively to the poor directly or through other religious institutions. This tax is imposed on the initial capital of the bank, on the reserves, and on the profits as described in the *Handbook of Islamic Banking*.

Haram

A strict code of "ethical investment" operates. Hence, it is forbidden for Islamic banks to finance activities or items forbidden in Islam, *haram*, such as trade of alcoholic beverage and pork meat.

Furthermore, as the fulfilment or materials needs assures religious freedom for Muslims, Islamic banks are required to give priority to the production of essential goods which satisfy the needs of the majority of the Muslim community, while the production and marketing of luxury activities, *israf wa traf* is considered as unacceptable from a religious viewpoint.

In order to ensure that the practices and activities of Islamic banks do not contradict Islamic ethical standards, Islamic banks are expected to establish a shariah supervisory board, consisting of Muslims schooled in jurisprudence, who act as advisers to the banks.

Profit-Sharing Agreements

Although the restriction against the use of interest might seem to be a binding constraint upon expansion, Islamic banks and financial institutions have, in fact, grown rapidly. Table 4.1 sets out the number of banks, paid-up capital, total deposits, and total assets of these Islamic banks, classified by region. It shows that the total assets of these reporting banks amounted to $155 billion in 1994, with employment in excess of 220,000 (data supplied by the International Association of Islamic Banks).

If the paying and receiving of interest is prohibited, how do Islamic banks operate? It is necessary to distinguish between the expressions "rate of interest" and "rate of return." Whereas, Islam clearly forbids the former, it not only permits, but encourages, trade. In the interest-free system sought by adherents to Muslim principles, people are able to earn a return on their money only by subjecting themselves to the risk involved in profit sharing. As the use of interest rates in financial

Table 4.1 Summary of Current Islamic Finance Products Offered in the UK

Financial Product	Fyshe Group	HSBC Amanah Finance	Islamic Bank of Britain	Lloyds TSB	Destini
Current Accounts		X	X	X	
Cash-Generating Arrangements			X		
Mortgages		X	X		X
Pension Funds		X			
Savings			X		
Stock Broking	X	X			

transactions is prevented, Islamic banks are expected to undertake operations only on the basis of profit-and-loss sharing (PLS) arrangements or other acceptable modes of financing. *Mudarabah* and *musharakah* are the two profit-sharing arrangements preferred under Islamic law.

Mudarabah

A *mudarabah* can be defined as contract between at least two parties whereby one party, the financier *(sahib al-mal)*, entrusts funds to another party, the entrepreneur *(mudarib)*, to undertake an activity or venture. This type of contract is in contrast with *musharakah*. In arrangements based on *musharakah*, there is also profit-sharing, but all parties have the right to participate in managerial decisions. In *mudarabah*, the financier is not allowed a role in management of the enterprise. Consequently, *mudarabah* represents a PLS contract where the return to lenders is a specified share in the profit-or-loss outcome of the project in which they have a stake, but no voice.

In interest lending, the loan is not contingent on the profit-or-loss outcome, and it is usually secured so that the debtor has to repay the borrowed capital plus the fixed-interest amount, regardless of the resulting yield of the capital.

Under *mudarabah*, the yield is not guaranteed in profit-sharing, and financial losses are borne completely by the lender. The entrepreneur as such loses only the time and effort invested in the enterprise. This distribution effectively treats human capital with equally financial capital.

Musharakah

Under *musharakah*, the entrepreneur adds some of his own to that supplied by the investors, thereby exposing himself to the risk of capital loss. Profits and losses are shared according to pre-fixed proportions, but these proportions need not coincide with the ratio of financing input. The bank sometimes participates in the execution of the projects in which it has subscribed, perhaps by providing managerial expertise.

Mudarabah and *musharakah* constitute, at least in principle, if not always in practice, the twin pillars of Islamic banking.

The two methods conform fully with Islamic principles in that, under both arrangements, lenders share in the profits and losses of the enterprises for which funds are provided and *shirkah* (partnership) is involved. The *musharakah* principle is invoked in the equity structure of Islamic banks and is similar to the modern concepts of partnership and joint stock ownership.

Two-Tiered *Mudabarah*

For banking operations, the *mudarabah* concept has been extended to include three parties: the depositors as financiers, the bank as an intermediary, and the entrepreneur who requires funds. The bank acts as an entrepreneur when it receives funds from depositors and as financier when it provides the funds to entrepreneurs. In other words, the bank operates a two-tiered *mudarabah* system in which it acts both as the *mudarib* on the saving side of the equation and as the *rubbul-mal* (owner of capital) on the investment-portfolio side. Insofar as the depositors are concerned, an Islamic bank acts as a *mudarib,* which manages the funds of the depositors to generate profits subject to the rules of *mudarabah.* The bank may in turn use the depositors' funds on a *mudarabah* basis in addition to other lawful (but less preferable) modes of financing, including markup or deferred sales, lease purchase, and beneficence loans. The funding and investment avenues are then listed.

Sources of Funds

Besides their own capital and equity, Islamic banks rely on two main sources of funds: (a) transaction deposits, which are risk-free but yield no return, and (b) investment deposits, which carry the risks of capital loss for the promise of variability. In all, there are four main types of accounts: current, savings, investment, and special investment.

Current Accounts

Current accounts are based on the principle of *al-wadiah,* whereby the depositors are guaranteed repayment of their funds. At the same time, the depositor does not receive remuneration for depositing funds in a current account, because the guaranteed funds will not be used for PLS ventures. Rather, the funds accumulating in these accounts can only be used to balance the liquidity needs of the bank and for short-term transactions on the bank's responsibility.

Savings Accounts

Savings accounts also operate under the *al-wadiah* principle. Savings accounts differ from current deposits in that they earn the depositors income; depending upon financial results, the Islamic bank may decide to pay a premium (*hiba*), at its discretion, to the holders of savings accounts.

Investment Accounts

An investment account operates under the *mudarabah al-mutlaqa* principle in which the *mudarib* (active partner) must have absolute freedom in the management of the investment of the subscribed capital. The conditions of this account differ from those of the savings accounts by virtue of: (a) a higher fixed minimum amount, (b) a longer duration of deposits, and (c) most importantly, the depositor may lose some or all of his funds in the event of the bank having losses.

Special-Investment Accounts

Special-investment accounts also operate under the *mudarabah* principle and usually are directed toward larger investors and institutions. The difference between these accounts and the investment account is that the special-investment account is related to a specified project, and the investor has the choice to invest directly in a preferred project carried out by the bank.

Uses of Funds

The *mudarabah* and *musharakah* modes, referred to earlier, are supposedly the main conduits for the outflow of funds from banks. In practice, however, other important methods applied by Islamic banks include:

Murabahah (markup). The most commonly used mode of financing seems to be the markup device. In a *murabahah* transactions, the bank finances the purchase of a good or assets by buying it on behalf of its client and adding a markup before reselling it to the client on a cost-plus basis profit contract.

Bai' muajjal (deferred payment). Islamic banks have also been resorting to purchase and resale of properties on a deferred-payment basis. It is considered lawful in *fiqh* (jurisprudence) to charge a higher price for a good if payments are to be made at a later date. According to *fiqh*, this does not amount to charging interest, since it is not a lending transaction but a trading one.

Bai'salam (prepaid purchase). This method is really the opposite of the *murabahah*. There the bank gives the commodity first and receives the money later. Here the bank pays the money first and receives the commodity later. This type of purchase is normally used to finance agricultural products.

Istissanaa (manufacturing). This is a contract to acquire goods on behalf of a third party where the price is paid to the manufacturer in advance and the goods produced and delivered at a later date.

Ijara and ijara wa iqtina (leasing). Under this mode, the banks buy the equipment or machinery and lease it out to their clients, who may opt to buy the items eventually, in which case, the monthly payments will consist of two components, i.e., rental for the use of the equipment and instalment toward the purchases price.

Qard hasan (beneficence loans). This is the zero-return type of loan that the Qura'n urges Muslims to make available to those who need them. The borrower is obliged to repay only the principal amount of the loan, but he is permitted to add a margin at his own discretion.

Islamic Securities

Islamic financial institutions often maintain an international Islamic equity portfolio where the underlying assets comprise ordinary shares in well-run businesses, the productive activities of which exclude those on the prohibited list (alcohol, pork, armaments) and financial service based on interest income.

3. ISLAMIC BONDS (SUKUK)

Sukuk have become a very hot topic and are becoming one of the most sought after Islamic financing vehicles (Bijur 2007). Sukuk can be defined as "asset-backed, shariah-compliant trust certificates" (Bijur 2007) that give the owner rights to owning part of the asset, the cash that arises from the asset, and responsibilities that go with it (MIFC 2008).

The closest conventional instrument similar to sukuk in the conventional financial system is a bond (mainly those issued in relation to a securitization). However, these bonds lead to usurious interest and are therefore forbidden for a Muslim to partake in such a thing under Islamic law (Bijur 2007).

Based on a range of Islamic values, sukuk can be structured in a number of ways to offer the issuing entity greater financial flexibility and options to meet its funding needs (MIFC 2008). Sukuk can be structured based on the principles of:

- **Contract of exchange,** such as *bai' bithaman ajil* (BBA), *murabahah, istisna,* and *ijarah*; or
- **Contract of participation,** such as *musyarakah* and *mudharabah*. (MIFC 2008).

Most commonly, sukuk are backed by assets and tend to be used in conjunction with an *ijara* structure (mentioned earlier), where the rental income from the lease earns a profit for the sukuk holder. Other sukuk forms use the *musharakah* structure, in which the profit share provides the holder with a decent return (Bijur 2007).

Having a sukuk signifies that the holder has a positive and valuable interest in the asset, as they partly own the underlying asset as well as the income that it produces (Bijur 2007).

Bijur (2007) also asserts that the sukuk bonds come with additional and tedious responsibilities, as the sukuk holder is also responsible for the maintenance of the asset, while in a conventional bond, the investor has no such responsibility and can only receive interest. Therefore, these additional responsibilities can be classed as a disadvantage of sukuk.

However, advantages are also high with sukuk, as according to MIFC (2008), sukuk are exempt from incurring any stamp duty.

4. Cases of Non-Muslim Sukuk Issuers & Investors

It was originally the domain of sovereign issues, but, more recently, corporations in domestic markets have begun to tap the sukuk market. Emirates Airlines, for example, launched a $500 million sukuk issue. The sukuk market is now no longer confined to predominantly Islamic countries, nor is it the sole domain of Islamic finance institutions. Increasingly, sukuk linked to assets based in the UK, continental Europe, and the United States are being structured as Islamic investors want to include securities with such profiles in their portfolios. Furthermore, non-Islamic issuers are currently seeking to capitalize on the increased liquidity in the Islamic world. For example, the German Federal State of Saxony-Anhalt issued a $100 million sukuk in 2004, for which the regional minister said the rationale for issuance was twofold: "On the one hand [for] economic reasons. There are investors out there and it makes sense to provide them with a product. On the other hand it is a matter of international courtesy. We want to send out a message of respect for other cultures that have different regulations on investing."

Sukuk investor demographics are becoming increasingly diverse with non-Islamic investors increasingly participating in the market. Middle Eastern credit risk, for example, has increasingly become appealing for offshore investors. In a recent sukuk issue, conventional investors purchased 48 percent of the issue (24 percent institutional investors, 13 percent central banks and government institutions, and 11 percent fund managers).

The Products and Structures

Islamic banks around the world have devised many financial products based on the risk-sharing, profit-sharing principles of Islamic banking. For day-to-day banking activities, a number of financial instruments have been developed that satisfy the Islamic doctrine and provide acceptable financial returns for investors. Broadly speaking, the areas in which Islamic banks are most active are in trade and commodity finance, property and leasing. Almost every Islamic bank has a committee of religious advisers whose opinion is sought on the acceptability of new instruments and services and who have to provide a religious opinion of the bank's activities for year-end accounts.

Britain and Islamic Finance

Community Banking

Muslims in Britain and throughout the world aspire to carry out their financial matters in accordance with the principles of Islamic law. Muslims are forbidden from obtaining the various conventional banking and insurance products and services in the forms currently offered, due to their incompatibility with the principles of Islamic law.

It is estimated by various surveys that over 2 million Muslims are permanently residing in the UK. The community is predominantly composed of people from the Indian subcontinent who have settled in Britain during the 1950s. Besides them, there are also Muslims of Middle Eastern and North African origins. Additionally, there is a growing population of indigenous Muslims.

The UK Muslim community has now reached the second-generation stage. The first wave of immigrants having settled down, the second-generation Muslims are now slowly penetrating the different strata of the British society. It is not uncommon to find successful Muslim lawyers, chartered (or certified) accountants, bankers, businessmen, and even Members of Parliament, both at the House of Lords and the House of Commons.

The third generations of Muslims are also emerging from the educational system and are projected to increase the Muslims' presence in all strata of British society, especially, the educated middle class.

The vast majority of Muslims are either living in rented houses or have taken conventional interest-based mortgages. The total number of Muslim households as estimated by the Muslim Council of Britain is around 500,000. Of the 500,000 households, it is estimated by various market researches that approximately 40,000 families seek financing for home purchases each year.

We have regularly received inquiries regarding the availability of Islamic finance products, in particular finance (compatible with Islam) to purchase both residential and commercial properties. It is believed that a large number of Muslims have abstained from taking the conventional mortgage because of its incompatibility with Islamic principles. The needs of these Muslims must be served immediately.

Beside the market represented by Muslims living in Britain, there is potential for overseas investors to be introduced by HSBC. We understand that a considerable number of Muslims living abroad (mainly in the Middle East) had expressed their desire to own properties in Britain (mainly as a holiday residence) but have been reluctant to embark on an interest-bearing financing facility. For these investors, an Islamic home-financing scheme will offer the opportunity to own a property in Britain.

Islamic Home Financing: The Structure

The potential customer, having identified the property, will approach the bank to finance the purchase of the property. The transaction structure will be as follows:

The customer chooses the property for purchase and agrees on the purchase price with the owner of the property ("seller"). The bank buys the property from the seller at the agreed price. The customer will be requested to provide a deposit against the purchase price, but the bank will remain the sole registered owner.

The customer signs a lease agreement with the bank. The lease will be for a period of up to 25 years with the lease rentals to be reviewed annually to reflect the capital repayment. The terms of the lease agreement will stipulate that, in the event of a default, the bank will have the right to repossess and sell the property.

The customer/lessee will give an undertaking (a pledge) that in the event of a default under the lease agreement, the bank/lessor will have the right to compel the customer to purchase the property for the purchase price, which shall equal the amount of the principal outstanding.

There will also be an undertaking (pledge) whereby the bank/lessor promises to sell the property to the customer/lessee at the end of the agreed lease period (i.e., when the whole of the principal portion has been repaid). There will also be a provision for certain other specified instances including when the customer desires to sell the property.

The above structure would allow British Muslims to get access to home financing without forcing them to choose between their religion and home ownership. It allows British Muslims to purchase homes without violating Islamic prescriptions on borrowing money on which interest is charged. Further, this initiative will be consistent with the well-established public policy of encouraging home owner-ship and making Muslim stakeholders in Britain.

Islamic Home Financing: Current Impediments

The three main impediments to Islamic home financing are risk weighting, taxation, and legal fees.

Risk Weighting

A key element, which will impact the pricing, is the Financial Services Authority's (FSA) approach to risk weighting for this product. FSA has provisionally ruled that the product is to be 100 percent risk weighted. This is essentially because the transaction is equivalent to a lease, and leases are weighted 100 percent. This assumes that the house remains the property of the bank throughout the term of the transaction and is treated as a fixed asset on its balance sheet. If we are obliged to weigh at 100 percent, then pricing will be significantly higher than the conventional mortgage rate. Good Muslims should not be penalized for being good Muslims. Muslims in the United States have approached the Office of the Comptroller of the Currency (OCC), Administration of National Banks, to seek the approval for Islamic home finance based on the above leasing structure. The OCC had in 1997 approved Islamic home financing based on the above leasing structure and ruled, inter alia, that the banks' risks under the Islamic leasing structure are similar to the risks on traditional mortgage loans (see OCC's Interpretive Letter #806). We hope that a similar approval would be granted in Britain.

Taxation

The transfer of ownership from vendor to bank at the commencement of the lease and from bank to customer at the end of the lease may attract the payment of two sets of stamp duty. The second set would arise at the end of the term of the lease at the rate of stamp duty then applicable. The second set of stamp duty needs to be exempted because the true effect of the transfer is similar to the redemption of a conventional mortgage or charge: when the property finally vests with the customer without any encumbrance. If the second set of stamp duty is not exempted, the uncertain cost of the second stamp duty would make Islamic home financing unattractive and cost prohibitive.

Legal Fees

Unlike the conventional mortgage, the proposed product would require the appointment of two sets of attorneys (solicitors), thereby making the product more expensive. It is suggested that the Law Society in the Commonwealth should consider giving a general exemption as is done for the mortgage product.

Current Islamic Finance Efforts in the UK

In the past three years, several major banks have entered the Islamic finance effort in the UK, offering a variety of shariah-compliant products, including current accounts, cash-generating arrangements, mortgages, pension funds, savings, and stock broking.

The Islamic Bank of Britain, the first of its kind in the UK, opened in 2004, offering current and savings accounts and cash-generating arrangements that take the place of borrowing. The bank uses what would otherwise be interest on customers' savings balances to buy commodities, mostly metals, and to sell them at a profit, a share of which goes monthly to the client. Instead of guaranteed savings income, it offers a target amount. There are rules on the way profits are split and redistributed, including a cap on how much the bank can take. Cash-generating arrangements work with the bank buying commodities and selling them to customers at a markup. The customer in turn sells them to a broker, who then releases the cash by selling the commodities on the market. The customer repays the bank over a set term.

Islamic mortgages, offered by the likes of HSBC Amanah, the Islamic Bank of Britain, and the independent financial adviser Destini, obey shariah law because the bank buys the home for the customer. He or she pays the price of the house in monthly installments plus a rent type of payment, eventually buying out the bank, when ownership then passes to the customer.

Lloyds TSB Bank has launched an Islamic current account, which does not pay interest or provide overdrafts. The bank heralded it by announcing that Islamic banking was coming into the mainstream.

Last April 2005, HSBC's Amanah arm became the first UK bank to offer trustees a pension fund aimed at Muslims. It does not hold shares in firms mainly involved in areas that create religious problems, including alcohol, gambling, pornography, pork products, tobacco, or conventional financial services. It tracks an index that includes the top 100 companies engaged in shariah-compliant activities. Dividends generated by unacceptable business, for example, part of an advertising agency's profits from an alcohol account, are given to charity.

The Fyshe Group offers a tailored stockbroking service, which advises Muslims on whether an investment complies with shariah law as well as providing stockbroking services, while HSBC Amanah offers portfolio management.

Major UK high-street banks have also invested in research and development of shariah-compliant products, including HSBC Amanah, Lloyds TSB, and NatWest, as well as smaller providers and foreign players.

The UK Securities and Investment Institute and Lebanon's Ecole Supérieure des Affaires have launched the Islamic Finance Qualification, which will initially be offered in the UK and Lebanon. It is designed specifically for providers of financial advice in the Islamic community. It is thought that it may become part of the FSA's requirements for advisers in the UK working with Islamic clients.

HSBC Introduced Islamic Mortgages in July 2003

In July 2003, giant HSBC launched their new Amanah Home Finance product with the backing of the Muslim Council of Britain and the blessing of several world-renowned Islamic scholars. At that time, there were thousands of mortgage products on the market, but prior to that, no high-street bank offered one that was acceptable to Britain's Muslims. Launched on 14 July of 2003 in just four locations, the product attracted more than 6,000 inquiries in its first two months, and it is now offered across Britain in around 25 centers.

The HSBC solution to the shariah prohibition on interest works as following:

• HSBC buys the property and leases it back to the customer over an agreed term, typically 25 years.

- The customer makes monthly payments made up of rent and payments toward the purchase price. HSBC owns the property until the customer has made his final payment.
- The customer can arrange for the property to be sold at any time, and the rent rate will be reviewed on 1 July and 1 January every year.
- In Islamic terms, the rent paid to the bank on top of the monthly payments toward the purchase price is not classified as interest; it is seen as a fair payment for use of the property rather than a charge for borrowing money.

Lease Back

Under the HSBC scheme, the bank buys the property and leases it back to the customer over an agreed term. The customer makes monthly payments made up of rent and contributions toward the purchase price. HSBC owns the property until the customer has made his final payment. Crucially, at no stage is the customer paying interest; the paying of "rent" is seen as a fair payment for use of the property rather than a charge for borrowing money.

In addition, HSBC is launching an Islamic-law-compliant current account, which has no overdraft or credit-card facility. Money paid into the current account will be administered in accordance with Islamic law and not used for generating interest. The current account and mortgage products are to be introduced in selected HSBC branches from 14 July.

Huge Market

Previously only relatively small institutions such as the National Bank of Kuwait and the West Bromwich Building Society have offered tailored Islamic financial products for UK customers. Last year a report from market-analyst data monitor estimated that demand for Islamic mortgages in the UK was so strong that gross advances could reach £4.5bn ($7bn) in 2006.

Halalmortgage.com (First Online Halal Mortgage)

Halalmortgage.com is an online Halal mortgage provider whose primary service is to assist potential homeowners to find and select available halal mortgage options that meet Muslims personal needs in line with their beliefs. Halalmortgage.com service is to provide necessary information on the available halal mortgage products and to assist with the application process.

Being the first website in the United Kingdom solely dedicated to halal mortgages, Halalmortgage.com provides convenient online services and e-finance solutions. The website is easy to use, enabling visitors to the site to gain advantageous knowledge in a quick and convenient manner twenty-four hours a day, seven days a week. These state-of-the-art technology solutions ensure easy accessibility of up-to-date information.

These full-service specialized agents can be contacted through online inquiry, email, or by telephone. They are experienced in the Islamic finance industry and are kept up to date on the latest terms available for halal mortgages, and they are just a phone call or a key-stroke away.

Unlike most online financial services, halalmortgage.com is a technology-focused company with a human face. This encourages phoning for a free one-to-one consultation with a professional. Agents are available to give impartial information and a person can be assured that he will be under no pressure or obligation by using this free service.

Therefore, this change toward Islamic finance shows that there are already strong Islamic finance initiatives under way both in Islamic countries and in the UK, and this should be considered when trying to ascertain whether sukuk Islamic bonds would be a suitable alternative to conventional bonds, in a Muslim country setting and in a non-Muslim country setting, such as the UK.

Governance Structures

These structures are a framework of corporate governance for the Islamic bank. Central to such a framework is the shariah supervisory board (SSB) and the internal controls that support it. The SSB is vital for two reasons. First, those who deal with an Islamic bank require assurance that it is transacting in accord with Islamic law. Should the SSB report that the management of the bank has violated shariah, it would quickly lose the confidence of the majority of its investors and clients. Second, some Islamic scholars argue that strict adherence to Islamic religious principles will act as a counter to the incentive problems outlined above. The argument is that the Islamic moral code will prevent Muslims from behaving in ways that are ethically unsound, and so minimizing the transaction costs arising from incentive issues. In effect, Islamic religious ideology acts as its own incentive mechanism to reduce the inefficiency that arises from asymmetric information and moral hazard.

Such matters are obviously basic to the successful operation of Islamic modes of finance, and they are assessed in the next section when I examine principles of Islamic banking.

According to Directgov (2008), corporate bonds are sold by companies as a way of raising money for their firm. They have nominal value (usually £100), which is the amount that will be returned to the investor on a fixed future date (the redemption date) (Directgov 2008). Similarly, they also pay out the interest rate annually, and the rate is usually fixed. Corporate bonds are bought and sold on the stock market and their price can go up or down (Directgov 2008).

Gilts are bonds issued by the government, which pay a fixed rate of interest to the bondholder two times a year. They are considered safe, low-risk investments as the government is unlikely to go bust or to avoid the interest payments (Directgov 2008).

However, you are not guaranteed to get all your capital back as gilts, like corporate bonds, are also bought and sold on the stock market where their price can go up or down (Directgov 2008).

Reasons a bond may be used is if a business wants to expand, one of its options is to borrow money from individual investors. The company issues bonds at various interest rates and sells them to the public. Investors purchase them with the understanding that the company will pay back their original principal plus any interest that is due by a set date (this is called the "maturity").

The interest a bondholder earns depends on the strength of the corporation. For example, a blue chip is more stable and has a lower risk of defaulting on its debt. When companies such as Exxon Mobile, General Electric, etc., issue bonds, they may only pay 7 percent interest, while a much less stable start-up pays 10 percent. Usually, when investing in bonds, it is well known that "the higher the interest rate, the riskier the bond."

Conventional bonds can be issued from governments, municipalities, a variety of institutions, and corporations. Obviously, as they are based on interest, this is one of the main reasons many Muslim customers reject them, because interest, or usury, is prohibited in Islam.

Methodology

The usual research procedure attempts to identify similarities, dissimilarities, and important economic and financial issues, both in principle and in actual practice. In this regard, most studies utilize the following methods, which we have drawn on for our own study:

Secondary data was the first step in obtaining data for research. This secondary data came from the review of the literature and the use of preexisiting case studies, which cover the most common forms of bonds issuance and sukuk, with at least one case study for each type of sukuk and bonds. The comparison will refer to the underlying financing mode of sukuk, mode of issuance (discussing the possible issuer of each type), structure, documentation, return, tradability, listing, collaterals, redemption, risks, and risk mitigation thereof.

The first phase of this research would rely mainly on secondary data collected from existing published literature on the subject, drawn largely from that found in published scholarly journals in Islamic finance and the sukuk field as well as books and reliable Internet sources. Gharry and Gronghaug (2002) have defined *secondary data* as data that has been collated by other parties for specific reasons, which may not necessarily be for the same reasons as those of another researcher. The secondary data can provide valuable initial information and a summary on the subject of sukuk and serve to highlight those areas in the literature that authors and analysts have indicated as being a cause for concern, and the data allow me to specifically direct my research toward areas that require needed attention or improvement. It makes sense to begin with secondary data. As Churchill (1999) recommends, embark on research by using secondary data, and only when the data begin to become scarce or irrelevant, does he recommend moving onto primary data sources. The advantage of this approach is that it can reduce the amount of time spent on research and help to ensure that the research topic and methodology remain relevant (Ghauri and Gronhaug 2002). However, secondary data do not come without problems; after all, these data are not written specifically for the next researcher's topic in mind (Ghauri and Gronhaug 2002). Therefore, the new researcher may find it difficult to make secondary data both relevant and applicable to his own research aims, so caution must be exercised when utilizing such sources (Ghauri and Gronhaug 2002). Furthermore, only reliable Internet sources, such as official websites, must be used in order to preserve the integrity and validity of this research.

5. RESULTS: A CASE STUDY OF SUKUK ISSUANCE ON MALAYSIA

Malaysia operates a dual banking system promoted by the government. This allows conventional financial institutions, investment banks, commercial banks, and finance companies to launch separate Islamic banking divisions, competing alongside two Islamic banks, Bank Islam Malaysia and Bank Muamalat Malaysia. Bank Negara Malaysia (Central Bank of Malaysia) has its own shariah advisory board, which sets the rules for the entire Islamic banking sector, ensuring uniformity of products and services.

Malaysia's impressive record in starting sukuk and issuing them is well known, as it has taken pioneering steps since 1990 when the first sukuk in Malaysia was issued. This got the ball rolling for more sukuk issuances, especially in the last few years where Malaysia has achieved several awards and recognition for being the first to do things in the sukuk field (MIFC 2008). As of 2007, the Malaysian sukuk market has become the biggest sukuk market in world, dealing in more than 68.9 percent or $62 billion of the global outstanding sukuk (MIFC 2008). Similarly, a Malaysian firm was the first to issue the largest sukuk amount in the world, which was to the sum of approximately $4.7 billion, and the demand for this was so high that they were oversubscribed twofold (MIFC 2008). The development of the sukuk market in Malaysia is supported by a sophisticated and all-inclusive infrastructure, including the reporting, trading, and settlement system for all sukuk transactions, and this has led to an active primary sukuk market with an average growth of 22 percent in the period 2001–2007 (MIFC 2008).

Looking at the dynamic development of Malaysia's sukuk market and infrastructure, it is evident that the country offers one of the most viable options for participation in this fast-growing asset class. Coupled with Malaysia's more than 30 years of experience in Islamic finance and its overall comprehensive domestic sector, Malaysia offers several value propositions for local and foreign sukuk issuers and investors.

Table 4.2, taken from MIFC (2008b), shows the major sukuk issuances that Malaysia has overseen.

The Malaysian government's inaugural sukuk issue in 2002 marks the beginning of a market that has grown to around $8 billion.

Malaysia can attract many foreign investors to its sukuk market because it has many incentives to encourage them to trade, because it provides a tax exemption for non-Malaysian residents, and also it exempts sukuk holders from stamp duty (MIFC 2008).

Malaysia has not only attracted external customers by incentives, but foreign investors are also extremely impressed by Malaysia's organized framework (MIFC 2008), which makes the whole process of buying sukuk clear and easy, and Malaysia can also issue sukuk in

Table 4.2 Major Sukuk Issuances Overseen by Malaysia

Issuer	Amount *Ringgits and U.S. Dollars*	Year	Transaction Highlights
Shell MDS	RM125 million (USD33 million)	1990	World's first ringgit sukuk issuance by foreign-owned, non-Islamic company
Kumpulan Guthrie Bhd.	USD150 million	2001	World's first global corporate sukuk
Government of Malaysia	USD600 million	2002	World's first global sovereign sukuk
International Finance Corporation (World Bank)	RM500 million (USD132 million)	2004	First ringgit sukuk issuance by supranational agency
Cagamas MBS Bhd.	RM2.05 billion (USD540 million)	2005	World's first Islamic residential mortgage-backed securities
PLUS	RM9.17 billion (USD2.86 billion)	2006	Complex and innovative structure—conversion of existing debts of PLUS info Islamic financing
Khazanah Nasional (Rafflesia Capital Limited)	USD750 million	2006	World's first exchangeable sukuk
AEON Credit Services	RM400 million (USD125 billion)	2007	First Japanese-owned company issuing sukuk
Nucleus Avenue (Malakoff Corporation)	RM8 billion (USD2.5 billion)	2007	First hybrid sukuk in the world
Khazanah Nasional (Cherating Capital)	USD850 million	2007	Largest equity-linked sukuk issuance and record highest over-subscription
Maybank Berhad	USD300 million	2007	World's first international subordinated sukuk
Binariang GSM	RM15.35 billion (USD4.8 billion)	2007	Largest-ever sukuk issue in the world

Source: MIFC 2008b, Notable sukuk issuances.

their own local currency (the ringgit) and other foreign currencies. Consider an excerpt taken from the Malaysian International Financial Centre (MIFC 2008) website, mifc.com, regarding the Malaysian framework for sukuk issuance. Malaysia provides a facilitative framework for sukuk issuance, both for local and international issuers. In addition to issuing ringgit sukuk, the current issuance framework allows for issuers to issue a non-ringgit sukuk in Malaysia (MIFC 2008):

- Facilitative approval process for issuance of ringgit-denominated sukuk:
  - Deemed approval granted to sovereigns, quasi-sovereigns, Multilateral Development Banks (MDBs), and Multilateral Financial Institutions (MFIs) rated "AAA."
  - 14 working days to foreign Multi-National Corporations (MNCs) and foreign corporations.

- Facilitative approval process for issuance of non-ringgit denominated sukuk:
  - Deemed approval granted to sovereigns, quasi-sovereigns, MDBs, and MFIs rated "BBB" on foreign rating scale.
  - Governing laws of Malaysia, England, or the United States may be used for bond documentation.

- For both ringgit and non-ringgit denominated sukuk:
  - Both resident and non-resident issuers are free to utilize proceeds from the issuance onshore and offshore.
  - The issuers are also free to hedge to the full amount of the underlying commitment.

Malaysia's sukuk framework has a proper infrastructure platform, which involves the use of an electronic trashing platform and real-time technology that enables the transferring of funds and securities. This helps investors and issuers alike to have transparency and helps to ensure that the sukuk market can easily remain liquid (MIFC 2008).

6. Discussion

The findings from both the literature review and the case studies examined appear to suggest the validity of sukuk in today's marketplace. The Malaysian government, known to be a Muslim country, has proven the success of sukuk and has done so by using the most up-to-date technology and by having an organized framework and system in place to oversee all sukuk transactions. This has lead to the Malaysia being the market leader in issuing sukuk, and for this, they are reaping immense rewards. With a long history in Islamic banking (they are an Islamic country), it is clear that Malaysia has seen a big opportunity and tapped into the demand for shariah-compliant bonds, with a great degree of success.

Furthermore, for those who believe that the sukuk bonds will only be attractive to Muslims is clearly mistaken; throughout the course of this research, it has clearly been emphasized that the non-Muslim issuers (such as a small state in Germany) is also cashing in on the financial gains to be had. By referring to the summary table that shows sukuk issuances made by Malaysia, it becomes clear that many of the companies, such as Shell, who are also issuing sukuk are non-Muslim. Similarly, the investor base for sukuk is clearly a diverse range of Muslims and non-Muslims alike, as Malaysia itself has attracted much foreign investment in sukuk by offering incentives, such as tax and stamp-duty exemption, and therefore, this clearly shows that sukuk have the potential not only to replace the common bond in Muslim countries, but it also shows that there is definitely a place for them in non-Muslim and European markets as well. London is one of the main wholesale transacting centers outside the Middle East for this market. Yet, it is ironic that little by the way of Islamic financial products are available to the Muslims in the UK. This community of between 1.5 to 2 million Muslims and some 350,000 households is a sizeable market and is unlikely to be ignored for long.

However, this research has demonstrated that sukuk bonds are not 100 percent foolproof, and this may be why many still prefer conventional bonds.

However, despite there being a lot of demand for such products, perhaps the countries of these banks are themselves not properly prepared for launching sukuk on a massive scale, and according to Sole (2008), many limitations to the development of a sukuk market exist in the Middle East, as there is an increasing interest by local investors and companies alike in the creation of a sukuk market as a potential alternative to conventional bonds. However, the use of sukuk may not be straightforward for entities unfamiliar with the legal underpinnings of these instruments. For instance, the issuance of sukuk certificates must be unequivocally linked to one or more underlying assets. These assets, in turn, are typically transferred to a special-purpose vehicle (SPV) for a period equal to the maturity of the sukuk. Although there is no explicit legal restriction on the creation of SPVs, Kuwait does not possess an unambiguous framework for the establishment, management, and accounting procedures of these vehicles. According to Sole (2008), the lack of a proper set of rules introduces a serious element of uncertainty in sukuk transactions, and thus, severely limits the attractiveness of these Islamic instruments because they are considered high risk.

Therefore, putting in place an explicit framework governing sukuk issuances and their management would certainly encourage their use by companies and investors alike. In a similar vein, an additional step that could be taken to bolster the sukuk market even further would be the introduction of a framework for the securitization of these instruments, to make them less risky (Sole 2008).

Therefore, in order to make sukuk more secure and to encourage more corporations to obtain them, Sole (2008) recommends that the authorities should consider developing a clear legal framework for the establishment, management, and accounting of SPVs, underpinning the issuance of sukuk and developing a legal framework for sukuk securitization (pool/funds of sukuk).

If these problems are to be overcome in the Middle East, then it appears that there is no explicit problem as to why sukuk cannot be used as a replacement for normal interest-bearing bonds. Similarly, this research also seems to suggest a positive reception of sukuk in non-Muslim countries, such as the UK.

A number of recent developments point to significant changes in the market place. Indications have emerged from UK regulators that they do not have any objections in principle to shariah-compliant financial products. As a result, major high-street players, like HSBC and some building societies, are seriously considering entering the market with an array of products. They have teamed up with Muslim institutions to try to address the regulatory issues that have so far discouraged the launch of Islamic housing finance and other products. A working party, comprised of practitioners and representatives of the Muslim Council of Britain (MCB) and Union of Muslim Organizations (UMO) has been formed with the blessing of the Governor of the Bank of England. This party has prepared a report on the issues of concern and has met several of the officials, regulators, departments, and ministries to work out acceptable solutions.

The last meeting of representatives of the working party was with Ruth Kelly, MP, Financial Secretary to the Treasury. In this meeting, the issue of levying of stamp duty was discussed. The way the shariah-compliant housing finance product is structured would mean that stamp duty would be levied twice on a single property purchase. This additional levy would obviously make the product uncompetitive. The British government is considering making changes to the stamp-duty legislation to recognize this problem and facilitate the levying of a single charge on what, in effect, is a single purchase. In a similar way, many other issues have been taken up with different departments and officials to enable a like-for-like competitive product to be launched.

In fact, recent changes in legislation in 2007, have meant now that the unfair taxation of sukuk is no longer a problem because the government in the UK has removed the tax disadvantage to UK sukuk transactions (Bijur 2007), which is another reason that sukuk bonds have the potential to work in non-Muslim countries.

Indeed, as one or two major institutions who lead the launch of these products make headway and gain market share, other institutions would follow to protect their market. Thus, if successful, in a short space of time, one may see a plethora of shariah-compliant financial products in UK high streets.

Many people have argued that Muslims have availed themselves of existing products and are unlikely to abandon them for the new shariah-compliant products. However, anecdotal evidence suggests that many people would switch to shariah-compliant products if they are properly structured and competitively priced. Certainly, new buyers would seriously explore these facilities. As the range and scope of these products builds up, the whole saving and borrowing patterns of UK Muslims are likely to change. And as the volume of financing builds up, the underlying ethical base of Islamic financial products would begin to make its mark on the market. At that point, many non-Muslims would also be attracted to these products. In time, these products may provide a valuable bridge between different communities and interest groups in the UK.

7. CONCLUSION

This research can positively support the notion that sukuk can be used as a suitable replacement for conventional bonds, both in a Muslim countries, such as those in the Middle East, and also potentially in a non-Muslim countries, such as the UK. However, This is no easy feat, and this research has identified that, in order for this to happen, there are some recommendations that can help to make sukuk issuances successful and prosperous so that they can form a viable replacement for conventional noncompliant interest-bearing bonds.

8. RECOMMENDATIONS

1. Using the latest and most up-to-date technology to create a framework or system which will help sukuk transactions to be easy to buy and sell, create transparency, and reduce the risks of any bad business deals tainting the name of the noble sukuk tradition. This has been proven to be highly successful in Malaysia and has consequently led to it being the key sukuk issuer in the world.

2. Countries need to set up a special task force or regulatory body to oversee all sukuk transactions and dealings, which will be specially assigned to sukuk issuance, and these task forces will liaise with countries or companies who wish to issue sukuk, so that they can also educate regulatory bodies to help make the whole process more streamlined and to ensure that sukuk are not unfairly taxed in comparison to conventional bonds since this will inevitably put sukuk in a weak position and discourage their uptake. Furthermore, having a regulatory body or task force will help to ensure that only reputable providers are issuing sukuk, and this will help to reduce the risk of the sukuk holder losing his investment or assets to which his sukuk are assigned, because they will ensure that all sukuk sellers meet a criteria and are legitimate, and this will help to protect sukuk holders and give them credence.

In addition, the Islamic finance markets within the United Kingdom and the United States are showing significant growth and a promising future. However, the obstacle of complex regulatory environments presents a difficult challenge to the development of Islamic finance products. Nevertheless, Deutsche Bank, as an innovator and leader in the structuring space, is clearly best positioned to design creative products that overcome regulatory obstacles. As such, the United Kingdom and the United States represent significant business opportunities for Deutsche Bank in the Islamic finance arena.

5

RISK-BASED SUPERVISION FOR ISLAMIC BANKING & AREAS OF CONCERN

1. INTRODUCTION

The problem in the U.S. subprime mortgage market was identified as one of the main causes that triggered the recent global financial crisis. Crotty (2009) further argues that the deep cause on the financial side could also be found in the flawed institutions and practices of the current new financial architecture (NFA) regime. The NFA, that forms a globally integrated system of giant bank conglomerates, comprise the so-called shadow banking system of investment banks, hedge funds, and bank-created special-purpose vehicles (SPA). These institutions are either lightly and badly regulated or not regulated at all, an arrangement defended by and celebrated in the dominant financial economics theoretical paradigm—the theory of efficient capital markets. However, studies by Cheung and Coutts (2001) and Wooly (2010), among others, show that the theory of efficient capital markets is weak. Therefore, the celebratory narrative of the NFA accepted by regulators is seriously misleading.

In addition, the NFA also contributed to: (a) the widespread perverse incentives embedded in the NFA-generated excessive risk-taking throughout financial markets; (b) mortgage-backed securities, which became central to the boom, were so complex and non-transparent that they could not possibly be priced correctly, and their prices were bound to collapse once the excessive optimism of the boom faded; (c) contrary to the narrative, excessive risk built up in giant banks during the boom; and (d) the NFA generated high leverage and high systemic risk, with channels of contagion that transmitted problems in the U.S. subprime mortgage market around the world.

Understanding the profound problems of the NFA should become a lesson for the regulators and players in the Islamic financial services industry, which has expanded substantially over the last three decades. A review of the development so far indicates that too much emphasis has been placed on transplanting substantive norms from Islamic law that have become the foundation of Islamic banking (among examples are Zaher and Hassan 2001; Tahir 2007; and Tohirin and Ismail 2010) and little attention (up to our knowledge, only limited to Errico and Farakbahsh 1998)[1] has been paid to discussing the framework of regulations and supervision.[2]

In this paper, therefore, the aim is to design a risk-based supervisory framework for Islamic banks. This paper is motivated by three factors. First, Islamic banks matter for human welfare. Most noticeably, Islamic banks matter when they fail. Indeed, the fiscal costs of banking crises might be transferred to taxpayers. Second, recent research also finds that Islamic banks matter for economic growth.[3] Islamic banks that mobilize and allocate savings efficiently, allocate capital to entrepreneurs with the highest expected social returns, and exert sound governance over funded firms foster innovation and growth. Third, recent work further shows that banks matter for wealth creation.

The remaining discussion of this paper is divided into four sections. Section 2 will cover the debate and current evidence related to seven policy issues in the field of regulation and supervision. The discussion in section 3 will be focused on the risk-based supervision (RBS) approach, framework, and process. Section 4 will highlight the areas of concern to the central bank in performing the supervisory task. And section 5 presents the conclusions.

2. THE DEBATES & CURRENT EVIDENCE

In this section, discussion focuses on the debate and current evidence related to seven policy issues in the field of regulation and supervision. These issues cover the regulations on Islamic bank activities and banking-commerce links; domestic and foreign Islamic bank entry; capital adequacy; deposit-insurance design; regulations on easing private-sector monitoring of Islamic banks; government ownership of Islamic banks; and supervision. For each issue, we will: (a) stress the theoretical and policy disagreements and (b) emphasize that specific regulatory oversights are inextricably interrelated, so it is important to examine them simultaneously. This discussion will motivate the use of various interaction terms in our proposed approach and empirical analyses that will be discussed in section 3.

Regulations on Islamic Bank Activities and Banking-Commerce Links

There are five main reasons for restricting the degree to which banks can engage in securities, *takaful,* and real-estate activities or own nonfinancial firms. Indeed, it is these regulations that help define what observers mean by the term *bank.* First, conflicts of interest may arise when Islamic banks engage in such diverse activities as securities underwriting and real estate investments. Islamic banks, for example, may attempt to "dump" securities on, or shift risks to, ill-informed investors so as to assist firms with outstanding debts or existing equities. Second, to the extent that moral hazard encourages riskier behavior by Islamic banks, they will have more opportunities to increase risk if allowed to engage in a broader range of activities. Third, broad financial activities and the mixing of banking and commerce may lead to the formation of extremely large and complex entities that are difficult to monitor. Fourth, large Islamic banks may become so politically and economically powerful that they become "too big to discipline." Finally, large financial conglomerates may reduce competition and hence efficiency in the financial sector. Based on these arguments, the government can ease market failures and thereby enhance Islamic bank performance and stability by restricting certain activities.

However, there are alternative theoretical reasons for permitting Islamic banks to engage in a broader range of activities. First, fewer regulatory restrictions on activities will allow them more scope in processing information about firms, managing different types of risk for customers, advertising and distributing financial services, enforcing contracts, and building a reputation with clients. This moves banks toward becoming Islamic investment banks, rather than simply "Islamic banks."

Second, fewer regulatory restrictions may increase the value of Islamic banks, and thereby, augment incentives for Islamic banks to behave prudently. Third, broader activities may diversify income streams and thereby create more stable Islamic banks. Finally, the approach to regulations suggests that governments do not restrict Islamic bank activities to ease market failure. So, regulatory restrictions promote government power, create a bigger role for corruption through the granting of exceptions to the rules, and thereby hinder Islamic bank performance and stability.

Most of the literature suggests there are positive benefits from permitting broader powers for Islamic banks. For instance, expanded

Islamic banking powers may reduce the cost of capital and cash-flow constraints. Unrestricted Islamic banks may also have higher levels of operational efficiency than Islamic banks with restricted powers. In terms of diversification, since profits from providing different financial services are not highly correlated, there are diversification benefits from allowing broader powers. Hence, the greater involvement of Islamic banks in different financial services can be expected to develop. This offers wider scope for Islamic financial services which are based on profit-sharing and markup methods.

Regulations on Domestic and Foreign Islamic Banks Entry

Islamic banks with monopolistic powers have stronger incentives to incur costs associated with overcoming informational barriers, which then facilitate the flow of financing to more worthy corporations. Furthermore, Islamic banks with monopolistic power may possess considerable value, which will enhance prudent risk-taking behavior. Thus, there may be a "helping-hand" role for the government in limiting competition. While there may exist valid economic reasons for regulating entry, this view stresses that placing such limits can cause corruption and impede economic efficiency. Politicians and regulators may use entry restrictions to reward friendly constituents, extract campaign support, and collect bribes.

Furthermore, an open, competitive Islamic banking sector may be less likely to produce powerful institutions that unduly influence policymakers in ways that adversely affect bank performance and stability. Greater restrictions on the entry of foreign and domestic Islamic banks make for less efficient and more fragile Islamic banking systems. And while not emphasized in formal theoretical literature, the impact of competition may depend on the degree of regulatory restrictions on Islamic banking activities and the mixing of Islamic banking and commerce, the quantity and quality of supervision, the features of any deposit-insurance scheme, capital-adequacy requirements, the degree of equity-market development, and the extent to which government-owned Islamic banks play a dominant role in the Islamic banking sector.

Regulations on Capital Adequacy

Traditional approaches to Islamic bank regulations emphasize the positive features of capital adequacy requirements. Capital, or net worth, serves as a buffer against losses and failure. When faced with limited liability, Islamic bank owners avoid higher risk activities, considering the amount of capital at risk relative to assets. With deposit insurance, the regulatory capital requirements play a crucial role in aligning the incentives of Islamic bank owners with depositors and other financiers. However, disagreement may exist over whether the imposition of capital requirements actually reduces risk-taking incentives. Moreover, it is difficult, if not impossible, for regulators and supervisors to set capital standards that mimic those that would be demanded by well-informed, undistorted private-market participants. For instance, actual capital requirements may increase risk-taking behavior. At the same time, capital requirements may also induce credit rationing that produces negative implications for economic growth.

Higher capital requirements may induce customers to shift to capital markets, and in the process, impair capital allocation, while raising capital requirements can increase the cost of capital. Thus, these provide conflicting predictions on whether capital requirements curtail or promote Islamic bank performance and stability.

Therefore, at a time when existing regulatory capital requirements are widely viewed as being arbitrary and inadequate, it seems especially important to examine whether they even matter, since capital adequacy standards have been introduced.

Deposit-Insurance Design

Countries often adopt deposit-insurance schemes to provide protection for unsophisticated and small depositors who face coordination and free-rider problems. If too many depositors attempt to withdraw their funds at once, an illiquid but solvent bank can fail. Moreover, monitoring banks is expensive, and there is an externality associated with monitoring to curtail risk-taking behavior. Therefore, depositors will have a tendency to free ride, so that there is a socially suboptimal level of monitoring. To improve these problems, a proponent of government intervention would favor deposit insurance to protect payment and credit systems from contagious bank runs *plus* a tight official overview to augment private-sector monitoring of banks. However, potential gains from a deposit-insurance scheme come at a cost. There are concerns that deposit insurance could encourage excessive risk-taking behavior.[4]

The moral-hazard problem, which is aggravated by deposit insurance, continues to be a concern today. Thus, even those subscribing to the helping-hand view of government may argue that the adverse-incentive costs of deposit insurance outweigh the benefits. On the other hand, many believe that regulation and supervision can control the moral-hazard problem, including an appropriately designed insurance system that encompasses coverage limits, scope of coverage or the extent of uninsured liabilities, coinsurance, funding, premium structure (flat fee or risk-based), that manages the funds and how they are motivated, and membership requirements.

In the case of Islamic banks, the intention of depositors to share the profit and losses might indicate that deposit insurance is not applicable. Furthermore, the current amount insured up to RM60,000 per depositor in Malaysia, per member institution, does not consider the risk-base of each member institution.

Regulations on Easing Private-Sector Monitoring of Islamic Banks

Many regulators encourage private monitoring of banks. For instance, regulators may require Islamic banks to obtain certified audits and/ or ratings from rating agencies. Regulators may also make Islamic bank directors legally liable if information is erroneous or misleading. Regulators may also compel Islamic banks to produce accurate, comprehensive, and consolidated information on the full range of Islamic bank activities and risk-management procedures. Furthermore, a country credibly imposes a no-deposit-insurance policy to stimulate private monitoring of banks.

Some economists have advocated greater reliance on the private sector and expressed misgivings with official regulation of Islamic banks. For instance, the grabbing-hand view of government regulations holds that banks will pressure politicians who, in turn, can unduly influence regulators. Furthermore, in some countries, regulators are not well compensated and hence, quickly move into banking, resulting in a situation in which regulators may have mixed objectives when it comes to strict adherence to the rules. Also, since regulators do not have their own wealth invested in banks, they have different incentives from those of private owners, or *rab al-mal*, when it comes to monitoring and disciplining Islamic banks. For example, the *rab al-mal*, who act as capital contributors via restricted deposits, are in a better position to monitor and discipline Islamic banks.

However, questions are raised about placing excessive trust in private-sector monitoring, especially in a system with poorly developed capital markets, accounting standards, and legal systems. A system with a weak institutional environment will benefit more from regulators containing excessive risk-taking behavior and thereby instilling more confidence in depositors than would exist with private-sector monitoring. This view argues that, in weak institutional settings, increased reliance on private monitoring leads to exploitation of small savers and hence less Islamic bank development.

Government Ownership of Islamic Banks

Economists hold sharply different views about the impact of government ownership of Islamic banks on financial and economic development. The argument is that government ownership of Islamic banks would facilitate the mobilization of savings and the allocation of those savings toward strategic projects with long-term benefits on an economy. According to this view, governments have adequate information and sufficient incentives to ensure socially desirable investments. Consequently, government ownership of Islamic banks helps economies overcome private capital-market failures, exploit externalities, and invest in strategic sectors. The government ownership of Islamic banks to promote economic and financial development may be relevant in an underdeveloped financial system.

However, governments do not have sufficient incentives to ensure socially desirable investments. Government ownership tends to politicize resource allocation, soften budget constraints, and otherwise hinder economic efficiency. Thus, government ownership of Islamic banks facilitates the financing of politically attractive projects, but not necessarily economically efficient projects.

Supervision

Islamic banks are generally supervised within the framework of the prevailing international commercial-banking supervisory systems. In some countries, special laws have been introduced to facilitate Islamic banking, while in others, no such laws have been introduced. Islamic banking operations in the latter group of countries are performed under the guidelines issued by their respective central Islamic banks.

Member countries covered in this review segregate banking functions from securities and *takaful* businesses, and distinct supervisory authorities are assigned the task accordingly. In Malaysia, where Islamic banks and *takaful* companies are supervised by a single authority, namely, the Central Bank of Malaysia (Bank Negara Malaysia or BNM), is the only exception. The global trend is also inclined toward the concept of universal banking with emphasis on supervision by a single mega-supervisor.

Islamic banks in member countries are supervised by central Islamic banks. However, the emerging trend in the world is to segregate the monetary-policy framework of macroeconomic management from the microeconomic considerations of bank soundness. As a result of this segregation, bank supervision is separated from monetary policy and assigned to a specialized authority. There are many examples of this segregation, the most recent and significant being the separation of supervisory functions from the Bank of England in 1998 and the establishment of the Financial Services Authority (FSA) in the UK to take up the responsibility of a mega-supervisor.

In cases where different supervisory authorities specialize in supervising different banking and non-banking financial institutions, the need for cooperation and coordination between these authorities increases. The available literature on banking supervision in member countries does not mention other sectors. This could perhaps be an indication of the absence of such coordination between the different supervisory organizations. Conventional Islamic banks are allowed to open Islamic windows in some member countries, while some other countries do not allow this. Only two member countries, Bahrain and Malaysia (Labuan), have offshore banking centers. In terms of compatibility with international banking standards, a study conducted by the Financial Stability Forum puts these centers in the moderately good second category.

3. SUPERVISION BY RISK—APPROACH, FRAMEWORK & PROCESS

Having discussed the debate on the current regulatory framework, the question arises as to how to produce an effective supervisory approach. An effective supervision, as discussed in Ismail (2010a) might produce a positive and negative influence. The positive influence might be seen in three areas. First, Islamic banks are costly to monitor. Private agents may not have the ability or incentive to supervise Islamic banks and will attempt to free-ride. Thus, there will be too little monitoring of Islamic banks, which implies suboptimal performance and stability. Supervisors can improve this market failure. Second, because of informational asymmetries, Islamic banks are prone to contagious and socially costly bank runs. Supervision in such a situation can serve a socially efficient role. Third, some countries choose to adopt a deposit-insurance scheme, and this situation: (a) creates incentives for excessive risk-taking behavior by Islamic banks, and (b) reduces the incentives for depositors to monitor Islamic banks.

Thus, strong supervision will help prevent Islamic banks from engaging in excessive risk-taking behavior and thus improve Islamic bank performance and stability. Alternatively, effective supervisors might exert a negative influence. Governments with powerful supervisory agencies may use this power to benefit favored constituents, attract campaign donations, and extract bribes. Effective supervisors would be less focused on overcoming market failures and more concerned with currying favor from political support and implementing their own narrow objectives. Therefore, supervision would be positively related to corruption and would not improve either Islamic bank performance or stability.

On the other hand, we should also recognize that Islamic banking is a business of taking risk in order to earn profits. However, risk levels must be appropriately managed and controlled. Islamic banking risks must also be evaluated in terms of their significance. Therefore, in this section, the discussion will be focused on the approach, framework, and process of risk-based supervision.[5]

The Approach

For an individual Islamic bank, supervision by risk leaves the responsibility for controlling risks with the Islamic bank management. The supervisor assesses how well an Islamic bank manages this risk over time, rather than only assessing the condition at a single point in time. With supervision by risk, the supervisor functions in more of an oversight than an auditing role. Supervision by risk allows the supervisor to supervise by concentrating on systemic risks and institutions or areas that pose the greatest risk to the system.

For the whole industry, the supervisor's supervision by risk identifies areas that, in aggregate, pose the potential for presenting an unacceptable level of risk to the Islamic banking system and the deposit-insurance fund. For those high-risk activities or activities that have become particularly risky because of market conditions, the supervisor's goal is to communicate with, and influence, the industry through direct supervision, policy, and regulation. In situations where an individual Islamic bank is not properly managing its risks, the supervisor's goal is to use appropriate means to influence the Islamic bank management to adjust its practices to conform with sound fundamental banking principles.

Some risks are inherent to Islamic banking. A wide body of knowledge exists within the industry on how to identify, measure, control, and monitor these inherent risks. Supervision by risk acknowledges those inherent risks and performs limited testing in examinations directed at confirming whether adequate controls are in place. Other risks in the industry are more diverse and complex. These more sophisticated risks require enhanced controls and monitoring by both the Islamic bank and the supervisor. The supervisor is committed to directing significant resources to these complex and evolving risks, especially where they present material, actual, or potential risks to the Islamic banking system.

Risks that large Islamic banks assume are generally diverse and complex and warrant a risk-oriented supervisory approach. Under this approach, supervisors do not attempt to prohibit appropriate risk-taking, but rather, they ensure that Islamic banks understand and control the levels and types of risks they assume. In situations where risk is not properly managed, the supervisor tries to direct the Islamic bank management to take corrective action so that the Islamic bank is managed in a safe and sound manner. In all cases, the supervisor's supervisory focus is to ensure that the Islamic bank management identifies, measures, controls, and monitors risks to ensure sufficient capital is present in light of the risks involved.

Risks that small Islamic banks assume are generally less diverse and complex than those of larger Islamic banks. Under this approach, supervisors verify the existence of adequate controls and risk-management systems by testing transactions. Supervisors will focus attention on the risk-management systems and the methods the management uses to identify, measure, control, and monitor risks in those small Islamic banks or in areas that are more diverse and complex. Supervision by risk allocates greater resources to those areas with higher risks.

The supervisor accomplishes this by:

- Identifying risks using common definitions. This set of risks forms the basis for supervisory assessments and actions.
- Measuring risk based on common evaluation factors. Risk measurement is not always quantified in ringgit terms; it is sometimes a relative assessment of exposure. For example, numerous internal control deficiencies may indicate an Islamic bank has an excessive amount of transaction risk.
- Evaluating risk management to determine if Islamic banking systems adequately manage and control the identified risk levels. The sophistication of the systems will vary based on the level of risks present and the size and/or complexity of the institution.

- Assigning greater resources to areas of higher or increasing risk, both within an individual institution and among banks in general. This is done through the supervisory strategy.
- Performing examinations based on the risks, reaching conclusions on risk profiles and conditions, and following up on areas of concern.

To accomplish the above tasks, supervisors should discuss preliminary conclusions of this risk-based supervisory strategy with the Islamic bank management and adjust conclusions and strategies based on these discussions, if appropriate. The supervisor can then focus supervisory efforts on significant risks, i.e., the areas of highest risk within an Islamic bank and within the Islamic banking system. Supervisors must focus on the consolidated company risk profile to fully implement supervision by risk. This consolidated approach recognizes that risks at individual institutions may be mitigated or increased on a companywide basis. However, individual Islamic bank-risk profiles must be determined for the lead Islamic bank and significant country bank affiliates for the supervisor to fully evaluate the consolidated risk profile.

In summary, the supervision by risk approach provides the supervisor and the Islamic banking industry with a high level of consistency in supervision because it sets and uses minimum core procedures; an allocation of resources based on risk; sufficient flexibility to allow supervisors to tailor the supervisory effort to the risks present; less supervisory intervention in areas of low risk; and help in determining the sufficiency of each Islamic bank's capital and risk management systems.

The Framework

To ensure effective supervision, the supervisor normally requires a common framework to document decisions. However, risks may threaten the Islamic banking institutions. Therefore, a framework that outlines the supervisory tools to mitigate them is required. This section will present the risk-based supervisory (RBS) framework. In the following discussion, we will introduce a series of structured stages that are designed to: (a) focus the supervisor's attention on the risks that threaten the achievement of supervisory objectives; and (b) enable the supervisor to devise a risk-mitigation program to address those risks. The framework is based on the three main supervisory objectives, namely, promoting stability and soundness of the Islamic

banking system, ensuring consumer protection, and reducing financial crimes.[6]

The framework involves six stages: the full-scope maiden examination; impact assessment; the risk assessment of Islamic banks (RAIB);
development of risk-mitigation programs; evaluation and validation;
communicating the results of the assessment and risk-mitigation program to the bank. Finally, the discussion will focused on the implementation of the risk-mitigation program, ongoing assessment of the
Islamic bank, and response to risk escalation.

Stage 1. Full-Scope Examination

A full-scope examination, covering the identification of risk elements
will be discussed in Stage 3. The identification will be conducted at the
commencement of the risk-based supervisory process. The risk elements
cover the full range of risks in an Islamic bank. This stage will be a one-
off event, as subsequent examinations will depend on the supervisors'
assessment and perception of the risks of individual Islamic banks.

Stage 2. Impact Assessment

The first step at this stage is to determine the potential impact of an
Islamic bank, in the event of distress, on the entire financial system by
appraising, quantitatively, balance sheet items such as total assets and
deposits against defined impact thresholds. This will indicate the scale
and significance of the problem, if it is to occur. Then, the Islamic bank
will be categorized into impact bands: Very High, High, Medium,
Low and Very Low. The impact threshold is as shown in table 5.1.

A bank's risk impact category is the higher of the two impact parameters. For example, if a bank, reviewing the table, has high impact rating, using the assets parameter, and has a medium or low rating, using
the deposits parameter, its impact classification will be high.

Stage 3. Risk Assessment

At this stage, the focus is to assess the likelihood of various Islamic
bank-specific risks crystallizing. The aim of risk assessment of Islamic
banks (RAIB) is to provide a concise method of communicating and
documenting judgments regarding the quantity of risk, the quality
of risk management, the level of supervisory concern (measured as
aggregate or composite risk), and the direction of risk. In achieving this, the first step is to identify the risk elements that threaten
the achievement of the supervisory objectives. Islamic banks will be
assessed based on a risk map, which takes into account external events
or threats (environmental risks) and Islamic bank-specific risk issues,

Table 5.1   Islamic Bank Impact Thresholds

Thresholds	Total Assets			Total Deposits		
	RM billion	Market Share	Number of Banks	RM billion	Market Share	Number of Banks
Very High	Above 114	Above 4%	1	Above 45	Above 3.2%	3
High	86–114	3%–4%	2	35–45	2.5%–3.2%	1
Medium	57–85	2%–3%	2	25–34	1.8%–2.5%	2
Low	28–56	1%–2%	5	14–24	1% –1.8%	5
Very Low	Below 28	Below 1%	12	Below 14	Below 1%	11
			22			22

and scores each of these risks in a common way. This will involve off-site assessments and on-site visits to complement available information on an Islamic bank.

Environmental Risks. These are risks that are external to the Islamic banks, which directly or indirectly affect the Islamic bank's business or control risks. Environmental risks will not be accessed directly under this framework, as their effect will be captured in the assessment of Islamic bank-specific risks and sector-wide assessment.

Islamic Bank-Specific Risk Assessment. The Islamic bank-specific risk assessment involves determining where the risks arise and which statutory objectives they may affect. The assessment will focus on the risk elements structured into four business-risk groups and five control-risk groups. Business risks are derived from the overall philosophy of the Islamic bank and include issues of strategy, target market, products and services, and the risk attached to the financial soundness of the institution. And control risks are the risks arising from the failure and/or inadequacies of systems, processes, and procedures as well as organization and culture. The main business-risk and control-risk elements adopted include the risks described in chapter 10.

Risk-to-Objectives. The risk-to-objectives (RTOs) are risk elements that threaten the achievement of supervisory objectives. The risk to the three supervisory objectives will include the following as shown in table 5.2.

In view of the fact that some RTOs are common threats to more than one supervisory objective, as indicated in table 5.2, they will be

Table 5.2 Risks to Supervisory Objectives

	Supervisory Objectives	Risk-to-Objectives
1	Promoting Stability and Soundness	Financial failure
		Poor corporate governance
		Widespread misconduct/Mismanagement
		Financial crime/Fraud or dishonesty
		Malpractices in operations
2	Ensuring Consumer Protection	Financial failure
		Widespread misconduct/Mismanagement
		Financial crime/Fraud or dishonesty
		Poor corporate governance
		Inadequate consumer understanding
3	Reduction of Financial Crimes	Financial crime/Fraud or dishonesty
		Money laundering
		Malpractices in operations

summarized under seven broad categories:

- Financial failure (objectives 1 and 2);
- Misconduct/mismanagement (objectives 1, 2, and 3);
- Poor corporate governance (objectives 1 and 2);
- Inadequate consumer understanding (objective 2);
- Financial crime/fraud or dishonesty (objectives 1, 2, and 3)
- Money laundering (objective 3)
- Malpractices in operations (objectives 1 and 3)

Scoring of Islamic Bank-Specific Risks. Having identified the risk elements, the risk assessment will involve measuring the threat of each Islamic bank's risk element against the RTO categories using the risk map, as shown in table 5.3. The measurement will be on a scale of 1 to 5, with 1 representing the lowest risk and 5 the highest. The risk bands will be as follows:

1—Very Low
2—Low
3—Medium
4—High
5—Very High

There might be situations where a risk element for a given Islamic bank does not have any correlation with a supervisory objective. In

Table 5.3 Islamic Bank-Specific Risk Map

Risk Groups	Risk Elements	Risk-to-Objectives						
		Financial Failure	Misconduct & Mismanagement	Poor Corporate Governance	Inadequate Government Understanding	Financial Crime/Fraud or Dishonesty	Money Laundering	Forex Malpractice
Strategy	Quality of corporate strategy/Nature of business	3	2	3	N/A	N/A	2.5	4
Strategy Score		3	2	3	N/A	N/A	2.5	4
Strategy OVERRIDE		3	2	3	N/A	N/A	3	4
Market, Credit & Operational Risks	Credit risk	4	3	1	N/A	1	N/A	1
	Market risk	2	1	N/A	N/A	N/A	1	4
	Operational risk	1	2	3	3	2	2	1
	Legal risk	1	1	1	1	1	3	3
Market, Credit & Operational Risks Score		2	1.8	1.2	2	1.3	2	2.25
Market, Credit & Operational Risks OVERRIDE		2	2	1	2	1	2	2
Financial Soundness	Adequacy of capital	5	5	5	N/A	N/A	N/A	N/A
	Liquidity/clearing settlement arrangement	5	5	5	N/A	N/A	N/A	N/A
	Earnings	5	2	3	N/A	N/A	N/A	N/A

Continued

Table 5.3 Continued

Risk Groups	Risk Elements	Risk-to-Objectives						
		Financial Failure	Misconduct & Mismanagement	Poor Corporate Governance	Inadequate Government Understanding	Financial Crime/Fraud or Dishonesty	Money Laundering	Forex Malpractice
Financial Soundness Score		5	4	4	N/A	N/A	N/A	N/A
Financial Soundness OVERRIDE		5	3	4	N/A	N/A	N/A	N/A
Nature of Customers & Products	Types of customers/Sources of business	2	2	N/A	4	1	2	1
	Types of products	2	4	N/A	2	N/A	1	N/A
Nature of Customers & Products Score		2	3	N/A	3	1	1.5	1
Nature of Customers and Products OVERRIDE		2	2	1	3	1	1.5	1
Treatment of Customers	Service delivery, training, recruitment, remuneration & security of customer	1	N/A	N/A	2	3	N/A	N/A
	Disclosure and adequacy of product literature	N/A	N/A	N/A	4	N/A	N/A	N/A
Treatment of Customers Score		1	N/A	N/A	3	3	N/A	N/A
Treatment of Customers OVERRIDE		1	1	N/A	3	3	N/A	N/A

Category	Item						
Organization	Clarity of ownership/group structure	2	3.5	3	N/A	N/A	N/A	N/A
Organization Score		2	3.5	3.5	N/A	N/A	N/A	N/A
Organization OVERRIDE		2	3	3	N/A	N/A	N/A	N/A
Internal Systems & Controls	Risk-management system	5	5	5	N/A	N/A	N/A	N/A
	Information communication technology	5	2	3	N/A	N/A	N/A	N/A
	Compliance/Internal audit	5	5	3	N/A	2	1	3
	Degree of outsourcing	4	1	N/A	N/A	N/A	2	N/A
	Money-laundering controls	5	4	1	N/A	N/A	1	5
Internal Systems and Controls Score		4.8	3.4	3	N/A	2	1.3	4
Internal Systems & Controls OVERRIDE		4	3	3	N/A	1	1	4
Board, Management & Staff	Corporate governance/Human resources	4.5	4.5	3	N/A	1	N/A	2
Board, Management, and Staff Score (Average)		4.5	4.5	3	N/A	1	N/A	2
Board, Management & Staff OVERRIDE		4	4	3	N/A	1	1	2
Business & Compliance Culture	Relationship with regulators	1	N/A	N/A	N/A	N/A	N/A	3
Business & Compliance Culture Score		3	N/A	N/A	N/A	N/A	2	3
Business & Compliance Culture OVERRIDE		2	N/A	N/A	N/A	N/A	2	3

that instance, the assessment will be categorized as "not applicable" (N/A). For situations where additional information is required to make an objective assessment, the assessment will be categorized as "additional information required" (AIR) and might require further supervisory action to obtain the required information. Table 5.3 illustrates a typical risk map.

The scores for each of the business-risk and control-risk elements in the risk map are aggregated to arrive at the average risk scores under the two risk groups as illustrated in table 5.4.

The assessment of the control risk will influence the assessment of business risks as low control risks will often mitigate the overall business risks and vice versa. For instance, where the aggregate score under the business risks is Very High and the control risk Very Low, then the overall score will be Medium. Conversely, when the business risk is Very Low but the control risk Very High, the aggregate rating should be considered High.

The overall Islamic bank-specific risk score will be derived as shown in the risk matrix in table 5.5.

The bank-specific risk scores for each RTO group will then be matched against the supervisory objectives that it is likely to affect, as illustrated in table 5.6.

Determining the Overall Risk. The next step will be to determine the overall risk. A combination of the bank-specific RTO score and the impact score gives a measure of the overall risk posed to the supervisory objectives, as represented in table 5.7.

The overall risk rating for any bank will be in accordance with the risk matrix in table 5.8.

The overall risk rating is a summary judgment that reflects the level of supervisory concern, considering both the quantity of risk and the quality of risk management, and then weighing the relative importance of each. The supervisor's assessment of aggregate risk may be impacted by mitigating factors, not necessarily considered in the quantity of risk and quality of risk-management decisions. An example of a mitigating factor is *takaful*. Aggregate risk is assessed as high. Aggregate risk assessments direct the specific activities and resources outlined in supervisory strategies. In addition, the Islamic bank's overall risk rating will be used to take informed decisions on the type and frequency of regulatory response to be adopted.

Direction of risk, which indicates the likely changes to the risk profile over the next 12 months, for example, and is assessed as decreasing, stable, or increasing. Decreasing direction indicates the supervisor anticipates, based on current information, that the

Table 5.4 Islamic Bank-Specific Risk-Map Summary

RTO Groups	Financial Failure	Misconduct & Mismanagement	Poor Corporate Governance	Inadequate Consumer Understanding	Fraud or Dishonesty	Money Laundering	Forex Malpractice
Risk Groups							
Strategy	3	2	3	N/A	N/A	3	4
Market, Credit & Operational Risk	2	2	1	2	1	2	2
Financial Soundness	5	3	4	N/A	N/A	N/A	N/A
Nature of Customers & Products	2	2	1	3	1	2	1
Total Business Risk Score	3	2	2	3	1	2	2
Total Business Risk Rating	Medium	Low	Low	Medium	Very Low	Low	Low
Treatment of Customers	1	1	N/A	3	3	N/A	N/A
Organization	2	3	3	N/A	N/A	N/A	N/A
Internal Systems & Controls	5	4	3	N/A	1	1	4
Board, Management & Staff	3	5	3	N/A	1	N/A	2
Business & Compliance Culture	2	N/A	N/A	N/A	N/A	2	3
Total Controls Risk Score	3	3	3	3	2	1	3
Total Controls Risk Rating	Medium	Medium	Medium	Medium	Low	Very Low	Medium
Bank-Specific Risk Score per RTO Group	Medium	Medium	Medium	Medium	Low	Very Low	Medium

Table 5.5   Risk Matrix for Bank-Specific Risk Score

Control	Business				
	Very High	High	Medium	Low	Very Low
Very High	Very High	Very High	High	Medium	Medium
High	Very High	High	High	Medium	Low
Medium	High	Medium	Medium	Medium	Low
Low	High	Medium	Low	Low	Low
Very Low	Medium	Low	Low	Very Low	Very Low

aggregate risk will decline over the next 12 months. Stable direction indicates that the supervisor anticipates that aggregate risk will remain unchanged. Increasing direction indicates that the supervisor anticipates that aggregate risk will be higher in 12 months in the future. When aggregate credit risk is moderate and the direction is decreasing, the supervisor can anticipate that the aggregate credit risk will be low or lower in 12 months. The direction of risk often influences the supervisory strategy. For the other two categories of risk, strategic risk and reputation risk, the supervisor's judgment of risk is less quantifiable. These risks affect the Islamic bank's value but are not direct risks that supervisors can precisely measure in an examination. These risks require supervisors to consult with supervisory offices to ensure that all elements are considered. Given the less explicit nature of these risks, the central bank's risk assessment and measuring process is modified.

Preliminary Feedback. At this stage, significant findings from the risk assessment will be discussed with the Islamic bank, following which the risk-mitigation program will be developed and formalized. The feedback will take the form of meeting with the Islamic bank management and will usually take place at the completion of the onsite risk-assessment work. It may, however, take place at a later time, particularly if additional time is required to arrive at conclusions on significant findings. Where issues identified are not material, a preliminary feedback meeting may not be necessary. The importance of the preliminary feedback is to allow the Islamic bank the opportunity to correct any errors of fact rather than to negotiate the supervisor's interpretation of the facts.

Stage 4. Development of a Risk-Mitigation Program
The risk-mitigation programs (RMPs) are regulatory actions designed to address the issues identified at the risk-assessment stage. The program will address the nature of the risk, intended outcome, actions

Table 5.6 RTO Score Sheet

Statutory Objective	Financial Failure 1	Misconduct & Mismanagement 2	Poor Corporate Governance 3	Inadequate Consumer Understanding 4	Fraud or Dishonesty 5	Money Laundering 6	Forex 7	SUMMARY
Stability & Soundness of the Financial System	Medium	Medium	Medium	–	Low	–	Medium	Medium
Consumer Protection	Medium	Medium	Medium	Medium	Low	–	–	Medium
Reduction of Financial Crime	–	Medium	–	–	Low	–	Medium	Low

Table 5.7   Overall Bank-Risk Rating Sheet

Statutory Objective	Derived Impact	Impact Override	Derived Bank-Specific Risk	Derived Bank-Specific Risk Override	Overall Risk	Override Comment
Stability & Soundness of the Financial System	Very High	Very High	Medium	Medium	High	
Consumer Protection	Very High	Very High	Medium	Medium	High	
Reduction of Financial Crime	Very High	Very High	Low	Low	Medium	
Summary	Very High	Very High	Medium	Medium	High	

Table 5.8   Risk Matrix for Overall Bank-Risk Rating

Derived Bank Impact	Derived Bank-Specific Risk				
	Very High	High	Medium	Low	Very Low
Very High	Very High	Very High	High	Medium	Low
High	Very High	High	High	Medium	Low
Medium	High	Medium	Medium	Low	Low
Low	High	Medium	Medium	Low	Very Low
Very Low	Medium	Medium	Low	Low	Very Low

to be taken by the supervisor and/or the Islamic bank, and the time frame within which to implement the program. This will involve the selection of regulatory tools, based on the severity and nature of the risk and the expected outcome.

Supervisory Tools. These are tools used to diagnose and mitigate risks. They consist of actions to be taken either by the supervisor or by the Islamic bank and are classified under four broad groups as shown in table 5.9.

The diagnostic tools will be used mostly to identify and/or measure risks, the monitoring tools will be used to keep track of risks on

Table 5.9 Supervisory Tools

Diagnostic	Monitoring	Preventive	Remedial
On-site examinations	Off-site surveillance	Disclosure	Compensation
Investigations	On-site visits	Consumer education	schemes
Sector-wide projects	External auditors	Public statements	Complaints resolution
Risk assessments		Regulatory standards	Holding actions
		Authorizations	Disciplinary actions
		Institution-specific standards	Interventions
		Contingency planning	Restitution
		Self-regulatory organizations (SRO)	Penalties
		Memoranda of understanding (MOU)	

an ongoing basis, the preventive tools are meant to mitigate or reduce risks, and the remedial tools will be used to address crystallized risks.

The selection of regulatory tools will depend on the overall risk rating of the Islamic bank. For Islamic banks rated Very High or High, remedial and preventive tools will mainly be applied; for those rated Medium, monitoring and preventive tools will be applied; while for those rated Low and Very Low, mainly diagnostic and monitoring tools will be applied.

Determining the Supervisory Period. The supervisory period is the time between one formal risk assessment and another, or the period for which the risk-mitigation program lasts. This will vary depending on the overall risk rating of an Islamic bank and will range between 12 and 24 months.

Islamic banks rated Very High and High should have a regulatory period of 12 months; those rated Medium and Low, 18 months; and those rated Very Low should have a regulatory period of 24 months. However, any bank that is rated as a Very-High-impact Islamic bank should have a supervisory period of 12 months.

Stage 5. Evaluation and Validation

Having completed the risk assessment and the risk-mitigation program, the next stage entails conducting an internal evaluation and validation before the results are adopted for implementation. The validation and testing process are expected to provide quality control and ensure consistency. A committee whose members will be independent of the risk assessment of a particular bank will conduct it. The process will cover the items listed in table 5.10.

Stage 6. Communicating the Results of the Assessment and Risk-Mitigation Program to the Islamic Bank

The results of the risk assessment and the threat it poses to achieving supervisory objectives, the on-site examination report, and the risk-mitigation program, will be formally communicated to the Islamic bank. The letter communicating the result of the risk assessment will contain the following: the Islamic bank-specific risk scores and impacts against each statutory objective; key findings that lead to the Islamic bank-specific risk scores of Very High or High; the length of the regulatory period; and a requirement that the Islamic bank should, at all times, communicate significant events that may affect the risk assessment to the supervisors.

The letter also will include findings of on-site visits, which should contain the following: (a) the supervisor's view of key environmental or external risks facing the Islamic bank (where appropriate) that provides the context for the Islamic bank-specific issues identified in the risk assessment; and (b) the detailed comments and observations of the supervisor.

Table 5.10 Evaluation and Validation Procedure

Type of Review	Reviewer
Review of the risk assessment for completeness and appropriateness of the scores assigned	Committee of group heads of relevant supervisory departments
Review of any business and control risk overrides	Central Bank Management (CBM)/ PDIM Executive Committee on Supervision
Review of the risk-mitigation program for completeness, adequacy, proportionality, and optimal allocation of resources	The director of the relevant supervisory department
Approval of the overall risk-rating and risk-mitigation program	CBM/ PDIM Executive Committee on Supervision

Finally, the letter will also inform the Islamic bank of the prescribed risk-mitigation program that will set out the following: the issues identified by the supervisors; the intended outcome the supervisors seek to achieve for each issue; the action to be taken to achieve the intended outcome, specifying whether the action is to be taken by the supervisor or the Islamic bank; and the timetable of the action.

The letter to the Islamic bank will be addressed to the board of directors to emphasize the importance placed on the board's responsibility for setting up and operating effective internal controls and running the Islamic bank's business in compliance with regulatory requirements. In line with this approach, there will be a bias in risk-mitigation programs (RMPs) for action to be taken by the Islamic bank rather than the supervisors, to achieve specific intended outcomes and make management responsible for ensuring that the action is taken. Where an Islamic bank is a subsidiary, a copy of the letter will be sent to the parent company.

The Islamic bank will be required to respond formally to the letter confirming that it will follow the prescribed risk-management program. If the Islamic bank declines to carry out the actions detailed in the RMP, the supervisor will consider the use of other supervisory tools. The supervisor will also consider whether the Islamic bank has breached any rule, principle, or threshold condition and whether other formal actions, consistent with the provisions of the Islamic Banking Act of 1983 (IBA) and Malaysia's Banking and Financial Industries Act of 1989 (BAFIA) as well as the Contingency Planning Framework for Systemic Distress and Crisis, should be taken. The issuance of the letter will trigger implementation actions, as specified in the RMP, by both the supervisory authorities and the Islamic bank.

Stage 7. Implementation of Risk-Mitigation Program, Ongoing Assessment and Response to Risk Escalation

Where an Islamic bank's supervisory period exceeds certain prescribed months or, say, 12 months, an interim review will be carried out before the expiration of the regulatory period to determine whether the earlier risk-assessment and risk-mitigation programs are still applicable to the Islamic bank. The review will also determine whether there has been an escalation of the risks and the appropriateness of the risk-mitigation programs. The review will be an off-site assessment, covering all the risk factors, issues, and the supervisory tools deployed.

Reviews could also be carried out when any of the following occurs: developments in the external environment that could materially affect the Islamic bank; changes in the bank's business, strategy, infrastructure, or management; where the supervisory tools deployed have not been effective; and successful achievement of desired outcomes in the RMP, which should ordinarily lead to an improvement in the risk profile of the Islamic bank.

Supervisory Process

This section details steps in off-site surveillance and on-site examination under the risk-based supervision framework. The new framework, based essentially on risk profiling of Islamic banks, would be largely carried out through baseline monitoring. Through analyses of information rendered by the Islamic bank, the supervisor would monitor, identify, and deal with Islamic bank-specific risks, and provide an insight into industry developments. Since supervisory action would be risk-driven, routine monitoring visits will not be a dominant feature of the new framework.

Off-Site Surveillance

The off-site function will principally be preemptive. It will aim at preventing, controlling, and mitigating risks. It will also aim at early identification of problems with a view to taking prompt corrective actions, thereby minimizing overall risk in the system.

In line with the framework, off-site supervisory activity will involve risk identification and assessment; implementing and monitoring ongoing corrective actions; providing statistical reports to operators; discussions with management and/or external auditors; collaboration with on-site examiners; and identification of high risk areas for on-site examination.

Pre-Conditions for Effective Off-Site Surveillance

There are several conditions needed for effective off-site surveillance; among them are data integrity, legal protection for compliance officers, legal protection for whistle-blowers, independent directors, fit and proper persons tests, and supervisory team formation.

Data Integrity. The efficacy of RBS relies heavily on the integrity of the data upon which informed and accurate analysis of risks are based. Where information and data are either false or unreliable, assessment from the analysis conducted on such data would also be unreliable and faulty. The need for zero tolerance for data and information unreliability is a *sin qua non* for effective risk based supervision. In order to further ensure the quality of data received from Islamic banks, proper validation tests should be carried out with adequate links to examination reports through the Electronic Financial Analysis Surveillance System (e-fass). *Legal Protection for Compliance Officers.* The compliance officers of the reporting Islamic banks will play a significant role under a risk-based supervision regime. Accordingly, there should be adequate legal protection for them. They are to ensure that returns comply with rules and regulations before appending their signatures. They should be made to operate within minimum operating standards. *Legal Protection for Whistle-Blowers.* The supervisor needs to be alerted on happenings in the Islamic banking institutions being supervised that constitute threats to the supervisory objectives. One source of such information would be the insiders of the Islamic banking institutions and others whose information could be relied upon. To assure adequate protection for those providing the information, appropriate legal backing will be necessary.

Independent Directors. In constituting the board of directors of Islamic banks, provision should be made for independent directors so as to promote transparency and reliability of information from the Islamic banks. Such persons must be of high integrity, have no equity interest in the Islamic bank, and should be professionals in their own fields. The Islamic banks should ensure that they are appointed as members of the major committees of the board.

Fit and Proper Persons Test. The process of carrying out the fit-and-proper persons test should be reviewed to make it more effective. The boards of banks should have proper combination of executive and non-executive directors. The chairman of the board should not serve as the chairman of board for committees while the posts of board chairman and managing director/chief executive officer should not be vested in one person.

Supervisory Team Formation. Risk-based supervision requires full collaboration between on-site and off-site supervision. In that regard, the roles of on-site examination and the off-site supervision teams need to be harmonized. This would entail the assignment of a group of Islamic banks to a particular on-site examination team with its equivalent off-site. This arrangement would facilitate continuous exchange of information, regular meetings, continuity, and specialization among supervisory personnel.

Off-Site Surveillance Processes

The process involves the same stages as discussed in the RBS framework, except these stages will be actually taken by supervisors in response to the information provided.

Impact Assessment of Banks. The off-site processes will commence with the impact assessment of banks. This entails determining the relative significance of a bank to the entire system if it becomes unsafe or unsound. Balance-sheet items, (i.e., total assets and total deposits) are compared against defined impact thresholds. This will indicate the scale and significance of the problem, if it were to occur. The bank will then be categorized into impact bands—Very High, High, Medium, Low, and Very Low. The impact threshold is as shown in table 5.11.

Bank-Specific Risk Assessment. This assessment will involve an off-site review of the bank-specific risk elements. Integrating the outcome of the on-site bank-specific risk assessment with that of the off-site will complete the bank-specific risk review.

Development of Risk-Mitigation Programs. Once the bank-specific risk assessment is completed, the risk-mitigation program (RMP) should be developed. The off-site and on-site examiners as detailed below will jointly develop this.

The risk-mitigation programs (RMPs) are regulatory actions designed to address the issues identified at the risk-assessment stage. The program will address the nature of the risk, intended outcome, actions to be taken by the supervisor and/or the bank, and the time frame within which to implement the program.

This will involve the selection of regulatory tools, based on the severity and nature of the risk and the expected outcome. The tools, which consist of actions to be taken either by the supervisor or the bank, are classified under four broad groups as shown in table 5.12.

Evaluation and Validation. Having completed the risk-assessment and the risk-mitigation program, the next stage entails conducting an internal evaluation and validation, before the results are adopted for implementation. The validation and testing process is expected to

Table 5.11   Impact Thresholds

Thresholds	Total Assets			Total Deposits		
	RM billion	Market Share %	Number of Banks	RM billion	Market Share %	Number of Banks
Very High	Above 114	Above 4%	1	Above 45	Above 3.2%	3
High	86–114	3%–4%	2	35–45	2.5%–3.2%	1
Medium	57–85	2%–3%	2	25–34	1.8%–2.5%	2
Low	28–56	1%–2%	5	14–24	1%–1.8%	5
Very Low	Below 28	Below 1%	12	Below 14	Below 1%	11

Table 5.12   Supervisory Tools

Diagnostic	Monitoring	Preventive	Remedial
On-site examinations	Off-site surveillance	Disclosure	Compensation schemes
Investigations	On-site visits	Consumer education	Complaints resolution
Sector-wide projects	External auditors	Public statements	Holding actions
Risk assessments		Regulatory standards	Disciplinary actions
		Authorizations	Interventions
		Institution-specific standards	Restitution
		Contingency planning	Penalties
		Self-regulatory organizations (SRO)	
		Memoranda of understanding (MOU)	

provide quality control and ensure consistency. A group whose members will be independent of the risk-assessment team of a particular Islamic bank will conduct this function. The process will include the items in table 5.13.

Communicating the Results of the Assessment and Risk-Mitigation Program to the Bank. The results of the risk assessment, and the threat it poses to achieving supervisory objectives and the risk-mitigation program, will be formally communicated to the Islamic bank.

Ongoing Assessment and Response to Risk Escalation. After communicating the results of the assessment and RMP to the Islamic bank, the next stage is the ongoing assessment and response to risk escalation. The ongoing assessment will also focus on prompt corrective actions and contingency plans to curtail possible escalation of risk. Apart from the risk assessment that is carried out for each Islamic bank during the supervisory cycle, an ongoing off-site assessment of the financial soundness of the Islamic bank will continue. The process would include off-site rating of Islamic banks, sending offsite reports to Islamic banks, and a review of compliance with prudent thresholds and guidelines.

On-Site Examination Process

The risk-based supervision will commence with a full-scope examination of an Islamic bank. Subsequently, the on-site examination will

Table 5.13   Evaluation and Validation Procedure

Type of Review	Reviewer
• A review of the risk assessment for completeness and appropriateness of the scores assigned. • A review of any business and control risk overrides. • A review of the risk-mitigation program for completeness, adequacy, proportionality, and optimal allocation of resources. • Approval of the overall risk-rating and risk-mitigation program.	• Committee of group heads of relevant supervisory departments. • CBM/PDIM executive committee on supervision. • The director of the relevant supervisory department. • CBM/PDIM executive committee on supervision.

range from a full-scope examination that will cover the various risk elements identified to a target examination, as may be determined by the supervisory program developed for each Islamic bank.

On-site visitation will be required at the following stages of the framework: risk assessment, development of RMP, implementation of the RMP, and commencement of a new assessment cycle. The examination process will include the following phases: examination planning, examination program, and examination procedures.

Examination Planning. The starting point for RBS is an understanding of the Islamic bank being examined. The process begins with the review of all available information on the bank. The examination team will prepare an institutional overview report in the form of an executive summary that concisely describes the Islamic bank's present condition as well as its current and prospective risk profile.

To define the examination activities as well as provide information for the conduct of risk-based examination, two important documents must be prepared. These are the examination planning memorandum and the entry letter.

The examination-planning memorandum (EPM) will summarize the activities to be performed during the on-site examination, as an integral part of the RBS. The document, which would be prepared before undertaking the on-site visit, should identify the specific objectives of the examination and ensure that the objectives and strategy are communicated to the team members. The focus of on-site examination identified in the EPM, should be oriented to a top-down approach that includes a review of the Islamic bank's risk-management systems and appropriate level of transaction testing. Transaction testing and asset review would be necessary to verify the integrity of the systems.

The primary purpose of the EPM is to document and convey examiners' conclusions regarding allocation of examination resources according to perceived risks. However, it should not serve as an off-site analysis of the Islamic banking institution to be examined. The EPM includes a discussion of all CAMELS (*c*apital adequacy, *a*sset quality, *m*anagement quality, *e*arnings, *l*iquidity, *s*ensitivity to market risk) rating-system components (and in some cases, ancillary areas), regardless of the risk involved or the volume of resources anticipated to be devoted to these areas. The EPM will also include data and discussion regarding examination hours (budgeted hours, average hours, and previous examination hours).

The EPM comments will be prepared on an exception-only basis, according to areas of higher-than-normal or lower than-normal perceived risk. It will also encourage brief, bullet comments, not necessarily of report quality; include high-level performance ratios and financial data; require the examiner's formal contact with the bank's off-site examiner during pre-planning, which will be documented in the EPM; define the deadline for submission to be the last five business days prior to the commencement of the examination. The examination planning process will generate concise pre-planning documents that are consistent with the stated examination objectives and detail allocation of resources according to perceived risks.

The entry letter is used to request an Islamic bank to supply specific information on its activities to the supervisor. It identifies information necessary for the successful execution of the on-site examination. The letter would be tailored to fit the specific character and profile of the Islamic bank to be examined and the scope of the activities to be performed. To eliminate duplication, the letter will not request any information that is provided on a regular basis to the regulatory authorities, such as the various types of financial information on the quarterly bank report.

Examination Program
The examination program will provide a comprehensive schedule of all examination activities to be conducted on an Islamic bank. The examination program should incorporate the following: targeted risk areas, low-risk areas subject to limited review, financing scope, staffing, documentation methodology, and submitting the examination planning memorandum.

Targeted Risk Areas. Targeted risk areas are defined as areas with more than normal risk, to which the examiner intends to devote additional or above normal examination resources. Targeted risk areas may include CAMELS components, specialty areas [e.g., e-banking], internal audit environment, and internal routine and controls. Targeted risk areas should not include discussions of areas that are perceived to present average or moderate risk. For areas of moderate or normal risk, the examiner will perform standard examination procedures. Specific discussion of these areas is, therefore, not necessary.

Low-Risk Areas Subject to Limited Review. Examiners will specifically discuss any areas of perceived low risk, where normal examination resources and procedures will be reduced or eliminated. Comments will include a brief explanation of why the area is considered low risk.

Financing Scope. The examiner will comment on the proposed financing scope, with emphasis on risk areas within the portfolio where financing file reviews will be concentrated. To the extent possible, examiners will disclose the target financing penetration percentage. The examiner will discuss financing scope with the off-site examiner during the pre-examination planning contact.

Staffing. The examiner will prepare a schedule of duties, apportioning tasks to members of the examination team. The job schedule should be accomplished within the specified time frame.

Documentation Methodology. The examiner is expected to indicate the specific examination modules that he or she anticipates using. The actual documentation methodology used may differ from that discussed in the EPM.

Submitting the Examination Planning Memorandum. The examination-planning memorandum (EPM) is expected to be submitted for approval not later than the last business day prior to the commencement of the examination. A copy of the EPM should also be forwarded to the relationship manager for comments.

Examination Procedures

Having developed the EPM, examination procedures will be tailored to the characteristics of each Islamic bank, bearing in mind the size, complexity, and risk profile. The procedures will cover the evaluation of areas of significant risk, documentation of findings and conclusions, exit discussion, and risk report.

Evaluation of Areas of Significant Risk. The field work will focus on developing appropriate documentation to adequately assess management's ability to identify, measure, monitor, and control risks.

Procedures will be completed to the degree necessary to determine whether the Islamic bank's management understands and adequately controls the levels and types of risks that are assumed. Full-scope examinations are expected to include the examiner's evaluation of all the risk elements, which usually are the common sources of significant risks. In addition, examiners are also expected to evaluate other areas of significant sources of risk to the Islamic bank. The examiner should hold formal meetings with the Islamic bank's management team to discuss and obtain commitment on their findings on each functional area.

Documentation of Findings and Conclusions. It is important for examiners to document their findings and overall conclusions after performing the procedures contained in the relevant examination manual. The comments are expected to be clear and well organized. The conclusions, as each relates to the functional area under review, should clearly communicate the examiner's assessment of the risk-management system, the financial condition, and compliance with laws and regulations

Exit Discussion. At the end of the examination, the examiners will arrange a meeting with the Islamic bank's management during which all findings will be discussed.

Risk Report. At the conclusion of each on-site visit, a risk map, as shown in table 5.3 will be produced. Accompanying the risk map, a detailed report will also be produced. It should clearly and concisely contain any supervisory issues, problems, or concerns related to the Islamic bank. All comments regarding deficiencies noted in the Islamic bank's risk management systems, as highlighted during the exit discussion, should be included in the report. Accordingly, the report should detail observations under each of the risk elements.

Stress Testing

Stress testing is developed to avoid the portfolio losses. In stress testing, supervisors are concerned that Islamic banks monitor their risk exposures with appropriate reference to unlikely events that could cause portfolio losses. They are interested in ensuring that stress-testing procedures are detailed in the Islamic bank's risk-management policies and that senior management actively uses the information, for example, in setting trading limits. Note that some supervisory concerns remain, including the need to improve financing and liquidity-risk stress-testing as well as the need to integrate market and financing risks across the Islamic banks. In addition to assessing Islamic banks' risk-management practices, supervisors have developed stress-testing tools for their own monitoring purposes.

The central bank in different jurisdictions use different stress-testing models to identify depository institutions that are potentially vulnerable to markets. For example, one model was calibrated to the financial crisis in 1997, which affected the health of several depository institutions. With regard to the benchmark rate risk, the central bank could maintain a duration-based valuation model that examines the impact of an increase in rates on bank-portfolio values. The model can be used to detect Islamic banks that would appear to be the most vulnerable to rising benchmark rates.

Recently, supervisors have been developing similar tools for assessing national financial systems overall. For example, macroeconomic stress-testing techniques are used to assess the vulnerability of a financial system to exceptional, but plausible, macroeconomic shocks. These stress tests have become an important component of the Financial Sector Assessment Program (FSAP), initiated by the International Monetary Fund in 1999 and conducted by national policymakers. There are two main methodological approaches here. The piece-wise approach evaluates the vulnerability of the financial sector to individual risk factors, such as nonperforming financing ratios, by forecasting their behavior under various macroeconomic stress scenarios. The integrated approach analyzes the sensitivity of the financial system to multiple risk factors by generating a distribution of aggregate portfolio losses that could occur under macroeconomic stress scenarios.

For example, one stress scenario could be based on the macroeconomic impact of a 35 percent decline in global stock prices while another scenario could be based on a 12 percent decline in domestic real-estate prices. The magnitude for these hypothetical macroeconomic scenarios would be compared with the range of historical estimates. The aim is to identify the probability that those two results move together.

4. Areas of Concern in Performing the Supervisory Task

Having discussed the approach and framework of RBS and the supervisory process, there are several areas of concern to the central bank. We will discuss each concern below.

Capital Adequacy and Earning Sustainability

An area of particular concern to the central bank in its supervisory role over Islamic banks is whether an Islamic bank has sufficient capital to support its operations, to provide an adequate base for the growth of the bank, and to act as a cushion to absorb unexpected losses incurred by the bank. Capital adequacy is a vital measure of the safety and soundness of the Islamic bank and a significant indicator of the level of protection the Islamic bank has against insolvency. Ensuring adequate levels of capital on a consolidated basis promotes public confidence in the particular Islamic bank and the entire banking system. The central bank's capital-adequacy guidelines include risk-based measures (based on the Basel I and capital-adequacy standard) and leverage measures.

The primary functions of the risk-based measure of capital adequacy are to: (a) sensitize regulatory capital requirements to differences in risk profiles among Islamic banks; (b) factor off-balance sheet exposures into the assessment of capital adequacy; (c) minimize disincentives to holding liquid, low-risk assets; and (d) achieve greater consistency in the evaluation of the capital adequacy of major Islamic banks throughout the world.

The risk-based capital guidelines set forth minimum ratios of capital to risk-weighted assets, but it is important to note that Islamic banks are expected to maintain capital well above these minimum ratios. Currently, the minimum ratio of total capital to risk-weighted assets is 8 percent, and the minimum ratio of Tier 1 capital to risk-weighted assets is 4 percent. Those bank-holding companies that intend to expand their operations are expected to maintain capital levels significantly in excess of these minimum ratios. Additionally, those bank-holding companies that engage in Islamic banking or Islamic non-banking activities that are prone to high levels of risk, such as engaging in underwriting and dealing in certain debt and equity securities through Islamic non-bank subsidiaries, must maintain capital ratios substantially above the minimum ratios. Islamic banks that fail to meet the minimum risk-based standard, or otherwise become inadequately capitalized, must develop and implement a capital restoration plan acceptable to the central bank.

The leverage measure of capital adequacy was formulated by the central bank to complement the risk-based measure in determining the overall capital adequacy of Islamic banks. The central bank has established a minimum ratio of capital to total assets of 8 percent. The principal objective of the capital leverage ratio is to limit the degree to which an Islamic bank can leverage its equity capital base.

As in the case of the earning sustainability, Islamic banks are expected to maintain an increasing trend of profit with a lower allowance. By doing this, Islamic banks are able to transfer reserves that could increase the total amount of capital.

Continuous Surveillance

Continuous surveillance can be judged by the use of various monitoring systems and risk-management tools or controls. This section will focus discussion on both.

Monitoring System

Over four decades, beginning in the 1970s, various monitoring systems have been developed, but their objectives have generally been the same: to identify developing financial problems at Islamic banking institutions; to identify the main areas of supervisory concern in those institutions; and to allocate the more experienced examiners to troubled institutions.

This discussion will concentrate on each monitoring system and highlight the limitations of each, which will later produce a combination of the Financial Institutions Management System (FIMS), the risk rank, and the risk-based supervision.

Uniform Bank Surveillance Screen. Since the mid-1970s, the central bank monitored the financial performance and condition of banking organizations by screening financial ratios calculated from the Call Report, filed quarterly by each banking organization. In an effort to improve this monitoring system, the central bank in the mid-1980s adopted the Uniform Bank Surveillance Screen (UBBS) as its primary surveillance system. With some changes, the UBBS remained in service until 1993, when it was replaced by FIMS. The UBBS used financial data from regulatory reports to identify individual institutions whose financial ratios had deteriorated relative to the averages of their respective peer groups, institutions with similar sizes of assets.

CAEL System. During the mid-1980s, the central bank developed a surveillance system known as CAEL, which is methodologically similar to the UBBS. The acronym CAEL refers to four CAEL-component ratings that the system evaluates: capital, asset quality, earnings, and liquidity. The system does not provide a management rating. Like the UBBS, CAEL is based upon quarterly bank Call Report data; but whereas the UBBS calculates a composite percentile ranking, CAEL calculates off-site surrogates for CAEL ratings.

CAEL ratings are calculated in a manner similar to that by which the surveillance scores are calculated in the UBBS, although the calculation of CAEL ratings is considerably more complex and involves many more financial ratios. Like the UBBS, the CAEL system divides banks into peer groups, based upon asset size, and calculates percentile rankings for four sets of financial ratios that correspond to the four component ratings. Each of the four component ratings is calculated as a weighted average of the corresponding set of financial ratios. The composite CAEL rating is calculated as a weighted average of the four component ratings. Both the ratios used to calculate the ratings and the weights associated with each ratio are determined by a panel of bank examiners. CAEL remains in place today as the central bank's off-site surveillance system.

Financial Institutions Monitoring System. The weaknesses of the above methods are identified around three areas. First, the weights assigned for each variable, which were fixed across estimation periods, were determined subjectively rather than by rigorous statistical testing. The CAEL applies equal weights to each of the four financial ratios used to construct the composite surveillance score. CAEL applies a system of weights determined by a panel of senior examiners.

Second, even if the selected financial ratios contained all the information necessary for an accurate assessment of risk, improper weighting of those ratios would reduce the accuracy of estimation. Moreover, even if optimal weights had initially been assigned, the failure to adjust for temporal shifts could also affect its accuracy.

Third, the weaknesses of these systems are the reliance upon peer-group analysis. Both systems divide banks into peer groups based upon asset size because the average values of key financial ratio are significantly different for banks of different sizes. Without a peer-group analysis, differences in the financial ratios associated solely with bank size could be mistakenly interpreted as differences in financial condition. Because performance is measured relative to that of other banks of similar size, however, systemic changes in the performance of the peer groups or of the banking system as a whole are not incorporated into the composite surveillance scores. Hence, if an entire peer group deteriorates, the percentile scores of individual banks within that peer group may not change, even though the banks have become riskier.

With peer-group analysis, an additional complication arises when the size of an institution changes in a manner that places it in a larger or smaller peer group than it was in during the previous quarter. In such a case, the institution's percentile scores may change significantly, even if its financial condition has not changed.

Addressing the weaknesses of the previous off-site bank-monitoring systems, the FIMS provides two complementary surveillance scores based upon two distinct econometric models—the FIMS rating and the FIMS risk rank. The FIMS rating is an assessment of a bank's current condition, whereas the FIMS risk rank is a longer-term assessment of the bank's expected future condition.

The FIMS rating represents an estimate, based upon the most recent data, of the financial health of the banks during the current quarter. Because the relationship between financial ratios and CAEL ratings may change over time, the FIMS rating model is updated each quarter. The updates reflect the most recent relationship between financial ratios derived from the two most recent quarters of the bank's financial statement and supervisory ratings based upon the most recent on-site examination. Empirical testing indicates that using data from the two most recent quarters to estimate the historical relationship maximizes the classification accuracy of the rating model.

On the other hand, the FIMS risk rank represents an estimate, based upon a bank's financial condition, as measured by the most recent data, of the probability that a bank will fail during the subsequent two years.[7] Like the FIMS rating model, the risk-rank model is updated quarterly to determine which ratios to include and how to weight these ratios. But the risk-rank model is updated using financial ratios derived from financial statements from the same quarter two years previously and information classifying banks as failing or surviving during the intervening period. This procedure enables the risk-rank model to incorporate change over time and produces a much longer-term assessment of a bank's financial viability than does the FIMS rating model.

Risk-Based Supervision. The dynamism of the global economic environment requires more robust tools and skills to mitigate risks arising from the rapid development of the financial sector. In response to the changing financial landscape as well as advancements in information and communications technology and its widespread use, a more effective approach is required. Although effective risk management has always been central to safe and sound banking activities, it has assumed added importance for two main reasons. First, new technologies, product innovation, and the size and speed of financial transactions have changed the nature of banking. Second, there is need to comply fully with the Islamic Financial Services Board guidelines and to prepare an enabling environment for the implementation of the new capital adequacy standards. The foregoing, among others, premised the imperative of the adoption of risk-based supervision (RBS) framework.

Risk-Management Tools

In promoting a stable and sound Islamic financial system, supervisory authorities place high priority on Islamic banks establishing effective risk-management processes. The processes put in place for the effective management of risks in any Islamic bank underscore the ability of the board and management of each Islamic bank to identify, measure, monitor, and control all risks inherent in its activities.

It is the overall responsibility of the board and management of each Islamic bank to ensure that adequate policies are in place to manage and mitigate the adverse effects of both business risks and control risks in its operations. Each bank should develop and implement appropriate and effective information systems and procedures to manage and control risks in line with the risk-management policies of the bank.

The supervisory authorities will appraise the adequacy of the risk-management processes of each Islamic bank. All the facets of the risk-management processes of the bank will be reviewed as the need arises to take account of changing circumstances. Each Islamic bank should submit a copy of its risk-management process (and any amendments thereto) to the central bank and the Malaysia Deposit Insurance Corporation for appraisal and review.[8]

The following issues need to be considered in developing the risk-management processes.

Self-Assessment. Each Islamic bank is expected to identify significant activities, types and levels of inherent risks, and the adequacy of its risk-management processes, and each Islamic bank should also assess itself to determine the level of risks inherent in its operations.

Risk Identification and Assessment. This process involves identifying the risks inherent in an Islamic bank's business activities, which may affect its business objectives. Each Islamic bank would also need to assess the likelihood of risks crystallizing from within the Islamic banks. The risk assessment entails the development of a risk map by Islamic banks, which should take into account external events and threats.

Risk-Measurement Methods. Islamic banks are required to score the risk elements identified in terms of size, duration, and probability of adverse consequences. The measurement should graduate risk levels, based on the scale or significance of the activities in relation to the Islamic bank's risk-management goals and objectives. Thus, a risk element may be scored Very High, High, Medium, Low, or Very Low.

Risk Mitigation and Control Program. The risk-mitigation program is a set of self-regulatory actions designed to address the impact of risks and its associated problems, if and when they occur. The type of risk-mitigation program that would be put in place would depend on the result of self-assessment carried out by the bank. Generally, risks viewed as Very High or High would require actions to be taken to mitigate such risks. The mitigation program from the individual Islamic bank's perspective would entail actions that are diagnostic, monitoring, preventive, or remedial. Actions are preventive when they are aimed at preventing the occurrence of an identified risk and remedial where they are to address crystallized risks. The risk-control process involves the establishment of risk-management standards. The standards to be set should be a deliberate policy of the Islamic bank to achieve its business objectives. The objective would be to minimize the occurrence of such identified risks and contain the effects of the risks when they occur.

Risk-Monitoring Process. Management should review the standards set for the Islamic banks on a continuous basis to ensure that they are appropriate in meeting the set objectives. This would be achieved by appointing specific risk managers who would review the adequacy or otherwise of the risk-management processes across the organization (see Appendix A). It is the duty of the senior management of the Islamic banks to ensure compliance with the risk controls put in place.

Supervisory and Enforcement Actions

The central bank may take both formal and informal supervisory enforcement action against an Islamic bank in response to violations of law or regulations, capital deficiencies, or other significant supervisory concerns. Generally, the central bank may take formal action only after informal action has failed to resolve the supervisory concerns. Informal actions include supervisory letters and formal discussions with the officers or directors of the Islamic bank. Formal actions include cease-and-desist orders, civil money penalties, criminal penalties, written agreements, and prompt corrective-action (PCA) directives. The central bank may take supervisory and enforcement action not only against the Islamic banks it supervises, but also against various persons affiliated with such Islamic banks, such as officers or directors.

Of the formal enforcement actions available to the central bank, PCA relates most directly to concerns regarding capital adequacy, as well as asset quality, management, earnings, and liquidity. PCA requires the central bank to administer timely corrective measures to Islamic banks when their capital position falls below certain thresholds that are considered unsafe and unsound. The five capital categories for PCA purposes are: (a) well capitalized; (b) adequately capitalized; (c) undercapitalized; (d) significantly undercapitalized; and (e) critically undercapitalized. Islamic banks falling into one of the last three categories are the primary candidates for PCA. PCA generally relies on the current total risk-based capital, Tier 1 risk-based capital, and Tier 1 leverage ratio thresholds to trigger specific actions to restore Islamic banks to appropriate capital levels. While these capital ratios are generally calculated from information submitted in the various regulatory reports required by the central bank, PCA may also be triggered by the finding of an unsafe or unsound condition or practice in an Islamic bank, irrespective of the Islamic bank's actual capital ratio. In such cases, the Islamic bank's measurable capital ratio may be reclassified to the next lower capital category.

PCA provides for increasingly stringent corrective provisions as an Islamic bank is placed in progressively lower capital categories. The PCA framework requires the central bank to take certain mandatory actions as well as to consider certain discretionary actions.

An important component of the PCA framework is the capital-restoration plan. Any Islamic bank that is undercapitalized, significantly undercapitalized, or critically undercapitalized must provide the central bank with a capital-restoration plan to bring capital ratios to at least the minimum level necessary for an adequately capitalized organization. These plans must be in writing and detailed in nature. Islamic banks submitting such plans for central-bank approval must adhere to established rules regarding the minimum substantive criteria for, and filing requirements of, capital restoration plans. Moreover, the central bank may not approve any capital-restoration plan unless each company or individual that controls the Islamic bank submitting the plan has guaranteed the Islamic bank's full compliance with the plan and has given the central bank reasonable assurances of performance. Failure to submit or implement an approved capital-restoration plan by an undercapitalized Islamic bank makes such an Islamic bank subject to the same PCA provisions applicable to significantly undercapitalized banks.

5. CONCLUSION

The aim of this paper is to produce effective supervision in Islamic banks. From the analysis, the findings suggest that the supervision by risk approach provides the supervisor and the Islamic banking industry: (a) a high level of consistency in supervision because it sets and uses minimum core procedures for an allocation of resources based on risk; (b) sufficient flexibility to allow supervisors to tailor the supervisory effort to the risks present; (c) less supervisory intervention in areas of low risk; and (d) help in determining the sufficiency of each Islamic bank's capital and risk-management systems.

6

IRAN'S ISLAMIC BANKING
EXPERIENCE & THE FUTURE

1. INTRODUCTION

The process of Islamization of the banking system in Iran had gone through two phases. In the first phase (1979–1982), the banking system was nationalized and reorganized in order to remove the weaknesses of the previous system. However, internal and external developments in this phase did not allow policymakers to build an adequate plan for the Islamization of the banking system. The second phase began in 1982 and lasted until 1986. In this phase, the law of *riba*-free banking (banking with no interest) was passed in 1983, which went into effect on March 20, 1984. The new banking law had these primary objectives: (a) the proper issue of money and credit for the creation of a just, healthy, and progressive economy; (b) the use of monetary tools to promote the country's national goals, including eliminating poverty and attaining national self-sufficiency; and (c) the preservation of the national currency value and the promotion of balance-of-payments stability.

With the passage of the Islamic banking law, the council on money and credit set the "minimum guaranteed profit return" (interest) for savings and time deposits at 7 to 8 percent. No interest was to be charged on loans and credits to private borrowers. Instead, a service fee and a contribution to the guaranteed profit were to be received, the rate differing according to the purpose. For example, 4 percent might be charged for housing, farming, and manufacturing and 8 percent for services. Despite drastic changes in economic conditions in the early years after the 1979 revolution, there were no major changes in the monetary and credit policy. While private deposits with the banking system increased more than 90 percent between 1979 and 1982, bank loans to the private sector rose by about 40 percent, because of stagflationary tendencies in the economy. To deal with the problem, the council on money and credit in 1982 raised the legal reserve requirement from 12 to 17 percent and placed ceilings on bank loans to various sectors. Nevertheless, the excess reserves of the commercial banks continued to mount due to government budgetary deficits, expansion of private deposits, and depressed conditions in the private sector. The fear of rising prices led the monetary authorities to raise the minimum reserve requirement on sight deposits from 17 to 27 percent in 1983. Private-sector liquidity was brought down to an annual growth rate of 17.2 percent (CBI 1985).

The central feature of the Iranian monetary system in the 1980s was that the money and credit-council-administered interest rates. The underlying purposes of such an administered structure of interest rates were the mobilization of savings and the provision of funds for productive activity to the preferred sectors at concessional rates of interest. Monetary policy was also influenced by the need to raise the domestic savings rate. If there is a larger proportion of savings in the form of financial assets, there is a need to offer depositors a positive real rate of interest[1]. The monetary authorities of Iran realized that low interest rates might not be able to generate savings. So they geared their policy toward encouraging deposits with long maturities.

The Islamic banking law gave the banks additional and more specific regulatory power. Of these regulatory powers, four instruments were the most effective. First, the Central Bank of Iran (CBI) had the power to set the minimum rate of return (i.e., interest charged by banks) in regular or limited partnerships in each sector. These rates effectively eliminated marginal and subpar projects. Second, by determining the profit-sharing ratio between the banks and their clients in each sector of the economy, the CBI could influence the amount of credit allocated by banks to various sectors. Third, by regulating and changing the rate of service fees (i.e., interest) charged by banks on forward transactions, installment sales, and lease-purchases, the CBI could regulate the allocation of credit financing for these traders. And, fourth, the CBI had the power to establish minimum limits for participation by banks in the capitalization of long-term investment projects; it thus had the power to influence the allocation of investment funds to different sectors of the economy.[2] The problems of slow growth of the banking-sector deposits worsened in the mid-1980s (when conversion of all operations to the new interest-free banking was completed), partly due to the lack of familiarity of lenders and borrowers with the new system. The sectoral loan rates, set administratively by the council on money and credit, were upwardly revised[3].

The priority sectors, like agriculture, had the lowest loan rates, and those for domestic commerce had the highest rates. The deposit rates were also upwardly revised, and certificates of deposit with different maturities were introduced. These changes were meant to reduce constraints on the banking system and increase its lending capacity by raising financial savings. This policy was successful in reducing cash holdings relative to deposits, increasing non-sight deposits and term investments in the banking system. Nevertheless, fiscal and monetary policies were inconsistent with the new deposits and loan rates. With a sharp increase in the rate of inflation in the early to mid-1990s, the real rate on five-year deposits began to decline substantially. The real return on five-year deposits had become positive again beginning in 1999. But short-term deposits have not enjoyed a positive real return for years. Perhaps the principal contributing factor to the weakness of Iran's financial reforms was the government's inability to produce definitive, rational, and cohesive policies in the financial and monetary sectors.

2. THE ISLAMIC BANKING LAW: DID THE BANKING SYSTEM IMPLEMENT IT?

The act of usury-free banking operations was ratified, and on that basis, the executive bylaws and directives were formulated. However, after a lapse of three decades from when the act was first put into effect, the phenomenon of interest has remained in the Iranian state-controlled monetary and banking system. Under the Islamic banking system, there are ten separate ways through which banks can make use of resources, such as deposits for financing personal, trade, and business needs as well as for longer term investments. Table 6.1 shows various methods of financing possible for each line of activity. The fact is that the performance of Islamic banking in Iran has not been much different from the previous Western style of banking. Since the early 1980s, installment sales have been on an upward trend, and this share has risen to one-third of credits. On the contrary, table 6.1 also indicates that another type of contract, such as the civil partnership, the share of *mozarebeh, qharz al-hassanh,*[4] were 29.4 percent in 1984, and had been reduced to 11.1 percent in 2006. However, Article 1 of the law of usury emphasizes the creation of necessary facilities for the extension of cooperation and *gharz-al-hassanh* among the people. The share of civil and legal partnership had experienced steady

Table 6.1   Islamic Modes of Financing in Iran (1984–2006)

Year	Gharz-al-hassaneh	Mozarebeh	Forward Transactions	Civil Partnership	*Joaleh*	Installment Sales	Hire Purchase	Legal Partnership	Direct Investment	Debt Purchase	Properties under Islamic Contract
1984	10.8	18.5	3.7	15.0	0.3	34.0	1.8	3.6	0.6	11.7	0.2
1985	10.8	15.9	3.2	13.2	1.4	32.6	0.9	7.3	3.6	10.1	1.2
1986	11.6	15.5	3.9	13.9	1.4	35.7	0.8	6.6	2.7	6.4	1.7
1987	10.6	12.6	3.9	13.9	1.8	42.7	0.8	7.1	1.7	3.1	1.8
1988	9.7	11.0	4.9	11.7	2.8	47.1	0.8	7.1	1.3	1.0	2.6
1989	7.5	10.7	6.7	12.8	5.1	46.8	0.5	5.8	1.3	0.6	2.2
1990	5.7	10.2	5.3	14.5	6.6	49.0	0.4	4.6	1.3	0.3	2.1
1991	4.2	9.7	5.0	17.8	7.0	47.0	0.7	4.8	1.3	0.1	2.4
1992	3.6	8.5	6.7	17.6	6.0	46.5	0.5	5.2	1.9	0.1	3.5
1993	4.6	7.5	6.9	17.4	6.0	45.0	0.7	4.8	2.6	0.1	4.3
1994	4.4	7.3	6.2	18.1	6.6	45.8	0.8	3.6	2.4	0.1	4.7
1995	4.7	6.8	5.5	19.4	7.0	45.0	1.0	2.7	1.7	0.0	6.2
1996	4.5	6.7	5.0	19.6	6.6	43.4	1.1	3.8	2.8	0.0	6.5
1997	4.6	6.4	5.2	11.6	1.6	56.0	0.8	4.7	2.5	0.0	6.4
1998	5.9	6.0	6.2	9.7	1.4	58.0	0.7	3.1	1.8	0.0	7.4
1999	4.6	6.3	6.7	10.3	1.7	28.3	0.6	2.7	1.5	0.0	0.9
2000	4.2	6.2	7.0	9.9	1.6	28.8	0.6	2.2	1.2	0.0	0.8
2001	4.5	5.5	7.5	8.6	1.6	31.4	0.7	1.6	0.9	0.0	0.5
2002	7.2	5.7	6.7	6.4	1.4	33.0	1.1	1.3	0.8	0.0	0.6
2003	5.8	6.2	6.1	6.7	1.6	35.5	1.2	1.6	0.9	0.1	0.6
2004	4.7	6.2	5.8	7.0	2.1	36.9	1.5	2.4	1.0	0.1	0.5
2005	4.4	6.9	5.2	7.5	1.7	33.6	2.4	2.5	1.0	0.1	0.4
2006	3.4	7.7	4.8	10.7	1.8	30.7	2.0	1.8	1.0	0.2	0.7

Source: Central Bank of Iran, annual and economic Reports, various years.

ⁱJoaleh (service contract), or an undertaking by the bank or the customer to pay a specific sum or service fee in return for a service as specified in a contract. Thus, the bank providing customary banking services (money transfers, cashing commercial paper, or handling other transactions) is entitled to a service fee.

growth. But for the last decade, this share has dropped to almost half of the previous amount. As a result, the share of civil and legal partnerships had reached 12.5 percent in 2006.

On the basis of the Usury-Free Banking Act in Iran, fiscal resources concerned with giving loans through the *mozarebeh* contract[5] necessarily must be provided by term-investment deposits, which are entrusted to banks by people for their utilization. The banks are authorized to insure the principal deposits and disburse the profit (which has not been specified in advance) accruing from permissible banking operations to the depositors after deducting the costs and advocates fees. According to this approach, the profit and principal deposit must not be guaranteed, because the profit appears to assume the nature of interest.

In effect, the purpose of the partnership contract with its Islamic tenor is to benefit from the investor's cash capital, and the *mozarebeh* agent's expertise and management in commercial affairs without the principal and profit thereof that is ensured by the agent in the *mozarebeh* contract. Indeed, in this kind of agreement, the party of the *mozarebeh* agent incorporates his work with the capital owner's cash capital, and if any profit accrues, the two parties have it divided between themselves as per the agreement. But if the trade incurs loss, the capital owner is not entitled to demand a profit or compensation from the opposite party. In this event, interest is not received or disbursed. But based on the bylaws and directives concerned with executing the *mozarebeh* contract, the contract between banks and the loan recipient is drawn up in such a way that this phenomenon emerges without its being directly named. In order to comprehend the argument behind this contention, it suffices to pay attention to the tenor of two of the articles associated with the *mozarebeh* contract between persons and the bank. The agent transfers to the bank the sum of expenses that he pays out of his/her own properties and resources in return for Iranian rials (RI)[6] 1,000, and while concluding the transfer contract (*solh* contract), the object of this article, he accepts all terms and obligations inserted in any of the prior and prospective articles of this agreement.

According to Article 15, while concluding the transfer contract, the object of Article 8, the agent necessarily accepts and undertakes to make up for any loss or decline that may be inflicted on bank principal out of his own properties. Because the party to the *mozarebeh* contract has transferred to the bank the amount that one should later pay on that account toward principal and profit expected by the bank (even when the agent incurs loss in his trade), the disbursement of the money is not tantamount to interest and usury because it has belonged to the bank itself all along. All contracts through which the bank resources confer loans to natural or legal persons out of the credit of investment deposits have similar attributes and are based on interest, though the rubric of interest has changed into bank profit. With regard to interest-free saving deposits (*gharz-al-hassaneh* deposits), by declaring various and precious prizes that are given to the winners via drawing lots, banks pave the way for attracting financial resources to these accounts, which, in turn, is a certain sort of deviation from the usury-free banking principle.

As apart of the implementation of the new banking law, the council on money and credit established the "minimum expected profit" in various economic sectors for lending or direct investment by the banks. Rates of charges on bank loans were determined by the central bank, according to the type of project and to the sectoral priorities. Thus, the rates in the agriculture sector were set at 4 to 8 percent and for services at 10 to 12 percent (CBI 1991). Beginning in 1990, these rates were raised to minimum 6 to 9 percent for agriculture and to a maximum of 17 to 19 percent for trade and service. As of early 1991, the market allowed the rates for the latter two sectors. In 1993, these rates again rose to 12 to 16 percent for agriculture and 18 to 24 percent for trade and services (CBI 1994). The rates of 9 to 16 percent for another sector also represented to the minimum payable and were calculated retroactively after the end of year, according to market conditions.

There has been a highly uneven expansion of credits to the service sector. The share of the service sector as a percentage of total credits paid to the economic sector has experienced an upward trend since late 1980s. Since 2000, this trend registered an increasing trend, which continued for the whole period. The aim of Islamic banking was to change the pattern of consumption and production in the economy through the reduction of credits to the service sector and increased credit availability to the agriculture sector. However, as table 6.1 indicates, agriculture's share as a percentage of total credits was the lowest. The share of agriculture rose from 14.2 percent in 1984 to 20.4 percent in 1989, but since then it had registered a declining trend for a decade. It was only between 1996 and 2000 that the agriculture share experienced a sign of improvement.

3. CONCLUSION

Under Islamic banking, the lender and borrower share the profits of enterprise and associated risk according to a previously agreed share.

Thus, the actual size of the profit to the lender can be determined only after completion of the projects. An increase in risk sharing, as entailed by Islamic banking, encouraged borrowers to adopt more risky projects. Naturally, this made the loan portfolios of banks more risky. Hence, banks were persuaded to ration credit more strictly and to divert a large proportion of their assets away from long-term investment loans to commercial and short-term loans.

Generally speaking, the record of Iran's banking system was unimpressive. Far from achieving the three-fold objectives of the 1983 banking act, namely, stimulating economic growth, promotion of social justice, and protecting the national currency, the economic sector was plagued by slow growth, a large portfolio of non-performing assets, and a narrow range of products and services[7]. As mentioned after the 1979 revolution, the stress laid on the Islamization of the system, policymakers of the economic system somehow had to eliminate the rubric of interest from the banking operations. However, most people in charge of economic affairs, impressed by the neo-classical approach, regarded interest as something that could not be omitted instead of probing into the real bases of interest and working out appropriate devices to eliminate it. For instance, in the *mozarebeh* contract, the bank and an agent agree to engage in some commercial activity and to earn a profit that would be shared between the bank and the agent (customer). However, the bank has received interest from the agent of the *mozarebeh* contract, and both parties treat the amount excess to the principal as a certain sort of interest.

The advocates of Islamic banking had exaggerated expectations of the benefits from the proposed law. Even if policymakers agreed on the elements of a program of policies, the transmission mechanism through which policies were adopted leads to complicated outcomes. Steps in that process of Islamization were subject to uncertainty and delay with the strong probability of adverse results. The adverse implications of poorly conceived policies exacerbated economic distortions.

7

ISLAMIC BANKING STRUCTURE & GROWTH IN THE SUDANESE ISLAMIC BANKING SECTOR

1. INTRODUCTION

The Islamic banking industry of Sudan is the backbone of the Sudanese economy. It emerged in 1977 with the establishment of Faisal Islamic Bank, the first Islamic bank to function in Sudan. In 1981 the West Sudan Islamic Bank and the Tadamon Islamic Bank set up their first branch in Khartoum, the Sudanese capital, followed by the creation of a cooperative Islamic development bank in 1982. In 1984 after the application of Islamic shariah as official law, the Sudanese government made it compulsory for all the banks in Sudan to conform to Islamic shariah principles. Since then, the entire banking system has converted to Islamic shariah principles, and many banks began to offer products and services that comply with Islamic shariah law.

In the 1940s and 1950s, many unsuccessful attempts were made to create an Islamic banking system as an alternative to conventional banking. But it was not until 1963 when the first Islamic bank was announced by Egypt, followed by the formation of the Dubai Islamic Bank (DIB) and the Islamic Development Bank (IDB) in 1975. After this initial period, openings of Islamic banks began to be announced in many Muslim countries, including Pakistan, Saudi Arabia, and Iran. Shortly after Malaysia's independence in 1963, the Malaysian government issued Tabbung Hajji as the first Islamic product designated to help Muslims to perform a pilgrimage (hajj) to Mecca and to Medina. Until late 1970s, there was only a limited range of Islamic products, but today with an estimated population of 1.6 billion Muslims, the interest-free Islamic banking industry is expanding rapidly with annual growth rates of 15 to 25 percent and around 250 to 300 establishments, operating from East to West. In the early 1990s,

Islamic banks started offering their services, which are driven by the profit-and-loss-sharing concept, to Western countries, including the United Kingdom, United States, and Germany, with a large selection of products for both Muslim and non-Muslim investors.

This chapter attempts to analyze the financial performance of three main Sudanese Islamic banks, i.e., the Faisal Islamic Bank of Sudan, Tadamon Islamic Bank, and Al-Baraka Bank, for the period between 2005 and 2008 and to highlight the subject bank's financial position, using financial statement analysis (FSA). To this end, we calculated numerous financial ratios and categorized them into five key groups by examining profitability, earnings, liquidity, credit risk, and assets activity. The numbers of the financial ratio used under the five main groups reached thirteen different financial ratios, including gross-profit margin, networking capital to sales, return on equity, and fixed-assets turnover.

According to O. Masood et al. (2008), the factors that affect the decision of customers when they are choosing whom to bank with begins with the bank's performance in terms of low service charges, followed by the bank's reputation and recommendations made by friends and family. Choosing their bank according to their faith was usually the least affecting factor of all. Hence, Islamic banks must not only rely on the fact that they are Islamic banks in order to market their products, but they must also take some measure to improve their efficiency and performance in order to survive in a highly competitive environment.

A large number of researchers in the Islamic banking performance area, such as M. Sabi (1996), Abdus Samad and M. Kabir Hassan (1997), A. Akkas (1996), M. Arif (1989), A. Samad (2004), and R. Libby (1975), have used financial ratios to determine the changes that occurred in the financial positions of these institutions, mainly because it is simple to understand and can be used for different sizes of banks or can match up a bank to an industry average in order to assist investment decisions. S. A. Rosly and M. A. Abu Bakar (2003) measured the performance of the Malaysian Islamic banking scheme (IBS) with Malaysia's mainstream banks during the period 1996–1999. They compared the performance of the banks' profitability using financial ratios, such as return on asset (ROA), return on deposit (ROD), asset utilization (AU), and operating efficiency ratio (OER).

According to B. Elliott and J. Elliott (2006), use of financial ratios while measuring performance has many advantages when investigating low performance areas and the changes that occurred during a specific period of time. In his research, A. Siddiqui (2008) used financial-ratios analysis to investigate the performance of two Pakistani banks, namely Al-Baraka Bank and Meezan Bank for the years 2003–2004. It was discovered that because of their unique nature, Islamic banks are generally more liquid than their conventional rivals. Two effective financial ratios to determine the liquidity position were identified as current ratio and quick ratio that related to the size of both assets and liabilities.

A. R. Belkaoui (1998) argued that due to the characteristic of the financial ratio in explaining links among the different financial statement entries, the analysis of financial statement accounts is much more complex than the analysis of financial ratios. This useful analysis involves comparing calculated ratios with the industry averages or with previous similar ratio analysis. The classification of financial ratios can be categorized into five key groups: (a) the business's capability to pay its immediate commitments, (b) its capability to meet its long-term commitments, (c) its mixes of funds, (d) business capital profitability and effectiveness, and (e) the effective usage of its assets.

For this chapter, we measured financial performance of selected Sudanese Islamic banks (Faisal Islamic Bank of Sudan, Tadamon Islamic Bank, and Al-Baraka Bank) and stressed their growth, using financial statement analysis (FSA). The procedure involved calculating numerous financial ratios and categorizing them info five key groups in order to identify profitability, earnings potential, liquidity, credit risk, and assets activity. The number of the financial ratio used under the five main groups reached thirteen further ratios which helped in calculating gross profit margin, networking capital to sales, return on equity, and fixed-assets turnover.

Using the ratios calculated, we made several contributions to the literature. First, we found that Sudanese Islamic banks are cost-effective in terms of generating reasonable profits. Second, the liquidity performances of all three selected banks were also found to be satisfactory with an average current ratio figure of 1.0 to 2.0. Moreover, the assets activity performance of three Sudanese Islamic banks measured by net-assets turnover suggested that all three banks are efficiently utilizing their net assets to generate profits. And finally, the credit-risk performance analysis implies that Sudanese Islamic banks are taking excessive risks.

The rest of the chapter is organized as follows. In section 2, we present a brief review of the Sudanese banking industry. Section 3 describes the methodology, research approach, and use financial statement analysis (FSA). Section 4 presents the empirical results and findings, and section 5 concludes.

2. Sudanese Banking Industry

A. E. Saaid, et al. (2003) has suggested that prior to the application of Islamic shariah and the discovery of Sudanese oil, the Sudanese banking industry suffered severe shortages of large profitable projects. Brutal civil war in many parts of Sudan led to a food crisis and economic deterioration. Although Sudan is the largest agricultural country in Africa, the farmers' immigration from rural to urban areas resulted in low production and loss of job opportunities. Other factors, such as political and economic instability, also reduced local and foreign trade. All these reductions had a direct effect on the Sudanese Islamic banking sector.

Recently, after the oil discovery in the last decade, large infrastructure projects were undertaken by the government, including building bridges, roads, and airports in order to link the production areas with local and foreign markets and in order to improve the efficiency of the internal trade between the various states of Sudan. All these efforts by the Sudanese government resulted in large foreign investments, and a considerable flow of liquid funds in the banking sector, creating more job opportunities. Although the entire banking industry in Sudan is Islamic, competition between banks is fierce. According to the central bank of Sudan (CBoS or simply called the Bank of Sudan, responsible for the country's bank regulations), there are over 30 Islamic banks currently operating in Sudan and all these banks are functioning within the rules and regulations of CBoS that conform to the Islamic shariah principle.

In an effort to improve Islamic banking performance and efficiency recognized in CBoS policies (2007 annual report, chapter 2), the central bank of Sudan motivated banks to keep 8 percent cash in balance from the total deposits (local and foreign currency) and 3 percent of the central bank's *ijara* as a legal reserve requirement. The current level of liquidity held by the banks is considered to be about 10 percent. This also resulted in an increase of banks' internal liquidity, which rose from 13.2 percent in 2006 to 18.5 percent in 2007, also in 2006 CBoS put into practice Basel II guidance for minimum capital adequacy.

3. Research Methodology

The annual reports of the Sudanese Islamic banks (Faisal Islamic Bank of Sudan, Tadamon Islamic Bank, and Al-Baraka Bank) are the main source of the secondary data for this research. Unfortunately, annual reports for Sudanese banks are not available for the period of more than one or two years at a time. Financial performances of Faisal Islamic Bank of Sudan for the years 2005–2008 are compared with financial performances of Al-Baraka Bank and Tadamon Islamic Bank for the periods 2005–2007 and 2006–2008, respectively.

For the purpose of this research, we have used five major types of ratios in order to measure profitability, earnings potential, liquidity, credit risk, and assets activity.

Profitability Performance Ratios

The assessment of the bank's earnings related to particular sale volume, assets size, or stakeholders' speculation can be achieved by using profitability ratios. While there are several profitability measures, we have considered four major ratios below.

Gross-Profit-Margin Ratio (GPM)

The gross profit margin points out the proportion of each sale per pound outstanding after paying the cost; the bank would consider it efficient and gainful if the ratio is on its highest level. The ratio can be calculated using the formula below.

Gross-profit-margin ratio = Gross profit * 100 / Sales

Cost-of-Sales Percentage Ratio (COS)

The cost-of-sales percentage ratio assesses the bank's efficiency in producing sales. The bank would consider it efficient if the ratio is at its lowest level. The cost-of-sales percentage ratio can be calculated using the formula below.

Cost-of-sales percentage = Cost of sales * 100 / Sales

Net-Profit-Margin Ratio (NPM)

The net profit margin indicates the efficiency and the financial position of the bank. The bank would be considered efficient and profitable if the ratio is at its highest level. This ratio can be calculated using the formula below.

Net profit margin = Net profit * 100 / Sales

Operating Profit Margin (OPM)

The operating profit margin determines the profit produced through bank operations; it's the pure profit after paying taxes and *zakat*

(PBTZ) for the Islamic bank. Operating profit margin can be calculated using the formula below.

Operating profit margin = Net profit before tax and Zakat /Sales

Earning (Principal) Performance Ratios

Earning or principal ratios measure the effectiveness of a bank in relation to the bank owner's equity level and total net assets. For the purpose of this research, we have considered using the two major earning (principal) ratios below.

Return-on-Equity Ratio (ROE)

The return-on-equity ratio simply appraises the return received for the bank's shareholders. The bank would be considered efficient and profitable if the ratio on its highest level is comparable to the market value. This ratio can be achieved by using the formula below.

Return on equity ratio = Net profit after tax and zakat /
Shareholders' book value

Return-on-Net Assets (RONA)

The return-on-net assets measures the effectiveness of bank management and how the existing resources have been utilized to produce reasonable earnings. The bank would be considered effective if the ratio is on its highest level. This ratio can be calculated by using the formula below.

Return on asset = Net profit after tax and Zakat / Total assets

Liquidity Performance Ratios

According to J. K. Shim and J. G. Siegel (2000), liquidity is the life-blood of business and a very essential part. It is extremely important to maintain the correct level of liquidity for any business in order to survive in the long run. While a lower level of liquidity may expose the business to financial and operational risks, a higher level of liquidity is not always a good thing because this may lead to minimum returns. For the purpose of this research, we will be considering two major liquidity ratios below.

Current Ratio (CR)
The current ratio examines the bank's safety margin to meet short-term obligations, the optimal ratio achieved when the total liabilities is less, or equal to, half of the total assets. This ratio can be calculated using the formula below.

Current ratio = Current asset / Current liability

Net Working-Capital-to-Sales Ratio (NCTS)
The net working-capital-to-sales ratio assesses the bank's outstanding balance after deducting the short-term commitments. This ratio can be calculated using the formula below.

Net working-capital-to-sales ratio = (Current assets − Current liabilities) / Sales

Credit-Risk Performance Ratios

Solvency can also be described as the ability of a corporation to meet its long-term fixed expenses and to accomplish long-term expansion and growth. The better a company's solvency, the better it is financially. We have considered three major credit-risk ratios below.

Equity-to-Asset Ratio (EQTA)
The equity-to-asset ratio measures the balance between the owner's total equity and the size of the total assets. This ratio can be calculated using the formula below.

Equity-to-asset ratio = Total equity / Total assets

Equity-to-Net-Loan Ratio (EQL)
This ratio of the equity to the net loan measures the balance between the owner's total equity and its total loans. It can be calculated using the formula below.

Equity-to-net-loan ratio = Total equity / Net loans

Debt-to-Equity Ratio (DER)
Debt-to-equity ratio, or gearing ratio, compares the owner's capital to borrowed funds. It can be calculated using the formula below.

Debt equity ratio = Debt / Equity capital

Assets Activity Performance Ratios

Assets-activity ratios give details on how effective a business is in utilizing their different types of assets (fixed and current). Moreover, the ratios simplify the link between total income and the existing level of assets. A bank would be considered effective if the ratio is on its highest level. For the purpose of this research, we have considered using the two major assets-activity ratios below.

Fixed-Assets-Turnover Ratio (FATR)

The fixed-assets-turnover ratio measures the efficiency of the bank and how the bank makes use of its total fixed assets to produce income. This ratio can be calculated using the formula below.

Fixed-assets turnover = Sales / Net fixed assets

Net-Assets-Turnover Ratio (NATR)

The net-assets-turnover ratio measures the efficiency of the bank and how the bank makes use of its total net assets to produce income. This ratio can be calculated using the formula below.

Total assets turnover a = Sales / Net assets

4. DATA ANALYSIS & FINDINGS

In order to analyze the data collected and draw the research findings, 13 ratios were calculated and divided into five groups in order to access (profitability, earning, liquidity, credit risk, and assets-activity ratios) for the period 2005–2008.

Profitability Ratios

Gross Profit Margin

Faisal Islamic Bank's gross profit improved during the fiscal year 2005–2006. During the period 2006–2007, the bank's gross-profit figure remained almost the same with only a marginal drop of 0.13 percent. This went to a huge drop of 12.22 percent during 2007–2008, due to a large increase in bank's total expenses, which had gone up by 64.29 percent.

Although Tadamon Islamic Bank's profit growth rate reached 13 percent in 2006–2007 from SDG 37.3 million to SDG 42.3 million (SDG stands for the Sudanese pound), a 16 percent increase in the bank's general expenses lead to an overall reduction in the bank's gross-profit ratio by 1.16 percent.

Al-Baraka Bank showed a reduction in the gross profit margin during 2005–2006 and 2006–2007. This was due to the massive increase in the bank's general expenditure by 38 percent from SDG 2,700 million to SDG 3,729 million in order to make use of the latest banking technology. Also the bank's efforts to strengthen its financial situation led to an increase in the bank's share of particular provisions, which included staff termination, reward provision, finance-risk provision, and bad-debt provision. Both increased in general expenditures, and provisions resulted in bringing the profit down by 13 percent from SDG 1,056 million to SDG 920 million.

Cost-of-Sales Percentage

Faisal Islamic Bank of Sudan showed a reduction in the bank cost-of-sales during 2005–2006 when total expenses declined from 45.90 percent to 16.12 percent. This went up again during the periods of 2006–2007 and 2007–2008, by 0.13 percent and 10.37 percent respectively, as expenses increased.

Tadamon Islamic Bank's cost of sales increased in the fiscal year 2006–2007, but reduced by 4.59 percent during 2007–2008 due to the bank's total expenses declining from 16.33 percent to 9.34 percent.

Al-Baraka Bank showed a continuous increase in the cost-of-sales percentage from 2005 to 2007, increasing its expenses in an effort to adopt the latest banking technology and to build up adequate provisions.

Net Profit Margin

Faisal Islamic Bank's net-profit ratio continuously increased during 2005–2006 and 2006–2007, due to the bank decline in sales from 76.20 percent to 15.99 percent that led to the decline in the bank's net profit from 119.12 percent to only 19.94 percent, respectively, but during 2007–2008, the bank's net-profit ratio declined by 11.85 percent as the result of sales that increased from 15.99 percent to 48.86 percent.

Tadamon Islamic Bank's net-profit ratio reduced from 2006 to 2007, but increased by 2.75 percent in 2007–2008, due to the bank sales declining from 14.76 percent to 14.61 percent as well as to the increase in bank net profit from 13.51 percent to 17.76 percent.

Al-Baraka Bank's net-profit ratio continuously was reduced from 2005 to 2006, and from 2006 to 2007, due to the bank's increase in general expenditures and provisions.

Net-Operating Profit Margin

Faisal Islamic Bank's operating profit increased from 2005 to 2006, due to bank sales declining from 76.20 percent to 15.99 percent. From 2006 to 2007, the bank's ratio was reduced by as little as 0.13 percent, but from 2007 to 2008, the bank ratio was reduced again by 12.22 percent as a result of the bank's sales increasing from 15.99 percent to 48.86 percent, compared with the bank's massive increase in expenditures from 16.12 percent to 64.29 percent.

Tadamon Islamic Bank's net-operating profit ratio from 2006 to 2007 was reduced by only 0.85 percent, and in 2007 to 2008, the bank ratio started to increase by 3.99 percent.

Al-Baraka Bank's net-operating profit ratio continuously declined from 2005 to 2006, and in 2006 to 2007, again due to the bank's uncompensated general expenditures but increased in relation to the bank's total sales level.

Earning (Principal) Ratios

Return-on-Equity Ratio

Faisal Islamic Bank of Sudan's return on equity continuously increased from 2005 to 2008.

Tadamon Islamic Bank's return on equity declined from 2006 to 2007, due to the bank owner's equity increase in 2006–2007 by 43 percent from SDG 97.2 million to SDG 193 million, and from 2007 to 2008, the bank shareholders' equity increased by 25 percent from SDG 139 million to SDG 175 million.

Al-Baraka Bank's return on equity declined from 2005 to 2006 due to the reduction in net profit before taxes and *zakat* as well as the increase in the bank shareholders' equity by 11.01 percent and again from 2006 to 2007, due to the bank's severe decline in net profit by 51.93 percent, compared with the bank equity growth of only 4.23 percent.

Return-on-Net-Assets Ratio

Faisal Islamic Bank's return on net assets increased from 2005 to 2006, and from 2006 to 2007 the bank ratio was reduced, due to the bank's net assets growth by 43.78 percent, compared with 19.94 percent growth in the bank profit after taxes and *zakat,* and again from 2007 to 2008, the bank ratio was reduced due to the bank huge growth in net assets by 50.29 percent, compared with 31.21 percent growth in the bank's profit after taxes and *zakat.*

Tadamon Islamic Bank's return on assets was reduced from 2006 to 2007 and from 2007 to 2008, due to the bank's net-asset growth of 24.87 percent and 23.04 percent, respectively, compared with growth in bank net profits after taxes and *zakat* of 13.51 percent and 17.76 percent, respectively.

Al-Baraka Bank's return on assets was continuously reduced from 2005 to 2006 due to the bank's reduction in profit after taxes and *zakat* by 12.92 percent from SDG 1,056,263 to SDG 919,735. The bank total assets also increased by 8.48 percent and again from 2006 to 2007.

Liquidity Ratios

Current Ratio

Faisal Islamic Bank's current ratio was reduced from 2005 to 2006 and from 2006 to 2007, due to the bank current liabilities, which increased by 75.20 percent and 47.90 percent, compared with current assets growth of 66.42 percent and 44.31 percent, respectively. From 2007 to 2008, the bank's current ratio increased dramatically by 71.14 percent due to the bank's current assets, which increased by 51.75 percent compared with the bank's current liabilities growth of 34.37 percent.

Tadamon Bank's current ratio reduced from 2006 to 2007, but in 2007–2008, it started to increase again.

Al-Baraka Bank's current ratio increased from 2005 to 2006 due to the bank's current liability, which increased by 33.65 percent compared with its current asset growth of 9.02 percent. From 2006 to 2007, the bank ratio was reduced due to the bank's current assets growth by 14.25 percent, compared with 17.25 percent growth in current liabilities.

Net Working-Capital-to-Sales Ratio

Faisal Islamic Bank's net working-capital-to-sales reduced from 2005 to 2006 due to the bank's superior current liabilities growth of 74.12 percent, compared with 47.90 percent and 34.37 percent from 2006 to 2007 and 2007 to 2008, respectively.

Tadamon Islamic Bank's net working-capital-to-sales continuously increased in 2006–2007 and in 2007–2008.

Al-Baraka Bank's net working-capital-to-sales ratio increased from 2005 to 2006, due to the bank's reduction in total revenue from 21.82 percent to 14.32 percent in 2006–2007, when the ratio began to decline.

Credit-Risk Ratios

Equity-to-Assets Ratio

Faisal Islamic Bank's equity to assets continuously reduced from 2005 to 2007 due to the bank equity reduction from 18.26 percent in 2005–2006 and to 15.70 percent in 2006–2007, and from 2007 to 2008, the bank ratio was reduced due to the bank's total assets increasing from 34.78 percent in 2006–2007 to 50.29 percent in 2007–2008, compared with a 15.70 percent and a 21.54 percent increase in the bank equity from 2006 to 2007 and 2007 to 2008.

Tadamon Islamic Bank equity-to-assets ratio increased from 2006 to 2007 and from 2007 to 2008, due to the bank total assets increase from 23.03 percent to 24.93 percent, respectively.

Al-Baraka Bank's equity-to-assets ratio increased from 2005 to 2006, and from 2006 to 2007, the bank equity-to-assets ratio was reduced due to the bank equity reduction from 11.01 percent in 2005–2006 to only 4.23 percent in 2006–2007.

Equity-to-Net-Loan Ratio

Faisal Islamic Bank's equity to net loan reduced continuously from 2005 to 2007, due to the bank's equity reduction from 18.26 percent to 15.70 percent in 2005–2006 and 2006–2007, respectively. From 2007 to 2008, the bank ratio increased due to the bank equity increase from 15.70 percent to 21.54 percent.

Tadamon Islamic Bank's equity to net loan increased from 2006 to 2008, due to the bank's reduction in net-loan level from 30.22 percent to 5.68 percent in 2006–2007 and 2007–2008, respectively.

Al-Baraka Bank's equity-to-net-loan ratio increased from 2005 to 2006 due to the bank's reduction in net-loan level from 49.12 percent to 3.78 percent in 2005–2006, and from 2006 to 2007, the bank ratio was reduced due to the bank's increased in net-loan level.

Debt-to-Equity Ratio

Faisal Islamic Bank's debt-to-equity ratio increased from 2005 to 2008, due to the bank's equity reduction from 18.26 percent in 2005–2006 to 15.70 percent in 2006–2007, and from 2007 to 2008, the bank ratio increased, due to the bank debt increase from 88.75 percent to 91.33 percent.

Tadamon Bank's debt-to-equity ratio declined from 2006 to 2007, and from 2007 to 2008, the bank ratio increased, due to the bank debt increase from 13.25 percent to 45.91 percent, as well as the bank reduction in equity from 42.91 percent to 26.02 percent.

Al-Baraka Bank's debt-to-equity ratio increased from 2005 to 2006, and from 2006 to 2007, the bank ratio increased due to the bank-equity reduction from 33.64 percent to only 4.23 percent.

Assets Activity Ratios

Fixed-Assets Turnover

Faisal Islamic Bank's fixed-assets turnover increased from 2005 to 2006, and from 2006 to 2007, the bank ratio was reduced due to the bank's sales reduction from 65.03 percent to 15.99 percent, and from 2007 to 2008, the bank ratio increased, due to the reduction in fixed assets from 44.10 percent to 34.50 percent as well the bank sales, which increased from 15.99 percent to 48.85 percent.

Tadamon Islamic Bank's fixed-assets turnover reduced from 2006 to 2007 due to the bank sales reduction from 22.46 percent to 18.01 percent as well as the increase in fixed assets from 1.45 percent to 61.34 percent, and from 2007 to 2008, the ratio was reduced due to the bank's sales reduction from 18.01 percent to 14.61 percent.

Al-Baraka Bank's fixed-assets-turnover ratio increased from 2005 to 2006 and in 2006–2007, due to the bank's fixed assets reduction, from 2.11 percent to -2.44 percent.

Net-Assets Turnover

Faisal Islamic Bank's net-assets turnover increased in 2005–2006 due to the bank's net assets reduction from 76.20 percent to 43.78 percent in 2006–2007, and in 2007–2008, the bank ratio was reduced due to the bank sales increase from 15.99 percent to 48.85 percent.

Tadamon Islamic Bank's net-assets turnover was reduced from 2006 to 2007 and from 2007 to 2008, due to the bank's sales reduction from 18.01 percent to 14.61 percent.

Al-Baraka Bank's net-assets turnover continuously increased from 2005 to 2006, and from 2006 to 2007, due to the bank's net assets superior reduction from 60.04 percent to only 8.48 percent.

5. PERFORMANCE MEASURES

Below are calculations of all the financial ratios mentioned above for the three Sudanese Islamic banks—Faisal Islamic Bank, Tadamon Bank, and Al-Baraka Bank.

FINDINGS

- Tadamon Islamic Bank is the most efficient bank in terms of generating profits as well as being cost effective, followed by Faisal Islamic Bank of Sudan, and Al-Baraka Bank, which continuously reduced its gross profit margin, net profit margin, and operating profit margin.
- The deteriorations in the selected Sudanese Islamic banks' profitability mainly emerge in 2007–2008, possibly because of the central bank of Sudan's (CBoS) policy to increase banks deposit with CBoS's lack of confidence in the international banking system.
- Tadamon Islamic Bank's return on net assets is better than that of the other two banks apart from Faisal Islamic Bank's performance in 2005–2006.
- In terms of the liquidity-ratio performance, all three Sudanese Islamic banks are performing satisfactory. The ratio ranges from +1 to +2 times. Tadamon Islamic Bank's liquidity level reached +2.24 times in 2007–2008.
- The equity-to-assets level of the three Sudanese Islamic banks is adequate with percentages from 4.59 percent to 10.30 percent of the total assets.
- The three Sudanese Islamic banks maintained different approaches on how much debt could to be used compared with their equity levels. Al-Baraka Bank used debt of less than 1.00 times to its equity to generate profits, while Faisal Islamic Bank used debt of between 1.00 to 4.5 times its owner equity.
- The three Sudanese Islamic bank net-loans level compared with the bank equity level range from 2 to 7 times. It's usually recommended to kept loan-to-equity level below 3 times, which shows that the banks are taking excessive risks.
- Credit-risk performance includes equity to assets, equity to net loans, and debt to equity. Of the three Sudanese Islamic banks, it is confirmed that there is no big difference in the bank's equity to assets, and equity to net loans. Faisal Islamic Bank of Sudan and Tadamon Islamic Bank's debt to equity suggested that both banks are more risky than Al-Baraka Bank, since the bank debt-to-equity ratio fluctuated between 0.5 and 1.0.

6. CONCLUSION

The financial performance investigation of the three major Sudanese Islamic banks' profitability revealed that the Faisal Islamic Bank of

Sudan and Tadamon Islamic Bank are performing more efficiently than Al-Baraka Bank, since Al-Baraka Bank planned to improve its banking service by using the latest banking technology, such as cash machines and electronic check clearance, and by assigning considerable provisions for different purposes, that mainly led to deterioration in the bank's profit after taxes and *zakat* from 12.92 percent in 2005–2006 to 51.93 percent in 2007–2008.

It can be concluded that all three banks are efficiently utilizing their net assets to generate profits. Tadamon Islamic Bank and Al-Baraka Bank have more liquidity to meet their short-term liabilities than Faisal Islamic Bank, although the later bank maintained a current ratio range between 1 to 2 times.

Apart from the risk taken by Sudanese Islamic banks, and if higher risk always means higher return, the overall performance of the three selected Sudanese Islamic banks is satisfactory regarding their size and authorized capital. The current banking crisis that began in 2007 also affected the profitability performance of Islamic banking and finance to some extent.

8

ISLAMIC MORTGAGES

1. INTRODUCTION

With the world economies encountering the effects of failed conventional banking practices, experts have already begun to look for alternatives in order to rectify this situation and to ensure that it does not recur in the future. Against the backdrop of the financial crisis and economic recession, world economies are increasingly becoming attracted to Islamic banking practices as an alternative to the conventional financial and mortgage system because of their unique element of interest-free transactions. There is so much attention to the Islamic mortgage that many see it as just what the Western world needs right now. The current credit crisis is the result of excessive lending and pure speculation, and many financial analysts believe that this would not have happened if Islamic financial principles had been followed.

The United Kingdom now has five fully shariah-compliant banks and another seventeen financial institutions offering the Islamic mode of home-finance mortgage. These include the Qatar Islamic Bank (QIB), with its London-based European Finance House in Berkeley Square, and the Islamic Bank of Britain, with its headquarters in Birmingham. In 2007, both answered Prime Minister Gordon Brown's call for Britain to become the global center for international Islamic finance system. A report by the International Financial Services, London, even states that Britain's Islamic finance sector is now larger than that of Pakistan (Wade 2008). But before we present Islamic finance as an alternative to conventional banking, it is very important to determine the primary cause of the current crisis.

The ongoing subprime mortgage crisis constitutes a financial market failure. This is because financing a home for a subprime borrower poses a dilemma in an efficient capital market (Fama 1970, 1991). The ingenious mortgage bankers had figured out an innovative way (which turned out to be disastrous, as explained below) to get financially strapped individuals to qualify for a home loan, using lax underwriting standards. This innovative way of awarding loans was through the use of exploding adjustable-rate mortgages (ARMs) with unusually low introductory (i.e., teaser) interest rates that later on climb to a much higher rate after the introductory period expires (Gapper 2007). This was supposed to facilitate access to a home for borrowers and to help them establish some credit history before qualifying for refinancing with a fixed-rate mortgage. The implicit assumption was that the eventual appreciation of the home would bail out the borrower prior to the expiration of the teaser rate, because he or she would be able to refinance and not be exposed to the shock of much higher mortgage payments. Unfortunately, the opposite happened, and not only did payments increase drastically with the termination of the teaser rate, but home prices also fell. This made it difficult for borrowers to keep up with their payments. Also, they could not refinance (or sell) their homes, as their values were significantly below their mortgage balance (leaving them with nega-tive equity). It also left them with no option but to default. It is esti-mated that more than 2.4 million American families have lost their homes through foreclosures (*Economist* 2007a; Paletta 2007; Mason and Rosner 2007).

According to Aziz Tayyebi (2008), "Islamic finance is any finance that is compliant with the principles of Islamic law" (shariah). In terms of finance, shariah explains in detail the ethical concepts of money and capital, the relationship between risk and profit, and the social responsibilities of financial institutions.

El-Qorchi (2005) also envisaged Islamic finance—financial insti-tutions, products and services designed to comply with the central tenets of shariah, Islamic law—as one of the most rapidly growing segments of the global financial industry. Starting with the Dubai Islamic Bank in 1975 and operations in the United Arab Emirates, Egypt, the Cayman Islands, Sudan, Lebanon, the Bahamas, Bosnia, Bahrain, and Pakistan, the number of Islamic financial institutions worldwide now exceeds over 300, with operations in seventy-five countries and assets in excess of USD $400 billion. Financial trans-actions are one of the more important dealings controlled by sha-riah, ostensibly to ensure the more equitable distribution of income and wealth among Muslims in Islamic economies. "As opposed to conventional finance, where interest represents the contractible cost for funds tied to the amount of principal over a prespecified lending period, the central tenet of the Islamic financial system is the pro-hibition of *riba,* whose literal meaning "an excess" is interpreted as any unjustifiable increase of capital, whether through loans or sales. The general consensus among Islamic scholars is that *riba* covers not only usury but also the charging of interest and any positive, fixed, predetermined rate of return that are guaranteed regardless of the performance of an investment" (Iqbal and Tsubota 2006; Iqbal and Mirakhor1987; Iqbal and Llewellyn 2002).

Since only interest-free forms of finance are considered permissible in Islamic finance, financial relationships between financiers and borrowers are governed by shared business risk and returns from investment in lawful activities (halal). Islamic law does not object to payment for the use of an asset, and the earning of profits or returns from assets are indeed encouraged as long as both lender and borrower share the investment risk together. Profits must not be guaranteed based on assumption and can only accrue if the investment itself yields income. Any financial transaction under Islamic law assigns to investors clearly identifiable rights and obligations for which they are entitled to receive commensurate returns. Hence, Islamic finance outlaws capital-based investment gains *without* entrepreneurial risk. In light of these moral impediments to passive investment and secured interest as form of compensation, shariah-compliant lending in Islamic finance requires the replication of interest-bearing, conventional finance via more complex structural arrangements of contingent claims (Mirakhor and Iqbal 1988).

Major Principles of Islamic Finance

The general principles are as follows:

a. The prohibition of *riba* (usury or excessive interest) and the removal of debt-based financing from the economy;
b. The prohibition of *gharar*, encompassing the full disclosure of information and removal of any asymmetrical information in a contract;
c. The exclusion of financing and dealing in sinful and socially irresponsible activities and commodities, such as gambling and the production of alcohol;
d. Risk-sharing, the provider of financial funds and the entrepreneur share business risk in return for shares of profits and losses;
e. Materiality, a financial transaction needs to have a "material finality," that is a direct or indirect link to a real economic transaction; and

f. Justice, a financial transaction should not lead to the exploitation of any party to the transaction.

Source: Gait and Worthington 2007

The rest of chapter is divided into five sections. In section 2 we review literature on Islamic banking, Islamic mortgages, and the principles of *murabahah*. In section 3 we present the Islamic mortgage market in the UK and the factors limiting the uptake of Islamic mortgages. A comparison between conventional and Islamic mortgages is also provided in this section. Section 4 describes data collection techniques and methodology. Section 5 presents the findings from primary and secondary sources, and section 6 concludes.

A number of theoretical works examined the implications of preferred Islamic modes of finance in the contemporary world. In their theoretical work, Siddiqui and Zaman (1989a and 1989b) have shown how the application of *mudarabah* and *musharakah* techniques of finance has the potential to enhance investment and could also generate a more equitable desirable income-distribution pattern. Their models confirm the intuitive point that, compared to a debt arrangement, both under a deterministic and probabilistic framework, *mudarabah* and *musharakah* finance could lead to higher level of investment as new (marginal) projects would be undertaken as long as they are expected to give a positive rate of return, however small those rates might be.

It also shows that under these Islamic techniques of finance, compared to a debt-management system, a greater portion of profits is allocated to the providers of funds if the economy is doing well. On the other hand, in bad conditions, the providers of funds receive a lower return, and in extreme cases, they may get a negative return. This has a stabilizing effect on the economy.

Siddiqui (1994) further discusses how an economy based on the institution of interest is inherently unstable (a proposition so elegantly presented and championed by prominent post-Keynesian economist, Hyman Minsky) and how the Islamic techniques of finance based on profit-and-loss sharing have the potential to provide financial stability.

It emphasises the point that *mudarabah* finance is particularly capable of attracting those potential capable entrepreneurs who are unable to provide any collateral. This possible increase in the supply of entrepreneurs would decrease the power of existing entrepreneurs and can lead to a desirable distribution of income by discouraging the concentration of wealth in fewer hands. Siddiqui (1994) also addresses the problems one would face under Islamic techniques of finance and argues that those problems are not insurmountable. He points out that any serious attempt to implement profit-sharing financing would require, at the initial stages, commitment and often supervision and intervention by the government (cited by Syed Assad 2007).

Islamic banks do not charge interest but rather participate in the yield resulting from the use of funds; investors also share in the profits of the bank according to a prearranged ratio. Hence, there is consequently a partnership between Islamic banks and its depositors, on one side, and between the bank and its investment client, on the other side, as the one who manages depositors' resources in a productive way. This is quite different from what happens in conventional banks, which mainly borrow funds at interest on one side of the balance sheet and lends funds at interest on the other. In other words, an Islamic bank is a banking institution whose scope of activities includes all currently known banking activities, excluding borrowing and lending on the basis of interest. On the liabilities side, it mobilizes funds on the basis of a *mudarabah* or *wakalah* (agent) contract. It can also accept demand deposits, which are treated as interest-free, guaranteed loans from clients to the bank. On the assets side, it advances funds on a profit-and-loss-sharing or a debt-creating basis, in accordance with the principles of shariah (Mabid and Munawar 2007).

Housing plays a vital role in any economy (Sheng 1997). This is due to its following attributes: First, a home is both a consumption good as well as an investment (Malpezzi 1990). The investment aspect of homeownership helps to increase wealth (Buckley 1994; Englehardt 1994; Sheng 1997; Haurin, et al. 2002). Second, homeowners support their neighborhood more than renters, as they participate in crime prevention and support public schools. They are better citizens and vote at a higher rate (Haurin, et al. 2002). Homeownership fosters investment in local amenities and social capital, thus enhancing the status and quality of the community (DiPasquale and Glaeser 1999).

As shariah law regards the practice of paying or receiving interest (*riba*) as unacceptable and forbidden, a shariah home loan provides a halal (permissible) alternative to an interest-based mortgage by allowing individuals to purchase their own homes without having to pay interest. Robin Matthews, et al. (2003) in case analyses shows that the principal difference between Islamic and conventional mortgages is that the former is equity-based and the latter is debit-based. In an Islamic mortgage situation, both the bank and the client share ownership (equity), and therefore, share the risk of equity ownership. In conventional banking, the client owns all the equity, and the bank's loan to the client is secured on the value of the property.

According to (Kuran 1995), *murabahah* is the most commonly used method of finance by interest-free banks. It is based on the use of a markup, or profit margin, which does not seem to differ much (in its calculation or application) from interest charges used by conventional banks (Brown 1994). This has subjected the interest-free banks to severe criticism.

Murabahah Contract (Markups on Sale)

Murabahah is an Islamic instrument for buying and reselling the purchase or import of capital goods and other commodities by institutions, including banks and firms. Under the *murabahah* contract, the customer provides the bank with the specifications and prices of the goods to be purchased or imported. The Islamic bank studies the application and collects information about the specifications and prices of the goods, focusing especially on the price and conditions for payment. When the bank and its client agree on the terms of the deal, the bank purchases goods or commodities and resells them to the customer. The profit that accrues to the bank is mutually agreed upon as a profit margin (markup) on the cost of purchase (Metwally 2006).

The fundamental principles attached to *murabahah* can be summarized as follows:

a. Goods must be classified, clearly identified according to commonly accepted standards and must exist at the time of sale;
b. Goods for sale must be in the ownership of the bank at the time of sale;
c. The cost price must be known at the time of sale and this should be declared to the client. This is especially the case when the bank succeeds in obtaining a discount where the profit margin is calculated on the net purchase price (this means discounts also provide benefits to the client); and
d. The time of delivery of the goods and the time of payment must be specified.

Source: Obaidullah 2005; Iqbal and Molyneux 2005; Lewis and Algaoud 2001; Kahf 1997

According to Obaidullah (2005), the *murabahah* contract is merely a two-party buying-and-selling contract between bank and customer involving no financial intermediation or financing. In other words, the bank offers this service to clients who should pay the cost of the goods plus a profit margin to the bank immediately following receipt. In addition, the client can pay for the goods and the bank's profit margin by deferred installments or a deferred lump sum without an increase over the original value. This type of contract is referred to as *bai muajjall-murabbah* or *baibithaman ajja*. The figure below shows how the *murabahah* contract is done.

2. MURABAHA CONTRACT

1. The customer identifies a property and agrees to all terms of the purchase with the vendor. The customer requests the Islamic mortgage provider to purchase the property and then sell it to the customer at the cost price plus a declared markup.
2. The Islamic mortgage provider purchases the property directly from the vendor and immediately sells it to the customer with a fixed markup profit. (This is calculated on the property value, length of finance, payment terms, and amount of deposit.)
3. The customer repays the Islamic mortgage provider the initial price and the agreed markup. (The customer's first payment to the Islamic mortgage provider in installments is made on the date of completion and is usually a minimum of 20 percent of the purchase price.)

Source: Islamic Finance *(Matthews, et al., n.d.)*

Murabahah *vs. Interest*

There is no unfairness involved in *murabahah* financing in so far as the relationship between the financier and the entrepreneur–buyer-on credit is concerned. On that count, it is superior to the financing arrangement based on interest. The financier is financing not a venture of uncertain results but the acquisition of a commodity of acknowledged utility and known current price. The markup on current price is tacked on the commodity, whereas in interest-based borrowing, it is tacked on money capital (the principal). By converting its money capital into a commodity, the financier has already given up liquidity and taken the risks associated with owning a real asset, e.g., a fall in its market price, destruction due to natural causes, or theft, etc. He or she also takes the risks associated with relying on the other party's promise to buy, such as the risk of bankruptcy of the would-be buyer or backing down on its promise to buy. Also, by selling on credit, the financier is taking the risk of default by the buyer as well as forgoing any other opportunities of using the money that could have arisen as time passes. Time, which is not recognized by shariah as a basis of claiming an excess over principal when making a money loan, becomes part of the justification for a markup in credit sale (Khan 1995). The fact that shariah does not allow any further increase in the contracted price, should more time elapse before the actual payment is made, clearly demonstrates that there is no price for the mere passage of time involving a sum of money.

The twin norms of justice in transactions, equivalence and reciprocity, which we found violated in interest-based lending, are not violated in sale on credit with a markup on current price. There is perceived equivalence between the commodity received by the buyer and the price received by the seller, as is the case in voluntary exchanges between commodity on the one side and money on the other. Reciprocity inheres in the seller's advantage of a markup (attached to which are the risks mentioned above) being matched by the buyer's advantage of getting the time and opportunity of using the commodity ahead of paying the price. As we have already seen above, no such claim can be made about exchanging money now for more money in future. Perception of equality is acceptable in place of objective equality in the exchange of dissimilar things, as money and commodity, but it cannot be acceptable between the same things, i.e., in exchange of money for money. It has to be measurable equality because there is no room for perception. There is no reciprocity either. What the lender gets is definite and known, but what the borrower gets is neither definite nor known, should we consider the point in time when the loan is repaid (Siddiqi 2004).

3. ISLAMIC MORTGAGE MARKET IN THE UK

The UK Islamic mortgage market has seen impressive growth over the last five years. Yet the market is still in its infancy and faces many obstacles. The Islamic mortgage market is now worth £164 million and is growing at an average rate of 68.1 percent per annum since 2000, in comparison to the total mortgage market growth of 16.2 percent.

With the Muslim community representing a substantial portion of the UK population, it is predicted that by 2009, the Islamic mortgage market will be worth £1.4 billion. In 2003 the Islamic mortgage market began to accelerate further, with the abolition of the payment of double stamp duty. Today, there are at least five lenders in the market actively offering Islamic products, including institutions such as HSBC and Lloyds TSB. The problem is that the Islamic mortgage market does not offer any real alternatives for customers unless they have a large amount of equity in a property or a substantial deposit. Islamic lenders recently increased their deposit requirements on products such as Alburaq to 35 percent and HSBC Amanah to 40 percent. Both these organizations, which have many innovative products, are leaders in the market.

Nevertheless, the Islamic mortgage market remains positive, with all lenders investing in marketing initiatives to drum up business. The Islamic Bank of Britain remains competitive and continues to develop its product portfolio, recently expanding into the Scottish market. But the average Islamic mortgage customer will still struggle to get a mortgage, with a minimum property value requirement of £150,000.

The Islamic mortgage is a trend that is broadening the home-ownership base, particularly among Muslims. However, you do not need to be a Muslim to take advantage of the Islamic mortgage schemes that exist. Muslims make up 5 percent of the UK population, and it is predicted by *Data Monitor* that the Islamic mortgage market could be worth £4.4 billion within the next two years. Islamic mortgage is one of the most rapidly growing segments of the Islamic financial industry, although it still has a huge market waiting to be fully explored. There are approximately 3 million Muslims permanently residing in the UK with an estimated saving of around £1 billion, while over half a million Muslims visited Britain in 2001, spending nearly £600 million.

Cumbo (2005) points out that one factor that appears to be limiting the uptake of the Islamic mortgage is that the cost is higher than for conventional mortgages. For Islamic financing worth £135,000 from Lloyds TSB over a period of 25 years, the monthly repayments were £883 plus £21 a month for building insurance in March 2005. This comprised a rental payment of £693 plus a capital repayment of £190. The total monthly payment was over £100 per month more than the cost of a Lloyds TSB conventional mortgage. This was further supported by Hassan and Lewis (2007), who state that with HSBC Amanah for the same loan of £135,000 over 25 years, the monthly repayments were £857, only £7 per month more than the bank's conventional mortgage, but the building insurance of £34 per month was obligatory with the Islamic financing, as the property itself is owed by the bank, unlike the case of a conventional mortgage, where the bank simply has a charge on the property so that it can be repossessed in the case of payment default. According to information from a publication by New Millennium Publishing (2004), a survey of 503 Muslims in ten cities throughout England, undertaken by Humayon Dar of Loughborough University, showed that many respondents had little knowledge of shariah-compliant finance, but those who had inquired about Islamic home finance were deterred from proceeding because of higher costs (Hassan and Lewis 2007).

Of course, the cost of a mortgage is not the only factor determining the level of business, as those Muslims who have signed contracts for Islamic finance are prepared to pay a premium. A further factor inhibiting the uptake of Islamic home finance is that a significant proportion of the Muslim population in the UK are in a low socioeconomic position and cannot afford to buy property. This has been true in areas such as East London, where many of those in the Bangladeshi community are quite poor, but property prices are relatively high. One solution might be co-ownership through Islamic housing associations, with the tenant, association, and bank all owning a share in the property, but at present, these do not exist in the UK.

4. DATA COLLECTION & METHODOLOGY

The people used for this research were all banking professionals with an in-depth knowledge of the banking industry. A total of 190 banking professionals completed the questionnaire. Initially, a test sample of 50 was carried out. The pilot questionnaire enabled the final questionnaire to be initially evaluated for design, format, and clarity in content, relevant to the research, questions, and structure. This is because it would be impossible to exactly predict how respondents would interpret the questions. After a favorable initial response, we proceeded to survey a population of 190. The first part of the questionnaire is related to views on the mortgage system consisting of six questions, based on a five-scale rating ranging from Strongly Agree (SA) to Strongly Disagree (SD). The purpose of this part was to assess the perception of banking professionals about what type of mortgage system they want in relation to interest, fees, choices, insurance, etc. The second part consists of demographic types of questions, like age, income, marital status, and, for the finance professionals, years in the profession. In total, ten questions were asked to analyze the bankers' views and expectations regarding the significance of the Islamic mortgage system. (A copy of the Questionnaire for Banking Professionals can be found in Appendix B; see pp. 281–282.)

The questionnaire included a two-line paragraph explaining the purpose of the study. Confidentiality, and to some extent secrecy, were assured to respondents so that they could give more honest and open answers to questions. A guarantee was also given that the collected data will only be used for academic purposes.

As this study aims at providing an insight into the significance of the Islamic mortgage to the UK finance industry and the practical view of those in industry, each duly filled and returned questionnaire was analyzed by using various software with good analytical capability. The analysis of the questionnaire offers insight about banking professionals' perception of the Islamic mortgage system and its principles.

5. EMPIRICAL ANALYSIS

There were a total of 190 questionnaires distributed because the researcher calculated that this was an appropriate sample. Data provided in table 8.1 divides and presents a profile of the respondents according to their income, age, and years of experience in the banking industry.

Table 8.1 Profile of Respondents

Demographic Variables		Number of Respondents	Percentage
Income	Less than £15,000	10	5.26
	£15,000–£20,000	50	26.3
	£20,000–£30,000	73	38.4
	£30,000–£40,000	47	24.7
	No Answer	10	5.26
	Total	190	100
Age	18–24	32	16.8
	25–34	43	22.6
	35–49	65	34.2
	50–64	38	20
	65 and above	12	6.32
	Total	190	100
Length in Banking Industry	1–9 years	38	20
	10–20 years	42	22.10
	21–30 years	59	31.05
	31–40 years	41	21.58
	41 years or more	10	5.26
	Total	190	100

Table 8.2 Views on the Mortgage System

Variables		Respondents	Percentage
Noninterest-based mortgages are better than interest based.	Strongly agree	45	23.70
	Agree	80	42
	Neither gree nor disagree	48	25.30
	Disagree	12	6.32
	Strongly disagree	5	2.63
	Total	190	100
Islamic mortgages are less risky than conventional mortgages.	Strongly agree	120	63.16
	Agree	50	26.32
	Neither agree nor disagree	15	7.89
	Disagree	5	2.63
	Strongly disagree	–	–
	Total	190	100
Its ethical foundations make the Islamic mortgage an increasingly serious alternative to the conventional mortgage.	Strongly agree	25	13.16
	Agree	75	39.47
	Neither agree nor disagree	40	21.05
	Disagree	37	19.47
	Strongly disagree	13	6.84
	Total	190	100
The Islamic mortgage has a market outside the Muslim community.	Strongly agree	103	54.21
	Agree	37	19.47
	Neither agree nor disagree	5	2.63
	Disagree	30	15.79
	Strongly disagree	15	7.89
	Total	190	100
There is great awareness in the UK about the Islamic mortgage and its principles.	Strongly agree	3	1.58
	Agree	7	3.68
	Neither agree nor disagree	25	13.16
	Disagree	58	30.53
	Strongly disagree	97	51.05
	Total	190	100
There is little or no difference between the choices offered in conventional and Islamic banks.	Strongly agree	76	40
	Agree	57	30
	Neither agree nor disagree	34	17.89
	Disagree	14	7.37
	Strongly disagree	9	4.74
	Total	190	100

Table 8.2 shows that 45 respondents (23.7 percent) of 190 strongly agree that the noninterest-based mortgage is better than the interest-based, 80 respondents (42 percent) strongly agree, 48 respondents (25.3 percent) agree, 12 respondents (6.32 percent) disagree, and 5 respondents (2.63 percent) strongly disagree. The result below indicates that the majority of respondents believe noninterest-based mortgages are better than interest-based; this might be because the interest-based mortgage system can be fundamentally unstable, and the recent subprime mortgage crisis witnessed in the United States, which also had an impact on the global economy, is a good example. Just (2.63 percent) of respondents strongly disagreed.

The results of table 8.2 indicate that, from the 190 respondents, 120 strongly agree that Islamic mortgages are less risky than conventional mortgages (63.16 percent), 50 agree (26.32 percent), 15 neither agree nor disagree (7.89 percent), 5 disagree (2.63 percent), and none strongly disagree. This result points toward the widely held view that the Islamic mortgage is less risky than the conventional mortgage, and many financial analysts believe the credit crisis would not have happened if Islamic finance principles were followed.

The results of table 8.2 demonstrate that 25 of the 190 respondents strongly agree that the Islamic mortgage's ethical foundation makes it an increasingly serious alternative to the conventional mortgage (13.16 percent), 75 agree (39.47 percent), 40 neither agree nor disagree (21.05 percent), 37 disagree (19.47 percent), and 13 strongly disagree (6.84 percent). Thirty-nine percent agree, probably because the Islamic principles of interest are concerned with issues of fairness and justice rather than with efficiency, narrowly defined, and the principles allow a more equitable distribution of income and wealth as well as increased equity participation in the economy. These principles focus on the necessity of sharing risk in a fair and stable society and on problems of exploitation in markets, where power is asymmetrical; this is the real *riba* (interest) issue.

Table 8.2 indicates that 97 of the 190 respondents (51.05 percent) strongly disagree that there is great awareness in the UK about Islamic mortgage and its principles, 58 disagree (30.53 percent), 25 neither agree nor disagree (13.16 percent), 7 agree (3.68 percent), and 3 strongly disagree (1.58 percent). While Wilson (2000) argues that the level of knowledge of Islamic finance methods is generally low among individual consumers as compared to the need, the Islamic finance industry is utilizing only a fraction of its true potential. A more professional approach has been recommended to penetrate into the untapped market; what is the easiest part of the market available has already been covered.

The results of table 8.2 indicate the responses when asked if there is little or no difference between the choices offered in Islamic and conventional banks, 76 respondents (40 percent) of 190 strongly agree, 57 agree (30 percent), 34 neither agree nor disagree (17.89 percent), 14 disagree (7.37 percent), and 9 strongly disagree (4.74 percent). This result is based on the fact that Islamic finance, so far has been free-riding on financial theories and instruments developed within the context of the conventional debt-based and interest-based system. Unless Islamic finance develops its own genuinely Islamic financial instruments, it cannot achieve the dynamism of a system that provides security, liquidity, and diversity needed for a globally accepted financial system that could prove to be a genuine alternative to the present interest-based international financial system.

According to evidence from both the primary and the secondary data obtained, it can be ascertained that there is no real difference between the two (Islamic and conventional) banking systems in terms of the organizational setup and products choice. It is quite clear that a disaster of such magnitude could not occur in markets governed by Islamic shariah because of the way transactions are made. Islamic law forbids usury and outlaws the selling of what you do not own except under strict conditions, such as the selling of commodities, where the full price is paid in advance while that which is valuated (the product) is postponed, which reduces the risks in the transaction. Islamic shariah also forbids the postponement of buying and selling (forward contracts), which is the case with derivative contracts and debt-trading, except under certain conditions that prevent usury manipulation and deceit. The above-mentioned facts also explain why Islamic institutions were not affected by the crisis.

6. CONCLUSION

The future is definitely dazzling and glorious for the Islamic banking and financial products like Islamic mortgages, *murabahah* and *ijara*. After detailed study of available literature and analyzing responses from respondents, researchers conclude that Islamic finance is convincing the world that it not only covers the ethical aspects of the society but also gives economic benefits. However, it is not a justified argument to portray Islamic finance as a real competitor for conventional banks, because Islamic banking industry is in its infancy, and it will take more time in order to prove over its conventional counterpart.

Islamic principles of interest are concerned with issues of fairness and justice rather than with efficiency narrowly defined. These principles focus on the necessity of sharing risk in a fair and stable society and upon problems of exploitation in markets where power is asymmetrical; this is the real *riba* (usury) issue.

Our survey shows that the principle differences between Islamic and conventional housing finance is that the former is equity-based and the latter is debit-based. In an Islamic mortgage situation, both the bank and the client share ownership (equity), and therefore, share the risk of equity ownership. In conventional banking, the client owns all the equity, and the bank's loan to the client is secured on the value of the property.

Putting aside the penetrating comment by Ahmed (1992), "It's not clear to whom we are cheating..." about hypocrisy in the current practice of Islamic banks, let us deal with the realm of the ideal. Consider an ideal situation in which Islamic principles of interest were adhered to by a substantial proportion of the world financial system. What they have in common is a prohibition of usury, or excessive interest rates. Could such an idealized system conceivably survive as a foundation of banking in a hypercompetitive global financial environment? Pure logic would dictate that this is not possible in a profit-maximizing world; that is, if "excessive" includes interest rates that reflect high-risk situations or situations of capital shortage, both of which would require high interest rates, that might be considered usurious. We remarked at the beginning of the chapter on the recurrent crises in the financial sector.

Maladministration, deception, and unethical behavior lie at the root of many of these problems: Enron and WorldCom are just two examples. The Islamic approach emanates from a foundation set of ethical principles. So, discussion of Islamic finance in connection with global financial practices introduces an ethical dimension that is welcome. Also as Khan (2002) points out an Islamic system of finance might create a more stable world financial market.

9

The Role of Islamic Mortgages in the United Kingdom

1. Introduction

Islamic banking began only three decades ago, but its growth has been phenomenal. El-Qorchi (2005) revealed that the number and reach of Islamic financial institutions indicates an increasing trend in their role globally, which has risen from a single institution in just one country in 1975 to over 300 institutions working in more than 75 countries. The activities of these institutions have had an effect on more than 20 to 30 percent of the world's population, and in certain countries, they handle more than 20 percent of financial flows.

In the early days when Islamic banking appeared with its ethical values, it was assumed by the financial circles in the world that it was impracticable. However, attitudes have changed gradually, and over the last few years, many new Islamic banks began their operations while other conventional banks also opened a separate division for an Islamic-style bank to attract more customers (Haqiqi and Pomeranz 2000).

The Islamic financial system employs the concept of participation in the enterprise, utilizing the funds at risk on a profit-and-loss-sharing basis. This by no means implies that investments with financial institutions are necessarily speculative. This can be excluded by careful investment policy, diversification of risk, and prudent management by Islamic financial institutions. Islamic finance as a concept is based on themes of community banking, ethical and socially responsible investments, and affinity marketing. These themes themselves are based on core ideas, which include individual responsibility, reliance on the market mechanism, commitment to economic and social justice, and mandatory care for the environment.

The time when the international financial market is rattled by sub-prime crises, Islamic banks have not yet felt it. Many experts and bank officials have confirmed that Islamic banks are untouched by the global financial crises, albeit, more and more people are coming toward ethically based banking. This can be credited to the ethics and values inherent within the Islamic banking system (Ahmed 1992).

Middle East Online explained that there are two main reasons that Islamic financial institutes were unaffected by the global crises. The first reason is their security from the liquidity problem, due to inter-bank lending in the money markets, mergers, and re-sales of debt companies. The second reason can be attributed to the rating of complete investment risks instead of mere credit risks. Owing to this, the liquidity-related problem can be avoided because interbank transfer is not permitted in the Islamic bank.

According to the rating of investment risks, Islamic finance has no problem with fluctuations in asset values; instead, it diverges according to actual business trends. Thus, there is no fear of subprime mortgages under Islamic banking principles; rather, Islamic banks counter the cutthroat competition in the financial sector to get more credit shares. In this way, Islamic banks offer stability and insulation in the financial market. However, if the right information and data are available for the consumer, the demand of justly motivated consumers toward Islamic banking would be quite high.

However, the Islamic economic principles of sharing risks and rewards and of participating in the wealth-creation activity via equity rather than through debt has provided a solution that eliminates debt in its existing interest-based form while continuing to promote entrepreneurship and creativity in the economic cycle. This requires equity participants to actively benchmark proposed projects against moral standards (social analysis) in addition to the financial parameters (risk analysis) leading to a clear comprehension of the wealth-creation process at an individual level. In the Islamic economic model, each individual is involved in the economic activity. In comparison, the debtor tends to be only remotely involved in scrutinizing the business proposal in the debt-bond model—broadly content with earning interest on the loan regardless of the social and financial implications of the project.

UK Shariah-Compliant Market Analysis

According to the International Association of Islamic Banks (IAIB), by 1998 there were 176 Islamic banks and financial institutions operating in 38 countries. These institutions had total assets of US $148 billion, paid-up capital of US $7.3 billion, and generated US $1.2 billion in aggregate net profits in the latest year of operation. Sir Howard Davies, chairman of the Financial Services Authorities (FSA) in the UK, said, "There was a gap in the market for retail-sector Islamic banking products, which would cater to nearly two million UK Muslims." There are approximately 3 million Muslims permanently residing in the UK (i.e., 50 percent of all UK ethnic minorities), with estimated savings of around £1 billion, while over half a million Muslims visited Britain in 2001, spending nearly £600 million. The 5,000 richest Muslims in the UK have liquid assets of over £3.6 billion. According to wealth analysts' Datamonitor, HSBC, the UK-listed bank, which has £2 billion assets under management and three Islamic funds, is predicting growth of assets under management of up to 40 percent for the year 2002. If we follow the Datamonitor Group (1999) research, then this indicates that out of their 1.65 million estimate, 300,000 Muslim adults in the UK have annual incomes in the range of £30,000 and above. This means that approximately 25 percent of all adult Muslims are excellent prospects for banking and financial products.

Islamic Modes of Financing

Islamic modes of financing are designed in such a way that they affect both the assets and liabilities of a bank's balance sheet and are divided into two major categories. They are based on profit-and-loss sharing (PLS), which is a core mode, as well as nonprofit-and-loss sharing, which is a marginal mode. According to Yaqubi (2006), these two modes of financing are central to formulating, designing, and structuring all the financial products and instruments of banking, insurance, and capital markets within the Islamic financial industry. From the onset, one can observe that these modes are performing tremendously different actions. This is because Islamic banking is based on Islamic law; hence, all transactions, product features, business approaches, investment aims, and responsibilities are purely based on shariah principles, which completely differ from those of conventional banking.

The reminder of the chapter is organized in five sections. Section 2 reviews the literature related to Islamic mortgage and Islamic finance. Section 3 describes the Islamic financial infrastructure and the role of corporate governance. Section 4 compares the Islamic and the conventional mortgage. And the study's conclusion is in section 5.

2. Literatre Review

Islam is a complete way of life that has a set of goals and values encompassing all aspects of human life (Al-Tamimi & Company 2004). In order to understand Islamic finance and banking, it is necessary to have certain knowledge about the history and tenets of Islam. It is not easy for individuals who are used to Western traditions to understand the teachings of Islam (Ibrahim 2000).

According to Dar and Presley (2000), Islamic banks (IB) act as an intermediary and trustee of people's money, just like a conventional bank, but the reimbursement to all depositors is done on a profit-and-loss-sharing basis. This basic difference establishes an element of mutuality in a wider socioeconomic context and provides the right of ownership to its customer. However, in practice, Islamic banks are similar to their conventional counterparts in terms of organizational setup.

Khan (1986) has noted that the abolition of interest-based transactions is not a subject alien to Western economic thought. Fisher (1945), Simons (1948), and Friedman (1969) have argued that the current one-sided liability, interest-based financial system can be fundamentally unstable. There are many such examples: the German hyperinflation of the 1920s; oil shock inflations in Europe of the 1970s; banking crises in Japan, East Asia, Russia, and Argentina; default and Enron bankruptcy; and so on. The occurrence of crises is the result of a complex of factors emanating from over-exuberance, greed, underestimating risk, overexposure, currency failures, asset depreciation, faulty regulation, illiquidity, macroeconomic shocks, and accountancy maladministration. Zarqa (1983), Khan (1986), Chapra (2000), El-Gamel (2000), and Abdul Gafoor (1997) have illustrated the macroeconomic stability that can form a profit-and-loss-sharing system, an Islamic form of banking would replace interest-based transactions that characterize Western transactions.

Islamic finance is based on shariah principles (Islamic laws and rules), which are also called as Islamic jurisprudence. "Shariah is not a codified body of commandments. It is a conceptual form of rules competent of adaptation, advancement, and interpretation. Shariah supervision may be thought of as the single most important distinction between a conventional and a truly Islamic financial venture, for it has no way of certifying that its services, products, and operations are actually shariah compliant" (Delorenzo 2003). Shariah manages all aspects of matters that include socioeconomic, political, and cultural aspects of Islamic societies. The main sources of shariah are the Qur'an (the holy book of Muslims), *hadith* (a narrative relating the deeds and statements of the Prophet Mohammad S.A.W.), *sunnah* (the practice of the Prophet Mohammad), *ijtihad* (the reasoning of shariah scholars), *qayas* (the use of assumptions by analogy to provide a judgment on a case not referred to in the Qur'an or *sunnah*), and *ijma* (the consensus among religion scholars about explicit issues not envisaged in Qur'an or *sunnah*).

The central feature of the Islamic financial system (IFS) is the elimination of the payment and receipt of interest (*riba*). One of the verses from Qur'an regarding interest is given below. The strong condemnation of interest by Islam and the fundamental role of interest in modern commercial banking systems led Muslim thinkers to discover ways and means by which banking could be prepared on an interest-free basis. Shariah mortgages are considered to be the only counterpart of conventional mortgages. Islamic home financing is the standard method for commercial and residential real-estate financing without paying the full value of the house upfront. In developed countries like the United Kingdom and the United States, where house prices are above average, people attempt to pay it off. Similarly, according to UK's Office for National Statistics, there are around 1.8 million Muslims living in the United Kingdom, so owing a house could be possible without compromising on religious beliefs. As a Muslim, the concept of a conventional mortgage with interest and debt-based financing is in conflict with Islamic principles and shariah.

In its early days, Islamic mortgages were considered painstaking, and there was a real dearth of *halal* mortgage providers in the UK, and until 2002, there were only two Islamic mortgage providers, i.e., United Bank of Kuwait (formerly known as Ahli United Bank) and West Bromwich Building Society. A major development in the market was seen after the removal of double stamp duty in 2003, when HSBC Amanah Finance and United National Bank emerged and in 2004 when Lloyds TSB and Alburaq Home Finance also entered the Islamic mortgages sector.

3. Growth of Islamic Financial Institutions

According to the report of Maris strategies and Karina Robinson (2007), the growth of Islamic financial institutions has increased significantly from 2006 to 2007. Table 9.1 shows the total figure of regional and global growth of Islamic financial institutions in

Table 9.1   Regional and Global Growth Totals

£ million	2007	2006	% Change
GCC	89064.78	63913.28	39.35%
Non-GCC MENA	88411.10	68078.82	29.87%
MENA total	177475.86	131992.09	34.46%
Sub-Saharan African	2353.99	1519.66	54.90%
Asia	59673.23	49534.78	20.91%
Australia/Europe/ America	10737.86	10150.12	5.79%
Global Total	250240.94	193016.65	30.88%

Source: Maris Strategies and the Banker *(2007)*

different regions, and it demonstrates the growing appeal of Islamic financing to non-Muslim institutions and investors.

Islamic Financial Infrastructure

The most significant sign of development of the Islamic financial institution is the complete infrastructure that has grown at an international level. Although they are still in initial stages, these institutions have been progressing satisfactory with the passage of time.

Shariah Governance

Islamic banks have the basic responsibility to make sure that all the products, instruments, operations, practices, management, etc. are in compliance with shariah principles. Shariah governance is another constituent that is exclusive to Islamic banks, and it serves as a backbone of Islamic banking and finance. It supports legitimacy and confidence for the general public and shareholders. The existence of a non-shariah-compliant constituent in Islamic bank finance introduces several risks, such as fiduciary and reputation risks. The compliance with the shariah principles will be achieved by having a proper shariah governance framework, which includes a shariah board (SB), corporate governance, regulators (FSA), taxation, and the role of auditors, which are discussed in later sections. Principle 3.1 of the Islamic Financial Services Board's (IFSB) "Guiding Principles on Corporate Governance" states that suitable methods must be shaped to ensure compliance with shariah principles. Similarly, Principle 7.1 of the IFSB's "Guiding Principles on Risk Management" states that Islamic banks shall have in place necessary systems and controls, including a shariah-board advisor, to ensure compliance with shariah principles (Hassan 2007).

The Role of the Shariah Board in Islamic Banking

"The shariah board is not just a codified body of directives; it is a theoretical form of proficient adaption, improvement, and a construal body" (Delorenzo 2003). Practically, the major responsibility of the shariah board is to review and verify the acceptability of Islamic contracts and products, which comes from two major sources, i.e., the Qur'an and *sunnah* (the practices of the Prophet Mohammad). Furthermore, it divides into two dependent sources: *ijma* (consensus) and *ijtihad /qaya*s (individual reasoning by analogy, or *hourani*).

The Accounting and Auditing Organization of Islamic Financial Institutions (AAOIFI) standard requires at least three individuals, but the legal or statutory requirement varies. In contemporary practice, most Islamic financial institutions appoint three to six members to their board. With regard to the reporting structure, the shariah board reports functionally to the bank's board of directors, which replicates the status of the shariah committee as an independent and autonomous body of an Islamic bank.

Role of Corporate Governance

Corporate governance is just another term for the accountability, transparency, and fairness of a company's management and board of directors to shareholders, depositors, and other stakeholders, which includes financial institutions, financial markets, supervisory authorities, and other providers of finance.

The issues of corporate governance arise because of the violation of the fulfilment of the promises. The basic issue is the principal/agent problem, because of the separation of management and finance, or of ownership and control. The principal-agent problem is very complex in banks because of high leverage and other systematic risks. The problem also lies in the *murabahah* contract where there might be a conflict of interest between financier and entrepreneur. Both parties want to enjoy the maximum share of profit, and it is only possible when the relationship is based on honesty, efficiency, and equity. So, in order to maintain the wider benefits of all the stakeholders and the economy, effective corporate governance needs to be evolved in Islamic financial institutes (Chapra and Ahmed 2002).

According to Al-Jarhi (2000), the corporate-governance mechanism for Islamic banks can be explained as below.

- **Shareholders.** The Islamic bank acts as a corporate entity; thus, they abide by the UK corporate law, which clearly defines the rights of shareholders, i.e., to monitor the performance of the Islamic bank through annual results and external auditing as well as sitting in the board of directors and annual general meeting.
- **Demand Depositors.** Regulators (FSA) always stand to insure that demand depositors are getting a guarantee of the value of their deposits and are able to transfer or withdraw their funds at reasonable costs.
- **Investment Depositors.** Sitting on the board of directors to monitor the banking operations in order to make sure that risks and other issues are managed with due care, and scrutinizing deposits so that people can sell and buy certificates of deposits at will. And finally, the rate of return on investment deposits should be calculated on the basis of total performance of the whole pool, which can increase investors' confidence.
- **Regulators.** The regulators of the Islamic bank monitor three types of supervision, i.e., shariah supervision to ensure that bank is providing quality products, financial supervision, which represents the financial position and management of the bank, and finally, operational supervision, which determines the applications of necessary procedures for the placement of funds.
- **Financial Market Authorities.** The authorities must ask for a proper procedure for standardization of Islamic financial instruments and contracts, set measurements of transparency and disclosures, and recognize rules of shariah-compliant trading.
- **Islamic Finance Community.** Standardization of Islamic financial contracts and products as well as unified shariah-compliant accounting, regulatory, and supervisory standards, which are internationally acceptable, increase the confidence of Islamic financial community.
- **Financial Community.** High standards of transparency and disclosure with a competitive behavior increase the overall confidence of the financial community in Islamic banking.
- **The Public.** The public is always interested in quality financial services and products at competitive prices, terms, and conditions.

According to Suleiman (2000), the corporate-governance structure, which drafts an intangible framework of corporate governance for any Islamic bank, the shariah supervisory board (SSB), and the internal controls are central to the framework. In promoting good corporate governance, Islamic banks are required to report their performance overview and corporate-governance practices. The performance overview requires the Islamic banks to disclose their review on performance, measures, business plans, and strategies, at the same time as the statement of corporate governance requires the bank to disclose the composition and responsibilities of the board, internal audit and control activities, and risk-management strategies and policies. These report requirements are vital in providing additional information to users in appraising the bank's performance and conduct.

The UK Islamic Mortgage Market

Although the Islamic mortgage industry is still young and facing obstacles, Islamic mortgage growth has been phenomenal. With over 1.8 million Muslims living in the UK and conventional mortgages hit by the subprime mortgage crisis, practitioners and academics expect that the Islamic mortgage industry will continue to grow. A survey conducted by Datamonitor.com suggests that the UK Islamic mortgage market could be worth approximately £1.4 billion by 2009. According to researchers, Islamic mortgages have been growing at an average of 68.1 percent per year since 2000; in contrast with the total mortgage markets, which have had an average growth of 16.2 percent, the Islamic mortgage market is now worth £164 million (www.allbusiness.com). The Datamonitor research (1999) reveals that out of their 1.65 million estimate, 300,000 Muslim adults in the UK have annual incomes in the capacity of £30,000/= and above. This means that approximately 25 percent of all adult Muslims have excellent prospects for Islamic mortgages.

A survey conducted by the U.S. Central Intelligence Agency (CIA) in 2007 estimated that the total population of Muslims was about 1.61 billion. Islam is the fastest emerging religion in Europe as well as in the world (CIA World Factbook 2007). There are about 1.8 million Muslims living in the United Kingdom and about 500,000 are frequent visitors to the UK. Twelve million Muslims live in the European Union (EU), mostly in France, Germany, and the United Kingdom, according to the Financial Service Authority of the UK (FSA).

Cost Involved in Shariah-Compliant Mortgages

Double stamp duty was the biggest issue up until 2003. Double stamp duty was the tax on the house that is paid once by the financier and then again by the mortgage holder. This led to the payment of stamp duty twice, and the final homeowner had to pay the cost. Thus, Islamic mortgages were becoming more expensive than conventional mortgages. However, this tentative block has now been removed in the UK; Gordon Brown, when serving as British chancellor of the exchequer in Britain, announced the change in his 2004 budget speech.

Another issue concerning the cost of Islamic mortgages is related to legal costs. In many cases, it has not been clear whether a single solicitor can advise both the financier and the purchaser of an Islamic mortgage, because the bank acts as an owner of the property.[1]

Another reason that shariah-complaint mortgages are costly is because the Islamic departments within the banks offering Islamic mortgages have had to allocate the funds that were not raised through investments in non-shariah industries, such as tobacco, drugs, pornography, and gambling.[2]

According to Paul Sherrin, the head of Islamic financial services at Lloyds, Islamic mortgages are costly because banks share more risk in a shariah-compliant mortgage. And to keep shariah rates competitive with lenders' standard variable rates is a tough job.

There was a dearth of competition before 2003, and Islamic mortgages were charged at a premium compared with interest-based mortgages in the market. But many high-street banks over the last few years have introduced shariah-compliant mortgages; therefore, the cost of Islamic mortgages has become competitive in the market. It is said by researchers and practitioners that, with the passage of time, removal of regulatory and supervisory obstacles, and increasing competition, Islamic mortgages would be more competitive and cheaper in the future.

Islamic Mortgage Structures in the UK

According to Ainley, et al. (2007), Islamic mortgages in the UK have been structured under two different shariah-compliant contracts, that is, *murabahah* and *ijara*. In *ijara*-based contracts *ijara* and diminishing *musharakah* are the most commonly used methods in the UK for home financing. These are available to all consumers and not just Muslims. In both types, the financial institution receives a rate of return on its investment, although both models are designed and structured in a pattern that avoids the use of interest payments.

Murabahah *Contract*

In this case of home financing, the bank purchases the asset/property at the request of a customer for a deferred price, which comprises an agreed profit, added to the actual cost. The bank retains the property until the final installments are paid. According to many ordinary Muslims, *murabahah*-based mortgages are similar to interest-based mortgages, but the *murabahah* is lawful through the consent of Muslim scholars. However, to make this transaction lawful under shariah, two separate transactions should be met by the Islamic financial institution: first, the bank must own a property and then, it must sell it to the customer. The table 9.1 demonstrates the application of this method to mortgages.

Apart from the complexity of Islamic banking in each transaction, the issue of security is common to all. Its advancement of money for sale in favor of the buyer must be supported by sufficient security. Current Islamic banks require the client to provide security other than that relating to the subject of the contract.

Default and Its Consequences in Murabahah

If the buyer defaults in payment at the due date, the price of the commodity cannot be increased. However, as mentioned above, the seller can charge a certain amount or certain proportion, like 5 percent, of the rental for charitable purposes.

Murabahah mortgages were offered by the Ahli United Bank (UK) and Manzil Home Purchase Plans. For the *murabahah* scheme, banks require a deposit of 17 percent to 25 percent, depending on the property value and residential status of the customer, the payment term is 5 to 15 years. Customers can repay the outstanding balance at any time, and payments are fixed for the term of the arrangement.

Ijara *Contract*

Ijarah literally means "to give something on rent," and in principle, it can be described as "transferring the usufruct of a particular property to another person on the basis of a rent claimed from him" (M. Lewis and L. Algaoud 2001). The person employing services is called *musta'jir,* and the person rendering his services is called *a'jir ijara.* This is the most attractive method of property finance, according to shariah scholars and practitioners. It is a more flexible than *murabahah* by allowing the customer to repay the mortgage early with one payment, or to make additional "overpayments." *Ijara* has many characteristics similar to lease financing and hire-purchase arrangements. It involves a lessor (usually a bank) purchasing a property and renting it to a lessee (customer) for a specific time period at an agreed rent.

There are two main types of models under the *ijara* structure. The first model is *ijara wa Iqtina*: "a longer term lease that usually ends with the transfer of ownership of the property to the lessee similar to a modern finance lease." And the second model is diminishing *musharakah*: "a shorter term lease which usually ends with the financial institution keeping possession of the property, which is similar to an operating lease," According to the *ijara* structure, the bank and customer jointly own a property, and the customer buys out the bank's share over time.

Regulatory Position of Islamic Mortgages

FSA chairman Callum McCarthy said: "Islamic finance is a fast-growing force in the world economy, and the FSA's open principle-based approach to regulation offers the right environment for it to flourish in the UK. There is huge potential for an expansion of Islamic offerings in the UK's financial markets, which will in turn boost London's position as an international financial center" (2007). And the UK government and the FSA had taken crucial steps to make an even playing field for both institutions. The Finance Act of 2007 was a breakthrough since the government brought *ijara*-based mortgages into the FSA regulatory framework; before that, only *murabahah* were regulated by the FSA.

According to the FSA[3], *ijara* mortgages are a type of equity-release product, and these products are generally designed for old-age homeowners to enable them to take advantage of the value of their homes without moving out of them. For regulatory purposes, these contracts are called Home Purchase Plans (HPP) and Home Reversion Plans (HRR). These two methods of financing home buying are acceptable under Islamic law. The other is the *murabahah*, which has already been regulated under the FSA's mortgage scheme since 31 October 2004.

According to Basel I, *murabahah*-based mortgages were considered to have the same risk as conventional mortgages with risk weighted at 50 percent. But the *ijara*-based mortgages, however, were risk weighted at 100 percent, which is another reason for the providers to make them slightly more expensive than conventional mortgages. Under the European Union Capital Requirements Directive, the risk weights of all three products (i.e., the HPP, HRP, and *murabahah*) are the same in the UK, which are set at 35 percent, under the standardized approach.

In the end, FSA has provided clear frameworks that can adapt to the change in the marketplace. It's now the responsibility of Islamic Financial Institutions to present innovative products because there is no hurdle with regulations as long as UK consumers are getting satisfactory benefits.

4. Comparison of Islamic & Conventional Mortgages

Comparison Analyses

Islamic banking has the same purpose as conventional banking, except that it operates in accordance with the rules of shariah, known as *fiqh al-muamalat* (Islamic rules on transactions). The basic principle of Islamic banking is the sharing of profit and loss and the prohibition

Table 9.2 Comparison of Islamic and Conventional Mortgages

Conventional Mortgage	Islamic Mortgage
The lender advances funds to the borrower and charges [interest] for the use of their money.	Based on trade [*murabaha*] and leasing [*ijara*], Islamic mortgages are interest-free.
Credit references, sources of income to be able to return the loan before 65 birthdays.	Credit references, sources of income to be able to return the loan before retirement age.
Most lenders have no lower limit on the property value.	Minimum property value £50,000.
Up to 125% of the property value.	Up to 80% of the property value.
Life insurance and building insurance are mandatory in most cases.	There is no compulsory life insurance, and building insurance is required.
Lender never owns the property. Payment term up to 40 years.	The bank puts itself in the position of owner of the property. Higher risks. *Murabaha* up to 15 years, minimum 5 years. *Ijara* up to 25 years, minimum 7.5 years.
Income multiples up to 5 times primary annual income of sole applicant.	*Murabaha* 2.5 times primary annual income. *Ijara* 3 times primary annual income for sole applicant.
Arrangement fee usually up to £500.	Arrangement fee of 0.75% of the property value less the first payment.

of *riba* (usury). Among the common Islamic concepts used in Islamic banking are profit sharing (*mudharabah*), safekeeping (*wadiah*), joint venture (*musharakah*), cost plus *(murabahah),* and leasing (*ijarah*) (see table 9.2).

According to Dar and Presley (2000), Islamic banks act as an intermediary and trustee of people's money, just like conventional banks, but the reimbursement to all depositors is done on a profit-and-loss-sharing basis. This basic difference establishes an element of mutuality in a wider socioeconomic context and provides the right of ownership to its customer. However, in practice, Islamic banks are similar to their conventional counterparts in terms of their organizational setup.

Conventional Mortgage

For example, if the price is £100,000.00, conventional banks require a 10 percent deposit if the bank agrees to give a 30-year mortgage of £90,000, at an annual interest rate of 8 percent, the monthly payments would be £660.39. Each payment will consist partly of interest due and partly the repayment of principal. The buyer will make 360 monthly payments, which add up to a total of £237,740.40 paid to the bank, accruing £147,740.40 in interest to the bank (see table 9.3).

Islamic Mortgage (Cooperative Bank)

Just as in the conventional arrangement, the cooperative bank will require some down payment. That will be client's initial equity share.

Table 9.3 Conventional Mortgage

Payment System	Monthly Payment	Interest	Principal	Balance after Payment
1	£ 660.39	£ 660.00	£ 60.39	£ 89,939.61
2	£ 660.39	£ 599.60	£60.79	£ 89,878.82
3	£ 660.39	£ 599.19	£ 61.20	£ 89,817.62
....				
120	£ 660.39	£ 527.13	£ 133.16	£ 78,951.84
....				
240	£ 660.39	£ 384.83	£ 295.56	£ 54,428.98
....				
359	£ 660.39	£ 8.70	£ 651.69	£ 653.09
360	£ 660.39	£ 7.30	£ 653.09	£ 0.00
Total	£ 237,740.40	£ 147,740.40	£ 90,000.00	

Source: Maris Strategies and the Banker *(2007).*

Let's assume that the client makes the same down payment of 10 percent, or £10,000. The coop bank puts up the remaining £90,000. Now client and the bank are co-owners. If client occupies the house, the client will be required to pay rent to the owners. But the clients are also allowed to increase their ownership share at any time by making additional payments to the coop bank, in effect, buying out the bank's interest in the house. As the client does so, his or her proportionate share increases while the co-op bank's share decreases, and the distribution of the rent payments will change accordingly.

The big question, of course, is what is a fair amount for the monthly rent? It might be reasonable to assume that it is equal to the monthly payments the client would have made under the conventional mortgage arrangement, in this case, £660.39. At the outset, the client will receive 10 percent of that rent as his/her ownership share, and the co-op bank will receive 90 percent. Let also assume that client can apply his share of the rental payments to increasing his share of the ownership. Table 9.4 is an abridged amortization table, which shows the respective returns to the client and the co-op bank. Under this arrangement, the client will own 100 percent of the property after making the 350th payment. The client will have paid a total rent of £231,018.30. The bank's total share will have been £141,018.30. This

Table 9.4 Shared-Equity Mortgage

Payment Number	Payment Amount	Client Share	Coop Bank's Share	Client Equity	Client Equity Percentage	Coop Bank's Equity	Coop Bank Equity Percentage
1	£ 660.39	£ 60.04	£594.35	£10,066.04	10.07	£89,933.96	89.93
2	£ 660.39	£ 60.48	£593.91	£10,132.52	10.13	£89,867.48	89.87
3	£ 660.39	£ 66.91	£593.48	£10,199.43	10.20	£89,800.57	89.80
...							
24	£ 660.39	£ 76.83	£583.56	£11,711.34	11.71	£88,288.66	88.29
...							
120	£ 660.39	£144.54	£515.85	£22,030.94	22.03	£77,969.06	77.97
...							
240	£ 660.39	£318.43	£341.96	£48,536.24	48.54	£51,463.76	51.46
...							
359	£ 660.39	£652.52	£ 7.87	£99,461.37	99.46	£538.63	0.54
360	£ 660.39	£538.63	£ 3.56	£100,000.00	100.00	£0.00	0.00
Total	£231,081.30						

is a saving of more than £6,000.00 or 4.1 percent over the amount of interest paid on the conventional mortgage.

With rent equal to the conventional mortgage at 8 percent, hte 30-year monthly payment owner's share is applied to repurchase. There are no additional principal payments.

Problems in the Provision of Islamic House Financing in the UK

Discussions took place with the Bank of England and the Financial Services Authority (FSA) on these issues, and Khan was confident that they would be resolved in time so that HSBC (Amanah Finance) could begin offering Islamic financial products in 2003. That was not inconceivable, because regulatory authorities had already approved Islamic mortgages in the United States. Khan believes that Islamic finance potentially can appeal to the mainstream as well as to Muslim consumers because of its ethical basis. "Islam teaches us that money should be channelled toward the 'real' economy, the production of real goods and services and not the 'financial' economy, such as hedge funds and derivatives," he argues. "It keeps us in touch with the real economy and away from speculation."

A document jointly prepared by Barclays Group, HSBC, Union Bank of Switzerland, Ihilal UK, and United Bank of Kuwait lists the following major barriers to the provision of Islamic house financing in the UK:

- Under current regulations on lease agreements, the product has to be 100 percent risk weighted. In other words, HSBC (Amanah Finance) says that it has to set aside the full amount of the property to cover the full value of the house in case the buyer cannot afford to pay the rent, whereas a conventional mortgage has a risk weighting of only 50 percent.
- Another impediment for the Islamic mortgage is the prospect of double stamp duty. The first would arise when ownership is transferred from the seller to the bank at the beginning of the lease. The second would occur at the end of the lease, when ownership is transferred from the bank to they buyer. For an Islamic mortgage to be viable for a bank, the bank needs to be exempted from the second set of stamp duties. Former Barclays boss Andrew Buxton chairs a working party on Islamic mortgages set up by the Bank of England. Buxton believes that a change in stamp-duty rules could result in 500,000 more mortgages.

- Unlike a conventional mortgage, the proposed product would require two sets of attorneys (solicitors). Islamic institutions would also want an exemption from a second set of solicitors.
- The inability to obtain financial assistance from the state in cases of financial hardship.

5. Conclusion

The future is definitely dazzling and glorious for the Islamic banking and financial products like the mortgage, *sukuk,* and t*akaful.* After detailed study of Islamic banks, this researcher concludes that Islamic banks are convincing the world that they not only cover the ethical aspects of the society, but they also offer economic benefits. However, it is not a justified argument to claim that Islamic banks are real competitors of conventional banks, because the Islamic banking industry is in its infancy and it will take more time to prove itself over its conventional counterpart.

The corporate governance is an effective tool in Islamic banking, and financial institutions because of their internal-controls system, facilitation of a risk-management culture, enhancing transparency of banking operations, proper selection and use of accounting standards, and disclosure about credit quality, external audits, shariah clearance, and shariah audits (Chapra and Ahmed 2002).

As far as Islamic mortgages are concerned, among the methods discussed above, the diminishing *musharkah* seems to be the solution to the problem for Muslims when buying a house because it more closely follows the principle defined in Islamic jurisprudence.

Islamic principles regarding interest are concerned with issues of fairness and justice rather than efficiency narrowly defined. These principles focus on the necessity of sharing risk in a fair and stable society and upon problems of exploitation in markets where power is asymmetrical; this is the real *riba* (usury) issue.

Our case analyses show that the primary differences between Islamic and conventional housing finance is that the former is equity-based and the latter is debit-based. In an Islamic mortgage, both the bank and the client share ownership (equity), and therefore, share the risk of equity ownership. In conventional banking, the client owns all the equity and the bank's loan to the client is secured on the value of the property.

Putting aside the penetrating comment by Ahmed (1992), "It's not clear to whom we are cheating..." about hypocrisy in the current practice of Islamic banks, let us deal with the realm of the ideal. Consider an ideal situation in which Islamic principles of interest were adhered to by a substantial proportion of people in the world financial system. What they have in common is a prohibition of usury, or excessive interest rates. Could such an idealized system conceivably survive as a foundation for banking in a hypercompetitive global financial environment? Pure logic would dictate that this is not possible in a profit-maximizing world. That is, if "excessive" includes interest rates that reflect high-risk situations or situations of capital shortage, both would require high interest rates that might be considered usurious. We remarked at the beginning of the chapter on the recurrent crises in the financial sector. Maladministration, deception, and unethical behavior lie at the root of many of these problems: Enron and WorldCom are just two examples. The Islamic approach emanates from a foundational set of ethical principles. So discussion of Islamic finance in connection with global financial practices introduces an ethical dimension that is welcome. As Khan (2002) points out, an Islamic system of finance might create a more stable world financial market.

10

THE ISLAMIC BANK OF BRITAIN:
A CASE STUDY

1. INTRODUCTION

Late in the nineteenth century when Muslim countries and Muslim populations were politically and economically at low ebb, the modern banking system was introduced. In order to have good, regular exports and imports from Muslim countries, under the rule of monarchies in distant home countries, the home-country main banks established local branches in the capitals of those countries under their sovereignty. As a result, local populations remained largely unaffected by this new banking system. This led to the local business communities beginning to avoid these "foreign" banks for patriotic as well as religious reasons. While this worked for short period, as time went on, it became more difficult to engage in trade and other activities without making use of commercial banks. Even then, many people limited their involvement to basic transaction activities, such as current accounts and money transfers. They strictly avoided borrowing from and depositing their savings with the bank in order to refrain from dealing in interest, which is prohibited under Islam (Zechmeister 2007).

To prevent interest on all sorts of personal, commercial, industrial, and agricultural loans, this led to the formation of Islamic banking. Islamic banking follows strict Islamic laws that prohibit interest in all sorts of business activities. Islamic banking is based on certain codes that do not allowed Muslims to pay or receive any interest in their business. These codes led to the formation of profit-and-loss sharing. By having this approach, Islamic banking attracted both the lender and borrower, who could work with each other under certain limits. Profit-and-loss sharing allows both lender and borrower to share any loss and profit. This profit-and-loss-sharing principle as its only base has led to Islamic banking in the modern era (Metwally 1997).

2. OBJECTIVES OF THE STUDY

This chapter's two major features are: first, to analyze financial performance and growth of the Islamic Bank of Britain, and second, to use survey methodology to obtain primary data and to assess the degree of customer satisfaction toward Islamic banking in the United Kingdom. Furthermore, this chapter reports on the extent to which Muslims in the UK are aware of the Islamic bank's products and services. The chapter discusses the implications for other Islamic banks in the UK.

3. LITERATURE REVIEW

The last two decades have witnessed that the Islamic banking system has increased momentum worldwide. This is quite clear from the growing number (180) of Islamic banks and other financial institutions based on Islamic principles operating in Asia, Europe, the Americas, and Africa. Collectively, they have over 8,000 branches throughout the world with estimated worth of US $170 billion (Alford and Sherrel 1996).

Regular growth along with modernization is going to convert a large number of customers from the conventional banking system to the Islamic banking system (Shepherd 1996). Through Islamic windows, Citibank, ANZ, HSBC and other major names from conventional banking today are also providing various Islamic financial services. Islamic banks are no longer the only institutions to provide Islamic financial services. Even conventional banks are better at providing those services to Muslims. This creates a lot of competition between the two financial institutions (Cunningham 1994).

Currently, Islamic banks have been going through developmental stages while conventional banking, on the other hand, has been in a boom period. This makes it more difficult for Islamic banks to compete with the conventional banking system in all areas (Nienhaus 1986). Also, it is easy for conventional banks, compared to Islamic banks, to attract more customers. The main reason behind that is that they are serving customers in various fields. This gives them the opportunity to present products and services to their customers very easily (Al Omar and Abdel-Haq 1996). The counter-argument, however, is that conventional banks' movement into Islamic banking is advantageous, since its wide-scale practice will make customers more aware of the system and diminish any apprehension they may have toward it (Al Omar and Abdel-Haq 1996). It is necessary for the conventional and Islamic banking systems to cooperate with each other in order to attain more profit from their products. This will also allow them to present their products in good shape (Kutty 1995). A new study reveals that the growth rate for the world's largest 100 Islamic banks was 26.7 percent, as compared to conventional banks' growth rate of 19.3 percent. The growth reported by Islamic banks is US \$350 billion (March 2008). The outstanding growth shown by Islamic banks not only belongs to Islamic banks, but this sector of the banking industry is also growing in non-Muslims countries as well.

Islamic Banking in the United Kingdom

The number of Muslims residing in the UK is about 1.8 million, which is about 3 percent of the population, and 50 percent of them are estimated to be residing in the London metropolitan area. The number of Muslims visiting the UK on a regular basis is about 500,000. Apart from these, 12 million Muslims currently live in the European Union with the majority in France and Germany (Moyer 2000).

United Bank of Kuwait and HSBC in London are the banks that have Islamic banking divisions in addition to conventional banking. Both banks, irrespective of their locations, regularly receive inquiries regarding the availability of Islamic finance products. The main inquiry is about Islamic-compatible financing to purchase residential or commercial properties. It is believed that a large number of Muslims have abstained from taking out conventional mortgages because these are seen as incompatibile with Islamic principles. The needs of these Muslims must be served immediately (Gambling 2004).

Many banks in the UK offer Islamic financial products. Their products range from savings accounts to home finance in the form of *ijara*. The Financial Services Authority (FSA) in the UK authorized the first retail bank based on the shariah principle under the name the Islamic Bank of Britain. This makes the UK the first country in the West to officially begin Islamic banking under Islamic shariah principles. A wide range of growth later forced the FSA to authorize the European Islamic Investment Bank.

Literature Review

The bank-selection criteria are expected to affect a customer's overall satisfaction toward his or her bank (Levesque and McDougall 1996). Various studies have investigated the bank-selection criteria, or the reasons that customers select specific banks: Mosad Zineldin (1996); Rita Martenson (1985); Jerry Rosenblatt, Michel Laroche, Alan Hochstein,

Ronald McTavish, Maureen Sheahan, (1986); Rosenblatt and Terrill Manning (1986); Allan K. K. Chan (1991); Tan and Christina Chua (1986); Mohammed Almossawi (2001); Huu Phuong Ta and Kar Yin Har (2000); Laroche and Terrill Manning (1984); Ross Jones (2002); Sudin, el al. (1994); Hegazy (1995); K. Chan (1991); Anderson, et al. (1976); Dentan and Chan (1991); Erol and El-Bdour (1989); Erol, et al. (1990); Khazeh and Decker (1992); Kaynak, et al. (1991); Laroche and Taylor (1988); and Levesque and McDoughall (1996).

These studies identified a number of factors that influence a customer's decision-making regarding bank-selection criteria, e.g., competitive interest rates, friends' recommendations, reputation of the bank, credit facility, cooperation of bank staff, convenient banking hours, quick services, availability of ATMs, parking arrangements, service charges, special services, and the quality of services on checking accounts. The significance of these factors varies from country to country and depends upon the age, gender, income, material status, occupation, and cultural background of the customers as well as the type of bank (Islamic or conventional).

For example, Jerry, Michel, Alan, Ronald, and Maureen's (1986) research in a Canadian bank indicates that key factors in this decision seem to hinge upon lower borrowing rates and higher interest rates on deposits as well as on better overall customer service. In spite of the trend of banks toward becoming one-stop-banking centers, Hegazy (1995) investigated bank selection criteria for both Islamic banks and conventional banks located in Egypt. He concluded that the selection attributes for the first are different from those for the latter. For Islamic banks, it was found that most important factor was the advice and recommendations made by the relatives and friends.

Anderson, et al. (1976) and Laroche and Taylor (1988) report that convenient locations is one significant factor influencing the choice of a bank by customers. However, Tan and Chua's (1986) findings show that convenient location was not an important factor for Singapore respondents. Rather, for Singapore respondents, courteous personal service was the most important factor in the selection of a bank, since Singapore is a small city and most banks are conveniently located. From these results, Islamic bank marketers can develop advertising that stresses the family or friend concept. On the basis of Tan and Chua (1986), who argued that, in an Eastern culture, customers desired to have a more intimate and close interaction with the bank personnel, Huu Phuong Ta and Kar Yin Har (2000) made a study of bank-selection decisions in Singapore, using the analytical hierarchy process.

Their findings indicate that undergraduates place high emphasis on the pricing and product dimensions of bank services.

The study of Erol and El-Bdour (1989) deals with the attitude of Jordanian people toward an interest-free bank. Their findings indicate that religiosity was not the main determinant of bank-selection criteria. Sudin, el al. (1994) undertook a study to determine the factors considered important by customers in selecting their financial instruments as well as other things. They used a sample of Muslims and non-Muslims living in three medium-size towns in Malaysia. The three most important criteria in bank selection for Muslims were the provision of fast and efficient service, the speed of transactions, and the reputation and image of the bank.

Kaynak, et al. (1991) reported differences in bank-selection criteria according to gender, age, and educational background of the bank customer in Turkey. They reported that factors like the bank's reputation and its image, business hours, parking facilities, a wide range of services offered, recommendation of friends and relatives, fast and efficient services, being able to pay utility bills, and financial counseling services were considered as more important by male customers than female customers in their selection of a commercial bank in Turkey. Furthermore, bank locations played a more important role for bank customers under the age of 40 as compared to the other age groups studied. Kaynak, et al. (1991) also reported that bank customers who had a more than primary-school education considered the friendliness of bank employees, fast and efficient service, the bank location, and availability of credit more important than the customers who only had a primary-school education.

Luther Denton, K. Allan, and K. Chan (1991) investigated multiple-banking behavior in Hong Kong and discovered statistically significant differences in the evaluation of the relative importance of these factors on multiple-banking behavior based on sex, age, marital status, income, and education. Levesque and McDoughall (1996) looked into the major determinants of customer satisfaction in the retail-banking sector in Canada. They collected information from 325 respondents, who rated their respective banks on various aspects, such as service quality, service-problem recovery, service features, product usage, satisfaction, and future intentions. Their study found that customer satisfaction in retail banking was driven by a number of factors. These factors included service quality, the bank's features (like location), the competitiveness of the bank's interest rates, the customers' judgement about the bank employees' skills, and whether the customer was a borrower or not. The study also found that whether the customer was a single or multiple-bank user was not significant factor. The study confirmed and reinforced the idea that unsatisfactory customer service would limit the willingness to recommend the service to a friend. This could result in increased switching by customers.

In the study by Metawa and Almossawi (1998), the bank behavior of Islamic bank customers in Bahrain was investigated with a sample of 300 customers. It reveals that there are two most important bank-selection criteria, adherence to Islamic principles, and the rate of return. Mohammed Almossawi's (2001) empirical analysis on bank-selection criteria used by college students in Bahrain suggests that it may be necessary to deal with male and female students as distinct segments with different priorities in their bank-selection process. Naser, et al. (1999) found that the most important bank-selection criteria for customers of Islamic banks was "the image of bank," followed by compliance to Islamic principles. The study of Erol and El-Bdour (1989), deals with the attitude of Jordanian people toward interest-free banking. For this aim, the author designed nine questions and statements, published in appendix of their article. It appears from this study that religiosity was not the main determinant of bank selection, whereas the level of profitability (return on investment) was one of the main factors in Jordan. The above studies were conducted almost a decade ago and not in the United Kingdom. Therefore, we felt it was appropriate and timely to investigate the bank-selection criteria adopted by the Islamic Bank of Britain, since it has been the only indigenous bank of its kind in the United Kingdom.

4. ISLAMIC BANK OF BRITAIN

The motive to form an Islamic bank based in the UK came from one of its nonexecutives from the Middle East in 2002. Initially, under the name Islamic House of Britain, the company began negotiations with the FSA to start operations within the UK. With the start-up capital of £14 million in August 2004, the FSA granted permission to the bank to begin operation under the name Islamic Bank of Britain. The Islamic Bank of Britain grew vigorously with the passage of time within the UK. The bank has shown enormous growth in a majority of fields. The number of customers for the year 2007 was 42,000, as compared to 30,814 for the year 2006 (see table 10.1). This shows a growth rate of 36.30 percent. The number of customer deposits in 2007 was £135 million, showing a growth of 60.91 percent as compared to the customer deposits £83.9 million for the year 2006. The amount of customer financing

Table 10.1   Islamic Bank of Britain—Analysis and Projection

	2007	2006	2005
Number of Customers	42,000.00	30,814.00	14,023.00
	36.30 % ↑	119.74 % ↑	
Customer Deposits	135,000,000.00	83,900,000.00	47,700,000.00
	60.91 % ↑	75.89 % ↑	
Customer Financing	15,800,000.00	10,400,000.00	4,500,000.00
	51.92 % ↑	131.11 % ↑	
Number of Accounts	64,000.00	51,032.00	25,403.00
	25.41 % ↑	100.89 % ↑	
Online Banking Customers	10,200.00	8,641.00	5,322.00
	18.04 % ↑	62.36 % ↑	
TOTAL ASSETS	164,936,827.00	118,012,095.00	89,289,500.00
	39.76 % ↑	32.17 % ↑	

for the year 2007 was £15.8 million, showing a growth rate of 51.92 percent as compared to 10.4 million for the year 2006. The number of accountholders for the year 2007 was 64,000, showing a growth rate of 27 percent as compared to the 51,032 bank customers for the year 2006. With the passage of time, the bank also began using modern technology to attract different customers. This urged the bank to start spending more money on information technology. This results in a quite reasonable increase in bank customers using Internet-banking facilities. The number of customers using online Internet banking for the year 2007 was 10,200, showing a growth rate of 91.66 percent as compared to the figure for 2005.

5. METHODOLOGY

The primary data for this research was collected from 200 customers of the Islamic Bank of Britain in early 2008, using face-to-face structured questionnaires. The methodology is in the spirit of studies based on questionnaires and personal interviews by Royal and Althauser (2002) on key indicators and performance drivers in the investment-banking industry; Collins (2002) and Bassi, et al. (2001) on human capital and the future financial performance of the firm; and Beaulieu (1994, 1996) with bank loan officers in relation to their commercial lending. Hussey (1997) also used questionnaire data collected from 12,000 customers. Data was gathered on a division basis as different divisions in the bank had different pricing, regulations, and tools used for customer satisfaction.

The main objective of the study was to investigate customers of the Islamic Bank of Britain, the only indigenous Islamic bank in the United Kingdom. The questionnaire focuses on reasons for selection criteria, customer awareness of different Islamic banking products as well as their perception of the quality of customer-service experience. The personal, face-to-face questionnaire has been shown to be effective for a survey because that makes it possible to gather and quantify qualitative information (Gray 2004). It was also important initially to analyze the demographic characteristics of the respondents. In total, 200 questionnaires were randomly distributed outside different branches of the bank throughout the United Kingdom.

6. RESULTS & ANALYSIS

By using primary and secondary data, this part of the research will evaluate the findings and explanations. The results are shown in table 10.2 and table 10.3. The focus was to get an answer to the research questions by using the findings from the research work. With the emergence of conventional banks offering Islamic financial products and services, the success and performance of banks depends on the satisfaction level of the customers involved. In a country where both conventional and Islamic banking systems operate, it is helpful to know about the factors that motivate a customer's bank selection. Furthermore, one also wants to know the level of customer satisfaction while dealing with Islamic banks, conventional banks, or both (Anderson 1976).

By collecting primary and secondary data, we conducted this study with an objective of knowing the extent of customer satisfaction for Islamic financial products within the UK. Research also focuses on knowing the awareness level of customers toward different Islamic products. While keeping in view that the customer-satisfaction level is on top, this report also aimed to find out the factors on which the customers based their banking selection, whether to maintain business with Islamic banks, conventional banks, or a combination of both within the United Kingdom.

The United Kingdom was chosen for a number of reasons. The number of Muslim residents within the UK is 1.8 million. The population of Muslims within the UK is almost 3 percent of the total population. Almost 500,000 Muslims visit the UK annually. The large number of Muslims based in the UK have forced financial

Table 10.2   Questionnaire Respondents' Profile

		Frequency	Percentage	Cumulative Percentage
Gender				
	Male	96	48.0	48.0
	Female	104	52.0	100.0
Age				
	20 or Less	9	4.5	4.5
	20–30	30	15.0	19.5
	31–40	87	43.5	63.0
	41–50	39	19.5	82.5
	51 or More	35	17.5	100.0
Religion				
	Muslim	109	54.5	54.5
	Non-Muslim	82	41.0	95.5
Martial Status				
	Single	117	58.5	58.5
	Married	74	37.0	95.5
Education				
	Up to primary school	9	4.5	4.5
	Up to high school	13	6.5	11.0
	College graduate	87	43.5	54.5
	Post-graduate school	65	32.5	87.0
	Professional	17	8.5	95.5
Job Type				
	Professional	13	6.5	6.5
	Management	43	21.5	28.0
	White Collar	26	13.0	41.0
	Blue Collar	26	13.0	54.0
	Business	79	39.5	93.5

institutions to begin thinking about the specific financial needs of the Muslim community. This led the FSA to authorize the Islamic Bank of Britain, the first of its kind within the West to begin providing basic Islamic financial products. Keeping in view the increasing demand for Islamic financial products, many conventional banks within the UK start providing Islamic financial products through the Islamic window system.

Table 10.3 Respondents' Selection Criteria

		Frequency	Percentage	Cumulative Percentage
Low Service Charges				
	Strongly Agree	74	37.00	37.00
	Agree	39	19.50	56.50
	Uncertain	26	13.00	69.50
	Disagree	35	17.50	87.00
	Strongly Disagree	26	13.00	100.00
Recommendation				
	Strongly Agree	96	48.00	48.00
	Agree	35	17.50	65.50
	Uncertain	26	13.00	78.50
	Disagree	26	13.00	91.50
	Strongly Disagree	8	4.00	95.50
Bank Based on Religion				
	Strongly Agree	30	15.00	15.00
	Agree	17	8.50	23.50
	Uncertain	5	2.50	26.00
	Disagree	61	30.50	56.50
	Strongly Disagree	87	43.50	100.00
Based on Fast Service				
	Strongly Agree	61	30.50	30.50
	Agree	47	23.50	54.00
	Uncertain	22	11.00	65.00
	Disagree	35	17.50	82.50
	Strongly Disagree	26	13.00	95.50
Based on Friendly Staff				
	Strongly Agree	48	24.00	24.00
	Agree	43	21.50	45.50
	Uncertain	26	13.00	58.50
	Disagree	43	21.50	80.00
	Strongly Disagree	40	20.00	100.00
Based on Unique Products				
	Strongly Agree	48	24.00	24.00
	Agree	43	21.50	45.50
	Uncertain	26	13.00	58.50
	Disagree	40	20.00	78.50
	Strongly Disagree	43	21.50	100.00
Bank Reputation				
	Strongly Agree	78	39.00	39.00
	Agree	52	26.00	65.00
	Uncertain	22	11.00	76.00
	Disagree	22	11.00	87.00
	Strongly Disagree	26	13.00	100.00

Continued

Table 10.3 Continued

		Frequency	Percentage	Cumulative Percentage
Parking Facility				
	Strongly Agree	74	37.00	37.00
	Agree	69	34.50	71.50
	Uncertain	17	8.50	80.00
	Disagree	9	4.50	84.50
	Strongly Disagree	22	11.00	95.50
Location				
	Strongly Agree	74	37.00	37.00
	Agree	57	28.50	65.50
	Uncertain	13	6.50	72.00
	Disagree	26	13.00	85.00
	Strongly Disagree	30	15.00	100.00

7. AUTHOR FINDINGS

- The findings of the author shows that bank service charges come first when customers make a bank selection.
- The second factor found by the author was the bank's reputation. This means that within the UK, customers place the bank's reputation as the second most important selection criteria, after low service charges. This may be due to the reason that, in a country like the UK, where there is strong competition among banks, customers are always looking for a bank with a good reputation both in the market and in customer views.
- Recommendation from friends and relatives to select an appropriate bank came third, according to the author's research.
- The author found from the study that customers place their religion as fourth when they are going to select their bank.
- The survey shows that respondents place fast and efficient services as their fifth selection criteria.
- The author also found that customers place the bank staff as their sixth top priority to select any bank.
- The author found that customers place unique products offered from bank, bank location, and parking facilities as their seventh, eight, and ninth, respectively, as their selection criteria.

As per table 10.4, only 24 percent of the respondents held accounts only in an Islamic bank. However, a majority, 61 percent, revealed that they held accounts in conventional banks only, whereas 30

Table 10.4   Respondents Using Islamic Banks, Conventional Banks, or Both

		Frequency	Percentage	Cumulative Percentage
Respondent's Bank				
	Islamic Bank	48	24.00	24.00
	Conventional Banks	122	61.00	85.00
	Both Islamic and Conventional Banks	30	15.00	100.00

percent indicated that they held accounts with Islamic as well as conventional banks.

8. SUMMARY & CONCLUSIONS

The reason for this study is the intensive competition and variety of products provided by the conventional banking system and the introduction of Islamic finance banks. In the United Kingdom, banking competition is due to many reasons. Many new players like the Islamic banking system, and others, like Tesco and Sainsbury, have entered into the banking market in the past. This strong competition from various suppliers has forced the banking sector to really focus on customer satisfaction and ways to attract customers.

The findings of this study indicate that, irrespective of the bank's nature and products, customers consistently prefer to select those banks that provide services with low charges. This selection is mainly based on an economic point of view, and this means that bank selection has nothing to do with demographic factors. The result also shows that in a country like the UK, with a number of financial services organizations that provide financial services to their clients, bank reputation plays an important role. The study also makes clear that friends and relatives also play an important role in the bank-selection process. This further suggests that word-of-mouth is the best source of advertisement in communities. Other communities, like Muslims in other European countries, do interact on a frequent basis. This frequent interaction results in the ability to influence and inspire each other in their daily-life decisions. So a financial advantage received from one's banking decision can be frequently communicated within the community and motivate others to adopt the same practice, accordingly. Decisions are rarely made totally on the basis of religion; however, this study revealed that religion is the fourth most important factor to affect the decision in selecting a bank. In today's rapid pace, any bank with good and fast services will be highly appreciated. However, the study reveals that customers place fast and efficient services fifth. The study also clarifies that the bank staff has an important role in attracting new customers to the bank. When asked about their ranking, the respondents keep friendliness and the behavior of the bank staff as their sixth selection criteria for a bank. The study also indicates that customers place the availability of unique products, bank location, and parking facility as their seventh, eight, and ninth best selection criteria, respectively, while selecting a bank.

It is quite clear from the study that, in order to attract more customers, banks have to keep their service charges at their minimum level. Today, where the credit crunch has been coupled with other financial crises, like soaring prices in the food market, a record decline in job availability, the worsening mortgage market, and the continuous increase in energy prices, consumers have been pushed to look for cheaper services and products. The second most important thing to attract more customers from the vast field of the customer-service industry is that banks must try to have a good reputation in the minds of customers and clients. This will lead to attracting more customers to the bank, which will in turn increase their business, and hence, their survival will be ensured. The third most important factor that came to be known was the role played by the word-of-mouth advertising. This is the main factor customers always use to select their financial-services providers.

9. RECOMENDATIONS

Islamic banks may only survive today when they provide good and reliable services to their clients. Islamic banks are very new in the market, and it is necessary for them to compete with conventional banks, which have been serving their clients for years and which have had a strong reputation. This makes it more difficult for Islamic banks to compete with them. Islamic banks cannot rely solely on religion as a basis to attract their customers, as our study shows that customers' first priority was always to choose their bank according to its low fees and charges, and not on a religious basis. In order to attract more customers to the Islamic banking system, Islamic banks have to do more work than do conventional banks, which are already more stable in financial markets. The main area on which Islamic banks should focus significantly is making their reputation appealing to customers. Islamic banks can take a number of steps in this regard, such as powerful advertising, utilizing all modes of media, and hiring an educated and friendly staff to attract more customers and retain current ones.

APPENDIX A

EXAMPLE OF FINANCIAL RISK–MANAGEMENT POLICIES OF AN ISLAMIC BANK

The guidelines and policies adopted by the bank to manage the following risks that arise in the conduct of the business activities are as follows. (This appendix relates to the discussion found in chapter 5.)

OPERATIONAL RISK

This risk is defined as the risk of loss arising from inadequate or failed internal processes, people, systems, and external events. In managing this risk, a dedicated team has been established. The team is responsible for identification, assessment and measurement, control framework, and monitoring and reporting of operational risks.

CREDIT RISK

Credit risk is the potential loss of revenue and principal in the form of specific allowances as a result of defaults by the customers or counter parties through financing, dealing, and investing activities. The primary exposure to credit risk arises from financing activities. Credit policy to govern the activities is rigorously being enhanced with the objectives of improving the quality of assets originated and preserved. This is in line with the ongoing organization transformation.

Under the credit-process flow, credit administration, and credit control, review and analysis are performed independently of individuals involved in the business origination. In addition, an independent evaluation of credit proposals before approval has been established for all proposals involving corporate and commercial sectors. This function is performed by the risk-management division.

Credit risk arising from dealing and investing activities are managed by the establishment of limits which include, counter-parties limits, permissible acquisition of not less than A-rated private-entities instruments. Furthermore, the dealing and investing activities are monitored by an independent middle office unit.

MARKET RISK

Market risk is the risk of loss arising from adverse movements in the level of market prices or rates. The market-risk components are foreign-exchange risk, profit-rate risk, and equity risk.

Foreign-Exchange Risk

This risk refers to adverse exchange-rate movements on foreign-currency positions taken by the bank. Foreign-currency open position is monitored against predetermined position limits and cut-loss limits.

Profit-Rate Risk

The profit-rate risk refers to volatility in the net-profit income as a result of changes in the levels of profit rate and shifts in the composition of the assets and liabilities. The profit-rate risk, however, is self-mitigated when most of the financing assets are based on fixed rates while profit paid to depositors is not contractual. Profit paid to depositors/investors depend on the profit generated from the bank's activities and the profit-sharing distribution. The bank is not exposed directly to interest-rate risk, because interest is prohibited under Islamic banking. The indirect interest-rate risk exists arising from competition with other banks. This is managed by regularly reviewing the bank's profit rates.

Equity Risk

Equity risk refers to the adverse movements in the price of equities on equity positions. Equity position is marked to market and the monitored risk management division and reported to the risk-management committee.

Liquidity Risk

Liquidity risk is related to the risk arising mainly from withdrawals of deposits. In managing this, the Bank is adopting the liquidity framework introduced by Bank Negara Malaysia which ascertains liquidity based on the contractual and behavioral cash flow of assets, liabilities, and off-balance sheet commitments.

Appendix B

Questionaire For Banking Professionals

The purpose of the current study is to provide an insight into the significance of the Islamic mortgage to the UK finance industry.

This questionnaire from chapter 8 was used to aid in the research and analysis of the views of banking professionals toward the growing sector of Islamic banking and finance.

Part A

Please use a (√) to indicate how strongly you agree or disagree with each of the following statements. Please make sure that you only check one response for each question. Remember that there are no right or wrong answers, so please be honest. Possible responses are:

SA—Strongly AgreeA—Agree
Neutral— Neither Agree nor Disagree
D—disagreeSD—Strongly Disagree

1. *Interest-based mortgages are better than non-interest based.*

_____ SA _____ A _____ N _____ D _____ SD

2. *Islamic mortgages are less risky than the conventional mortgages.*

_____ SA _____ A _____ N _____ D _____ SD

3. *Its ethical foundations make Islamic finance an increasingly serious alternative to conventional finance.*

_____ SA _____ A _____ N _____ D _____ SD

4. *Islamic mortgages have a market outside the Muslim community.*

_____ SA   _____ A   _____ N   _____ D   _____ SD

5. *There is great awareness in the UK about Islamic mortgages and their principles.*

_____ SA   _____ A   _____ N   _____ D   _____ SD

6. *There is little difference between the mortgages offered by conventional and Islamic banks.*

_____ SA   _____ A   _____ N   _____ D   _____ SD

Part B

We need some background information in order to classify your responses. I would like to remind you that all the information collected will remain confidential and will be used only for academic research purposes.

1. *Which age group do you fall in?*

_____ 18 to 24 years   _____ 25 to 34 years
_____ 34 to 49 years   _____ 50 to 64 years
_____ 65 years or more

2. *What is your total household income (before taxes)?*

_____ Less than £15,000   _____ £15,001 to $20,000
_____ £20,001 to £30,000   _____ £30,001 to £40000
_____ No Answer

3. *How long have you been in the banking industry?*

_____ 9 years or less   _____ 10 to 20 years
_____ 21 to 30   years   _____ 31 to 40 years
_____ 41 year

Notes

1 Islamic Banking, Finance & Financial Intermediation: Developments & Risk Management

1. Prohibition of interest is directly prohibited by the divine order in the Qur'an. Certain verses of the Qur'an clearly prohibit dealing with *riba* but do not define it precisely. Such omission is often attributed to the fact that the concept was not vague at the time of prohibition, so there was no need to provide a formal definition.
2. Cihak and Hesse, 2010. The authors argue that Islamic and commercial banks can coexist in the same system without substantial "crowding out" effects through competition and deteriorating soundness.
3. More up-to-date data confirm that the Islamic share of total assets has not increased all that much in recent years. Looking at the important GCC market, Islamic banks accounted for roughly one-fifth of regional bank assets in 2008, up only marginally from their share eight years earlier (S&P 2010).
4. These conclusions, as noted, are extremely tentative and sensitive to the way the data are measured. The authors note that outliers are extremely important, and thus they present stability measures that include and exclude them. Based on the unadjusted data, there are no statistically significant differences between Islamic and commercial banks, reversing the conclusion based upon data adjusted for outliers. A similar reversal occurs when assessing the stability of large Islamic and commercial banks, with the former now shown to exhibit less stability than the latter, a difference that is statistically significantly. Finally, a similar reversal occurs for small Islamic banks, though here the differences are not significant.

2 Productivity Growth in the GCC Banking Industry, 1999–2007: Conventional vs. Islamic Banks

1. This chapter is written by Samir Abderrazek Srairi, associate professor of finance at Riyadh Community College, King Saud University, Kingdom of Saudi Arabia.
2. For example, Saudi Arabia in the last few years has granted licenses to ten branches of Gulf-country banks and international banks (e.g., BNP Paribas, J. P. Morgan, and Deutsh Bank).

3. There are three financial centers in this region: the first off-shore banking centre established in Bahrain in 1974, the Dubai International Financial Center created in 2004, and the Qatar Financial Centrer founded in 2005.

4. It is possible to measure changes in productivity by employing an econometric method. This requires the estimation of a production, cost, or revenue function.

5. For a more detailed explanation, see Fare, et al. (1992) and Grifell-tatjé and Lovell (1996).

6. In this approach, we estimate the frontier in terms of the maximum level of outputs that can be achieved with a given set of inputs. The Malmquist index can also be defined by input-oriented approach where the frontier is the minimum set of inputs required for a given level of outputs.

7. An output distance function is defined as the reciprocal of the maximum proportional expansion of the output vector, y^t, given input vector, x^t, under period t technology (Shephard 1970).

8. This decomposition has been subject to a number of criticisms (see, for example, Ray and Desly 1997; Coelli 2005).

9. All Malmquist indices are computed by using the program Deap version 2.1 (Coelli 1996).

10. Using panel data, this technique produces unbiased and consistent estimates of the coefficients.

11. In some studies, such as Casu, et al. (2004), Pasiouras (2008a), and Sufian (2009b), off-balance-sheet items is used as a proxy to nontraditional business.

12. The variable of diversification or specialization can also be measured by the Herfindahl index of outputs which is calculated as a sum of the squared shares of each output in total output.

13. Two methods are used in the literature to construct the Malmquist index. The adjacent method calculates the Malmquist index for each period (e.g., adjacent periods t+1, t, adjacent periods t+2, t+1, ...). In the second approach, fixed-based period, the Malmquist index is computed for all periods relative to a fixed-base period (for details, see Grifell-Tatjé and Lovell 1996).

14. For example, in Saudi Arabia, the number of ATMs was increased by 240 percent to 7,531 in 2007, compared to 2,222 in 2000. Also the number of POS has multiplied by three in the same period.

4   The Development & Scope of Islamic Bank Bonds (Sukuk)

1. Janachi (1995), p. 42.
2. Janachi (1995), p. 28.
3. Janachi (1995), p. 29.

5   RISK-BASED SUPERVISION FOR ISLAMIC BANKING & AREAS OF CONCERN

1. This paper only discusses the appropriate and effective regulatory system.
2. Although the subject of regulation and supervision of Islamic banks was first mentioned at the Organization of the Islamic Conference (OIC) Meeting held in Khartoum on 7–8 March 1981, nothing much was done after that. Then, it was in November 2002, that IFSB was established to serve as an international standard-setting body of regulatory and supervisory agencies that have vested interest in ensuring the soundness and stability of the Islamic financial services industry. IFSB will also serve a similar role as BIS.
3. See Said, F. F. and A. G. Ismail. 2008. "Monetary Policy, Capital Requirement and Lending Behaviour of Islamic Banking in Malaysia." *Journal of Economic Cooperation*, 29 (3): 1–22.
4. Indeed, this argument helped develop the Malaysia Deposit Insurance Corporation Act of 2005. The act enables the establishment of Malaysia Deposit Insurance Corporation (PIDM) in 2005.
5. The RBS has been practiced in three jurisdictions, namely, the Federal Reserve System of America (FRS), the Office of the Superintendent of Financial Institutions (OSFI) Canada, and the Financial Services Authority (FSA) UK. In this paper, however, the unique characteristics of Islamic banks become crucial elements in the RBS approach.
6. These objective become part of maqasid shariah.
7. *Failure* is defined as encompassing not only those institutions declared equity-insolvent by their primary regulator during the two-year period but also those that are classified as "critically undercapitalized" at the end of the period. The latter group is included to identify institutions for which the central bank mandates "prompt corrective action." In general, that legislation requires the central bank to close critically undercapitalized institutions within ninety days. *Critical undercapitalization* is defined as a ratio of tangible equity to average assets of less than 2 percent.
8. The latter is only applicable if the central bank introduces a policy of deposit insurance based on the risk-exposure level of each Islamic bank.

6   IRAN'S ISLAMIC BANKING EXPERIENCE & FUTURE

1. If deposits rates rise over the course of the loan because of financial liberalization, then the bank may suffer a loss because it cannot increase the interest rate on the loan. Banks usually reduce this interest-rate risk

associated with maturity mismatching by lending at floating interest rates. Nevertheless, where banks have been subjected to directed credit allocation, naturally, they have a large proportion of their loans on a fixed-interest-rate basis, leaving them vulnerable in the period following deregulation.

2. For the proper functioning of the monetary and credit system, the Central Bank of Iran is empowered to intervene in, and supervise, the monetary and banking activities through the following instruments:a. Fixing a minimum and /or maximum ratio of profit for banks in their joint venture and *mozarebeh* activities; these ratios may vary for different fields of activity.b, Designation of various fields for investment and partnership within the framework of the approved economic policies, and fixing of a minimum prospective rate of profit for the various investment and partnership projects. The minimum prospective rate of profit may vary with respect to different branches of activity.c. Fixing a minimum and maximum margin of profit as a proportion to the cost price of goods transacted, for banks in installment and hire-purchase transactions.d. Determination of the types and the minimum and maximum amounts of commissions for banking services (provided that they do not exceed the expense of service rendered) and the fees charged for putting to use the deposits received by the bank.e. Determination of the types, amounts, as well as the minimum and maximum bonuses subject of Article 6 and the establishment of guidelines for advertisement by the banks in the cases referred to.f. Determination of the minimum and maximum ratio in the joint venture, *mozarebeh,* investment, hire-purchase, installment transactions, buying or selling on credit, forward deals, *mozarebeh, mosaqat, joalah,* and *gharz-al-hasaneh* for banks or any thereof with respect to various fields of activity; also fixing the maximum facility that can be granted to each customer.

3. Under Islamic banking, interest-paying deposits with the banking system are viewed as participation in the investment activities of the banking system. Such deposits are subject to two profit rates. An initial rate, known as the provisional rate, which is announced at the time deposits are placed with the banks, and a final rate, which is computed on the basis of the bank operations at the end of the of the year. However, in practice, the provisional and actual returns are very close (Pourian 1995).

4. *Mozarebeh* (limited trade partnership), whereby the bank provides initial capital to commercial traders, individuals and companies, preferably cooperatives, who engage in trade and business, other than imports. Profits from the undertaking are divided under specified terms at the end of the contract.

5. *Gharz-al-hassaneh* or interest-free loans to individuals, for the purpose of meeting the objective of paragraph (b) and (i) of Article 43 of the 1980 constitution (e.g., providing tools of trade for workers who lack these means; meeting urgent and unexpected needs of individuals; and

facilitating production of agricultural, livestock, and industrial goods). The expenses of making such loans are borne by borrowers as fees or charges.

6. *Rial* (RI) is a monetary unit of Iran.
7. For instance, in 1987, 62.4 percent of all lending by the banking system to the private sector was for short-term ventures (Mazarei 1995, 300).

9   THE ROLE OF ISLAMIC MORTGAGES IN THE UNITED KINGDOM

1. www.fiscusmortgages.co.uk
2. www.mortgageman.co.uk
3. Source:(www.islamicmortgageadvice.co.uk).
4. www.fsa.gov.uk/pages/library/communication/pr/2006/041.shtml

REFERENCES

1 ISLAMIC BANKING, FINANCE & FINANCIAL INTERMEDIATION

Accounting and Auditing Organization for Islamic Financial Institutions (AAOIFI). 1999. "Statement on the Purpose and Calculation of the Capital Adequacy Ratio for Islamic Banks." Bahrain, March.

Bellalah, Mondher. 2009. "Exotic Derivatives," In *Derivative, Risk Management & Value.*, London: World Scientific Publishing. Foreword by Nobel Laureates Myron Scholes and Harry Markowitz.

Bellalah, Mondher. 2008. *Derivatives, Risk and Exotic Derivatives.* London: World Scientific Publishing. Foreword by Nobel Laureates Myron Scholes and Harry Markowitz.

Bellalah, Mondher; et al. 2008. *Risk Management& Value: Valuation & Asset Pricing*, World Scientific Studies in International Economics. London: World Scientific Publishing. Foreword by Nobel Laureate Harry Markowitz.

Bellalah, Mondher; et al. 1998.*Options, Futures & Exotic Derivatives.* Hoboken, NJ: John Wiley & Sons. Foreword by Vasicek Olrich and Nobel Laureate Robert C. Merton.

Čihák, Martin, and Heiko Hesse 2008. "Islamic Banks and Financial Stability: An Empirical Analysis," IMF Working Paper No. WP/08/16 (January).

Finley, M. I. 1985. *The Ancient Economy.* London: Chatto & Windus.

Hasan, Maher and Jemma Dridi 2010. "The Effects of the Global Crisis on Islamic and Conventional Banks: A Comparative Study," IMF Working Paper WP/10/201 (September).

Islamic Development Bank (IDB). 2005. http://www.isdb.org/irj/go/km /docs/documents/IDBDevelopments/Internet/English/IDB/CM /Publications/Occasional%20Papers/Islamic%20Banking%20and%20 Finance/Regulations_Supervision_of_Islamic_Banks.pdf

Imam, Patrick, and Kangni Kpodar. 2010. "Islamic Banking: How Has it Spread?" IMF Working Paper, forthcoming (Washington: International Monetary Fund).

International Monetary Fund (IMF). 2004. *Compilation Guide for Financial Soundness Indicators*. Washington, D.C.: IMF.

Islamic Financial Services Board (IFSB). 2005a. "Capital Adequacy Standard for Institutions (Other than Insurance Institutions) Offering Only Islamic Financial Services." Exposure Draft 2. Kuala Lumpur, Malaysia: IFSB. (Text reference is IFSB 2005a.)

Islamic Financial Services Board (IFSB). 2005b. "Guiding Principles of Risk Management for Institutions (Other Than Insurance Institutions) Offering Only Islamic Financial Services." Exposure Draft 1. Kuala Lumpur, Malaysia: IFSB. (Text reference is IFSB 2005b.)

Iqbal, Zamir. 2005. "Impact of Consolidation on Islamic Financial Services Industry," 2nd International Seminar on Challenges Facing the Islamic Financial Services Industry, Tehran, Iran, April 6–7.

Iqbal, Zamir, and Abbas Mirakhor. 1999. "Progress and Challenges of Islamic Banking." *Thunderbird International Business Review* 41 (4–5, July–October): 381–405.

Iqbal, Zamir, and Abbas Mirakhor. 2002. "Development of Islamic Financial Institutions and Challenges Ahead." In *Islamic Finance: Growth and Innovation, edited by* Simon Archer and Rifaat Abdel Karim. London: Euromoney Books.

Iqbal, Zamir, and Abbas Mirakhor. 2004. "A Stakeholders Model of Corporate Governance of Firm in Islamic Economic System." *Islamic Economic Studies* 11 (2, March): 43–63.

Iqbal, Zamir, and Abbas Mirakhor. 2007a. *Introduction to Islamic Finance: Theory and Practice*. Hoboken, NJ: John Wiley & Sons.

Iqbal, Zamir, and Abbas Mirakhor. 2007b. "Qard Hasan Mircofinance." *New Horizon* No. 64, (April–June).

Iqbal, Zamir, and Hiroshi Tsubota.2005. "Emerging Islamic Markets." *The Euromoney International Debt Capital Markets Handbook*. London: Euromoney Publishing.

Jabbari, A. Nadia. 2006. "Capital Adequacy Standard for Institutions Offering Islamic Financial Services." Paper presented at Islamic Financial Services Board 2nd International Research Conference on Islamic Banking: Risk Management, Regulation & Supervision, Kuala Lumpur, Maylasia, February 7–8.

Kahf, Monzer. 1999. "Islamic Banks at the Threshold of the Third Millennium." *Thunderbird International Business Review* 41 (4–5, July–October): 445–60.

Khan, M. Fahim. 1994. "Comparative Economics of Some Islamic Financing Techniques." *Islamic Economic Studies* 2 (1, December): 81–102.

Khan, Mohsin. 1987. "Islamic Interest-Free Banking: A Theoretical Analysis." In *Theoretical Studies in Islamic Banking and Finance, edited by* Moshin Khan and Abbas Mirakhor. Houston: IRIS Books.

Khan, T., Ahmed, H. 2001. Risk Management: An Analysis of Issues in Islamic Financial Industry: Islamic Development Bank.

Kose, M. Ayhan and Eswar Prasad. 2010. Emerging Markets *Resilience and Growth Amid Global Turmoil. Developing Countries, Global Economics* Washington: Brookings Institution Press, 2010.

Masood, Omar. 2010. "Shariah Compliant Screening Practices," University of East London working paper.

Merton, R. C. 1987. "A Simple Model of capital market equilibrium with Incomplete Information." *Journal of Finance* 42, 483–510.

McMillan, John, 2002. *Reinventing the Bazaar: A Natural History of Markets.* New York: W.W. Norton & Company.

Standard & Poor's (S&P). 2010. *Islamic Finance Outlook. 2010.*

van Greuning, Hennie, and Amir Iqbal. 2008. "Risk Analysis for Islamic Banks." World Bank document.

2 PRODUCTIVITY GROWTH IN THE GCC BANKING INDUSTRY, 1999–2007

Al-Jarrah, I., and P. Molyneux. 2007. "Efficiency in Arabian Banking," *Jordan Journal of Business Administration* 3: 373–390.

Al-Muharrami, S. 2007. "The Causes of Productivity Change in GCC Banking Industry." *International Journal of Productivity & Performance Management* 8: 731–743.

Al-Obaidan, A. M. 2008. "Efficiency Effect of Openness in the Banking Industry of Emerging Markets." *International Research Journal of Finance & Economics* 17: 91–104.

Angelidis, D., and K. Lyroudi. 2006. "Efficiency in the Italian Banking Industry: Data Envelopment Analysis and Neutral Networks," *International Research Journal of Finance & Economics* 5: 155–165.

Ariss. R. M., R. Rezvanian, S. M. Mehdian. 2007. "Cost Efficiency, Technological Progress and Productivity Growth of Banks in GCC Countries." *International Journal of Business* 12: 471–491.

Asmild, M., J. C. Paradi, V. Aggarwall, and C. Schaffnit. 2004. "Combining DEA Window Analysis with the Malmquist Index Approach in a Study of the Canadian Banking Industry." *Journal of Productivity Analysis* 21: 67–89.

Avkiran, N. C. 2000. "Rising Productivity of Australian Trading Banks Under Deregulation 1986–1995." *Journal of Economics & Finance* 2: 122–140.

Berger, A. N., and D. B. Humphrey 1997. "Efficiency of Financial Institutions: International Survey and Directions of Future Research." *European Journal of Operational Research* 98: 175–212.

Berger, A. N., and D. B. Humphrey. 1992. "Measurement and Efficiency Issues in Commercial Banking." In *Measurement Issues in the Service Sectors,* edited by Z. Griliches. National Bureau of Economic Research, Chicago: University of Chicago Press, pp. 245–279.

Berger, A. N., and L. G. Mester. 2003. "Explain the Dramatic Changes in Performance of U.S. Banks: Technological Change, Deregulation, and Dynamic Changes in Competition." *Journal of Financial Intermediation* 12: 57–95.

Berger, A. N., and R. De Young. 1997. "Problem Loans and Cost Efficiency in Commercial Banks." *Journal of Banking & Finance* 6: 849–870.

Carvallo, O., and A. Kasman. 2005. "Cost Efficiency in the Latin American and Caribbean Banking Systems." *International Financial Markets Institution & Money* 15: 55–72.

Casu, B., C. Girardone, and P. Molyneux. 2004. "Productivity Change in European Banking: A Comparison of Parametric and Non-Parametric Approaches." *Journal of Banking & Finance* 28: 2521–2540.

Casu, B., and C. Girardone. 2004. "Financial Conglomeration: Efficiency, Productivity and Strategic Drive." *Applied Financial Economics*, 14: 687–696.

Caves, D. W., L. R. Christensen, and W. E. Diewert. 1982. 'The Economic Theory of Index Numbers and the Measurement of Input, Output and Productivity." *Econometrica* 6: 1393–1414.

Chan, V. L., and M. Liu. 2006. "Effects of Bank Efficiency and Productivity in Taiwan." *Academic Economic Papers* 34: 251–300.

Charnes, A., W. Cooper, A. Lewin, and L. Seiford. 1994. "Data Envelopment Analysis: Theory, Methodology, and Application." Boston: Kluwer Academic Publishers.

Chiou, C. C. 2009. "Effects of Financial Holding Company Act on Bank Efficiency and Productivity in Taiwan." *Neurocomputing* 16–18: 3490–3506.

Coelli, T. 1996. "A Guide to DEAP Version 2.1, A Data Envelopment Analysis." (Computer program), CEPA, Working paper 96/08, University of New England, Armidale, NSW, Australia, http://www.uq.edu.au /econometrics/cepa/

Coelli, T., D. S. P. Rao, C. J. Donnell, and G. E. Battese. 2005. *An Introduction to Efficiency and Productivity Analysis,* 2nd ed. New York: Springer.

Das, A. and M.S. Ghosh. 2006. "Financial Deregulation and Efficiency: An Empirical Analysis of Indian Banks During the Post Reform Period." *Review of Financial Economics* 15:193–221.

Daniels, K. N., D. Tirtiroglu, and E. Tirtiroglu. 2005. "Deregulation, Intensity of Competition, Industry Evolution and the Productivity Growth of the U.S. Commercial Banks." *Journal of Money, Credit & Banking* 2: 339–360.

Delis, M. D., P. Molyneux, and F. Pasiouras. 2009. "Regulations and Productivity Growth in Banking," Munich personal RePEc Archive, Paper no.13891, http://mpra.ub.uni-muenchen.de/13891/.

Dogan, E., and D. Fausten. 2003. "Productivity and Technical Change in Malaysian Banking: 1989–1998," *Asia-Pacific Financial Markets* 10: 205–237.

Drake, L. 2001. "Efficiency and Productivity Change in UK Banking," *Applied Financial Economics* 11: 557–571.

Drake, L., M. J. B. Hall, and R. Simper. 2006. "The Impact of Macroeconomic and Regulatory Factors on Bank Efficiency: A Non-Parametric Analysis of Hong Kong's Banking System." *Journal of Banking & Finance,* 30: 1443–1466.

Elyasiani, E., and S. M. Mehdian. 1995. "The Comparative Efficiency Performance of Small and Large U.S. Commercial Banks in the Pre- and Post-Deregulation Eras." *Applied Economics* 27: 1069–1079.

Elton, M. N. 2003. "Quantitative Measures of Financial Sector Reform in the Arab Countries. Working Paper, Arab Planning Institute, Kuwait.

Esho, N. 2001. "The Determinants of Cost Efficiency in cooperative Financial Institutions: Australian Evidence." *Journal of Banking & Finance* 25: 941–964.

Fare, R. S. Grosskopf, B. Lindgren, and P. Roos. 1992. "Productivity Changes in Swedish Pharmacies 1980–1987: A Non-Parametric Approach." *Journal of Productivity Analysis* 1–2: 85–101.

Fare, R., S. Grosskopf, and C. A. K. Lovell. 1985. *The Measurement of Efficiency of Production.* Boston: Kluwer Academic Publishers.

Fare, R., S. Grosskopf, M. Norris, and Z. Zhang. 1994. "Productivity Growth Technical Progress and Efficiency Change in Industrialized Countries." *American Economic Review* 1: 66–83.

Fisher, I. 1922. *The Making of Index Numbers.* Boston: Houghton.

Fukuyama, H., and W. L. Weber. 2002. "Estimating Output Allocative Efficiency and Productivity Change: Application to Japanese Banks." *European Journal of Operational Research* 137: 177–190.

Fries S, and A. Taci. 2005. "Cost Efficiency of Banks in Transition: Evidence from 289 Banks in 15 Post-Communist Countries." *Journal of Banking & Finance* 29: 55–81

Tung, M. K. 2006. "Scale Economies, X-Efficiency, and Convergence of Productivity among Bank Holding Companies." *Journal of Banking & Finance* 30: 2857–2874.

Goddard, J., P. Molyneux, S. Wilson, and M. Tavakoli. 2007. "European Banking: An Overview." *Journal of Banking & Finance,* 31: 1911–1935.

Grifell-Tatjé, E., and C. A. K. Lovell. 1997. "The Sources of Productivity Change in Spanish Banking." *European Journal of Operational Research* 98: 364–380.

Grifell-Tatjé, E., and C. A. K. Lovell. 1996. "Deregulation and Productivity Decline: The Case of Spanish Savings Banks." *European Economic Review,* 40: 1281–1303.

Grigorian, D. A., and V. Manole. 2005. "A Cross-Country Nonparametric Analysis of Bahrain's Banking System." IMF Working Paper No. 05/117.

Iimi, A. 2004. "Banking Sector Reforms in Pakistan: Economies of Scale and scope, and Cost Complementarities." *Journal of Asian Economics* I (15): 507–528.

Isik, I. 2008. "Productivity, Technology and Efficiency of de Novo: A Counter Evidence from Turkey." *Journal of Multinational Financial Management* 18: 427–442.

Isik, I., and M. K. Hassan. 2003. "Financial Disruption and Bank Productivity: The 1994 Experience of Turkish Banks." *The Quarterly Review of Economics & Finance* 43: 291–320.

Islam, M. M. 2003. "Development and Performance of Domestic and Foreign Banks in GCC Countries." *Managerial Finance* 7: 42–71.

Islam, M. M., and A. Mushtaq. 2003. "Regulation and Supervision of Financial Institutions in GCC Countries." *Managerial Finance* 7: 17–42.

Jabsheh, F. Y. 2001. "The GATS Agreement and Liberalizing the Kuwaiti Banking Sector." Working paper, Kuwait Institute for Scientific Research.

Jaffry, S., Y. Ghulam, S. Pascoe, and J. Cox. 2007. "Regulatory Changes and Productivity of the Banking Sector in the Indian Sub-Continent." *Journal of Asian Economics* 18: 415–438.

Kaparakis, E. I., S. M. Miller, and A. G. Noulas. 1994. "Short-Term Cost Inefficiency of Commercial Banks: A Flexible Stochastic Frontier Approach." *Journal of Money, Credit & Banking* 26: 875–893.

Koutsomanli-Filippaki, A., D. Margaritis, and C. Staikouras. 2009. "Efficiency and Productivity Growth in the Banking Industry of Central and Eastern Europe." *Journal of Money, Credit &Banking* 33: 557–567.

Kyj, L., and I. Isik. 2008. "Bank X-Efficiency in Ukraine: An Analysis of Service Characteristics and Ownership." *Journal of Economics & Business* 60: 369–793.

Leightner, J. E., and C. A. K. Lovell. 1998. "The Impact of Financial Liberalization on the Performance of Thai Banks." *Journal of Economics & Business* 50: 115–131.

Maniadakis, N., and E. Thanassoulis. 2004. "A Cost Malmquist Productivity Index." *European Journal of Operational Research* 154: 396–409.

Maudos, J., J. M. Pastor, F. Perez, et al. 2002. "Cost and Profit Efficiency in European Banks." *Journal of International Financial Markets Institution & Money* 2: 33–58.

Mester, L. J. 1987. "Efficient Production of Financial Services: Scale and Scope Economies." *Business Review*, Federal Reserve Bank of Philadelphia (January/February): 15–25.

Mukherjee, K., S. C. Ray, and S. M. Miller. 2001. "Productivity Growth in Large U.S. Commercial Banks: The Initial Post-Deregulation Experience." *Journal of Banking & Finance* 25: 913–939.

Pasiouras, F. 2008a. "Estimating the Technical and Scale Efficiency of Greek Commercial Banks: The Impact of Credit Risk, Off-Balance Sheet Activities, and International Operation." *Research in International Business & Finance* 22: 301–318.

Pasiouras, F. 2008b. "International Evidence on the Impact of Regulations and Supervision on Banks' Technical Efficiency: An Application of Two-

Stage Data Envelopment Analysis." *Review of Quantitative Finance & Accounting* 30: 187–223.

Pastor, J. M., F. Perez, and J. Queseda. 1997. "Efficiency Analysis in Banking Firms: An International Comparison." *European Journal of Operational Research* 98: 398–407.

Peterson, E. R. 1988. *The Gulf Cooperation Council: Search for Unity in a Dynamic Region*. Boulder, CO: Westview Press.

Ramanathan, R. 2007. "Performance of banks in countries of GCC." *International Journal of Productivity & Performance Management* 2: 137–154.

Park, K. H., and W. L. Weber. 2006. "A Note on Efficiency and Productivity Growth in the Korean Banking Industry, 1992-2002." *Journal of Banking & Finance* 30: 2371–2386.

Ray, S. C., and E. Desli. 1997. "Productivity Growth, Technical Progress, and Efficiency Change in Industrialized Countries: Comment." *International Advances in Economic Research* 3: 531–543.

Rebelo, J., and V. Mendes. 2000. "Malmquist Indices of Productivity Change in Portuguese Banking: The Deregulation Period." *American Economic Review* 5: 1033–1039.

Rezitis, A. N. 2006. "Productivity Growth in the Greek Banking Industry: A Non-Parametric Approach." *Journal of Applied Economics* 1: 119–138.

Rezvanian, R., N. Rao, and S. M. Mehdian. 2008. "Efficiency Change, Technological Progress and Productivity Growth of Private, Public and Foreign Banks in India: Evidence from the Post-Liberalization Era." *Applied Financial Economics* 18: 701–713.

Rogers, K. E. 1998. "Nontraditional Activities and the Efficiency of U.S. Commercial Banks." *Journal of Banking & Finance* 22: 467–482.

Saab G. 2007. "A Study of Financial Development, FDI and Growth in the GCC Area." *Competition Forum* 5: 53–57.

Saidi, N., and R. Kumar. 2007. "Corporate Governance in the GCC." Working paper, Hawkamah Institute for Corporate Governance, DIFC, Dubai.

Sathye, M. 2002. "Measuring Productivity Changes in Australian Banking: An Application of Malmquist Indices." *Managerial Finance*, 28: 48–59.

Shephard, R. W. 1970. *Theory of Cost and Production Functions*. Princeton, NJ: Princeton University Press.

Srairi, S. 2009a. "A Comparison of the Profitability of Islamic and Conventional Banks: The Case of GCC Countries." *Bankers, Markets & Investors* 98: 16–27.

Srairi, S. 2009b. "Cost and Profit Efficiency of Conventional and Islamic Banks in GCC Countries." *Journal of Productivity Analysis* doi: 10.1007/s11123-009-0161-7.

Sturm, J. E., and B. Williams. 2004. "Foreign Bank Entry, Deregulation and Bank Efficiency: Lessons from the Australian Experience." *Journal of Banking & Finance* 28: 1775–1799.

276 References

Sufian, F. 2009a. "Antecedents of total factor productivity change: Empirical evidence from the Chinese banking sector." *Transition Studies Review* 16: 114–126.

Sufian, F. 2009b. "The Impact of Off-Balance Sheet Items on Banks' Total Factor Productivity: Empirical Evidence from the Chinese Banking Sector." *American Journal of Finance & Accounting* 3: 213–238.

Sufian, F., and R. Haron. 2008. "The Sources and Determinants of Productivity Growth in the Malaysian Islamic Banking Sector: A Non-Stochastic Frontier Approach." *International Journal of Accounting & Finance* 2: 193–215.

Tornqvist, L. 1936. "The Bank of Finland's Consumption Price Index, Bank of Finland." *Monthly Bulletin* 10: 1–8.

Tortosa-Ausina, E., E. Grifell-Tatjé, C. Armero, , and D. Conesa. 2008. "Sensitivity Analysis of Efficiency and Malmquist Productivity Indices: An Application to Spanish Savings Banks." *European Journal of Operational Research* 184: 1062–1084.

Worthington, A. C. 1999. "Malmquist Indices of Productivity Change in Australian Financial Services." *Journal of International Financial Markets, Institutions & Money* 9: 303–320.

Wu, S. 2005. "Productivity and Efficiency Analysis of Australia Banking Sector under Regulation." Paper presented in the Proceedings of the Australian Conference of Economists, Blackwell, Carlton, Vic, Australia, pp. 1–43.

3 ANALYSIS OF THE GROWTH & RISE OF SMALLER ISLAMIC BANKS IN THE LAST DECADE

Abreu ,M., and V. Mendes. 2002. "Commercial Bank Interest Margins and Profitability: Evidence from E.U. Countries." Porto working paper series.

Afanasieff, T., P. Lhacer, and M. Nakane. 2002. "The Determinants of Bank Interest Spreads in Brazil." Banco Central di Brazil Working Papers.

Allen, Franklin, and Douglas Gale. 2004. "Competition and Financial Stability." *Journal of Money, Credit & Banking* 36 (3): 453–80.

Archer, Simon, and Rifaat Abdel Karim,eds. 2002. *Islamic Finance: Growth and Innovation* London: Euromoney Books.

Aggarwal, R. K., and T. Yousef. 2000. "Islamic Banks and Investment Financing." *Journal of Money, Credit & Banking* 32 (1): 93–120.

Boyd, John H., and David E. Runkle. 1993. "Size and Performance of Banking Firms." *Journal of Monetary Economics* 31: 47–67.

Berger, A., D. Hanweck, and D. Humphrey. 1987. "Competitive Viability in Banking: Scale, Scope and Product Mix Economies." *Journal of Monetary Economics* 20: 501–20.

Berger, A. N., and Humphrey, D. 1997. "Efficiency of Financial Institutions: International Survey and Directions for Future Research." *European Journal of Operational Research* 98: 175–212

Buser, S., A. Chen, and E. Kane. 1981. "Federal Deposit Insurance, Regulatory Policy, and Optimal Bank Capital." *Journal of Finance* 35: 51–60.

Choudhry, Nurun, and Abbas Mirakhor. 1997. "Indirect Instruments of Monetary Control in an Islamic Financial System." *Islamic Economic Studies* 4 (2): 27–66.

Ertugrul, A., and F. Selcuk. 2001. "A Brief Account of the Turkish Economy." *Russian & East European Finance & Trade* (37): 6–28.

El-Hawary, Dhalia, Wafik Grais, and Zamir Iqbal. 2004. "Regulating Islamic Financial Institutions: The Nature of the Regulated." World Bank Working Paper 3227, Washington, DC: World Bank.

Hesse, Heiko, and Martin Čihák. 2007. "Islamic Banks and Financial Stability." IMF Working Paper No. 08/16, International Monetary Fund.

Isik, I., and Hassan M.K. 2002. "Technical, Scale and Allocative Effiencies of Turkish Banking Industry." *Journal of Banking & Finance* 26: 719–766.

Iqbal, Munawar. April 2001. "Islamic and Conventional Banking in the Nineties: A Comparative Study." *Islamic Economic Studies* 8 (2): 1–27.

Iqbal, Munawar, and David T. Llewellyn, eds. 2002. "Islamic Banking and Finance: New Perspective on Profit-Sharing and Risk," Cheltenham, UK: Edward Elgar Publishing.

International Organization of Securities Commissions. 2004. "Islamic Capital Market: Fact-Finding Report." Report of the Islamic Capital Market Task Force of the International Organization of Securities Commissions, Madrid.

Guru B., J. Staunton, and Balashanmugam. 2002. "Determinants of Commercial Bank Profitability in Malaysia." University Multimedia, Malaysia, Working Papers.

Keeley, M., and G. Zimmerman. 1985. "Competition for Money Market Deposit Accounts." *Federal Reserve Bank of San Francisco Economic Review* 1: 5–27.

Meeusen, W., and van den Broeck. 1977. "Efficiency Estimation From Cobb-Douglas Production Functions With Composed Error." *International Econometric Review* 18: 435–444.

Maechler, Andrea, Srobona Mitra, and DeLisle Worrell. 2005. "Exploring Financial Risks and Vulnerabilities in New and Potential EU Member States." Second Annual DG ECFIN Research Conference, "Financial Stability and the Convergence Process in Europe," October 6–7.

Mishkin, Frederic S. 1999, "Financial Consolidation: Dangers and Opportunities." *Journal of Banking & Finance* 23: 675–91.

Moktar, Hamim S., Naziruddin Abdullah, and Syed M. Al-Habshi. 2006. "Efficiency of Islamic Banks in Malaysia: A Stochastic Frontier Approach." *Journal of Economic Cooperation among Islamic Countries* 27 (2): 37–70.

Naughton, S. A. J., and M. A. Tahir. 1988. "Islamic Banking and Financial Development,. *Journal of Islamic Banking & Finance* 5(2).

Tartisma Tebligleri Serisi, 2000/1 P. Molyneux, and J. Thornton. 1992. "The Determinants of European Bank Profitability." *Journal of Banking & Finance* 16: 1173–1178.

Rogers, K. E. 1998. "Nontraditional Activities and the Efficiency of U.S. Commercial Banks." *Journal of Banking & Finance* 22 (4): 467–482.

Street, James O., Raymond J. Carroll, and David Ruppert. 1988. "A Note on Computing Robust Regression Estimates via Iteratively Reweighted Least Squares." *The American Statistician* 42: 151–154.

Shaffer, S. 1985. "Competition, Economies of Scale, and Diversity of Firm Sizes." *Applied Economics* 17: 467–76.

Smirlock, M. 1985. "Evidence of the (Non)Relationship Between Concentration and Profitability in Banking." *Journal of Money, Credit & Banking* 17: 69–82.

Street, James O., Raymond J. Carroll, and David Ruppert. 1988. "A Note on Computing Robust Regression Estimates via Iteratively Reweighted Least Squares." *The American Statistician* 42: 151–154.

Yildirim, C. 1999. "Evaluation of the Performance of Turkish Commercial Banks: A Non-Parametric Approach in Conjunction with Financial ratio Analyses." International Conferences in Economics III, METU.

Yudistira, Donsyah, 2004. "Efficiency in Islamic Banking: An Empirical Analysis of Eighteen Banks." *Islamic Economic Studies* 12 (1): 1–19.

Yolalan, R. 1996. *"Turk bankacilik sektoru icin goreli mali performans olcumu."* TBB Bankacilar Dergisi, Sayi 19.

Zaim, O. 1995. "The Effect of Financial Liberalization on the Efficiency of Turkish Commercial Banks." Economic Research Forum for the Arab Countries, Workshop on Financial Market Development.

4   THE DEVELOPMENT & SCOPE OF ISLAMIC BANK BONDS (SUKUK)

Abdi, Sameer. 2005. "Survival of the Fittest: The future of Shari'a-compliant retail banking in the GCC", *Islamic Retail Banking and Finance,* Ed. Jaffer, S., Euromoney Books, London, UK.

Abdul Gafoor, A. L. M. 1995. *Interest-Free Commercial Banking.* Groninigen, Netherlands: Apptec Publications.

Ahmed, Z., M. Iqbal, and M. F. Khan. 1983. *Money and Banking in Islam.* Jaddah: International Centre for Research in Islamic Economics, King Abdual Aziz University.

Algaoud, L. M., and M. K. Lewis. 1997. "Bahrain as an International Centre for Islamic Baking." Proceedings of International Conference on Accounting, Commerce & Finance. The Islamic Perspective, University of West Sydney, Macarthur, Australia.

Alhi United Bank. 2007. http://www.iibu.com. December.

Arrif, M., ed. 1982. "Monetary Policy in an Interest-Free Islamic Economy: Nature and Scope." *Monetary and Fiscal Economic of Islam.* Jaddah: International Centre for Research in Islamic Economics.

The Banker, http://www.thebanker.com/news/fullstory.php/aid/1000 /Islamic_Bank_of_Britain_launch_imminent.html. December 2007.

Bijur, D. 2007. "Islamic Finance—From Niche to Mainstream." http://news.bbc.co.uk/1/hi/business/6483343.stm doa: 11/11/08.

Churchill, G.A. 1999. *Marketing Research: Methodological Foundations,* 7th ed. Fort Worth: Dryden.

Directgov. 2008.Corporate Bonds and Government Bonds. http://www.direct.gov.uk/en/MoneyTaxAndBenefits/ManagingMoney/SavingsAndInvestments/DG_10013986 date viewed:15/11/08.

Ghauri, P., and Gronhaug, K. 2002. *Research Methods in Business Studies: A Practical Guide,* 2nd ed. Harlow, UK: Prentice Hall, pp.76–78.

Handbook of Islamic Banking, 1977–1986. Cairo: International Association of Islamic Banks. (Six volumes in Arabic.)

International Herald Tribune, http://www.iht.com/articles/2005/09/08/news/sp-pri-05.php. January 2008.

Islam Online, http://www.islamonline.net/English. January 2008.

Islamic Banking, http://www.islamic-banking.com/aom/ibanking/ia_khan.php. December 2007.

Box, T. and Mohammed, A. 2005. "Islamic Finance Market Turns to Securitization." *International Financial Law Review,* No. 24, pp. 21–4.

"Islamic Finance: Turning the Prophet's Profits." 1996. *Economist* 340 (7980, August 24): 58.

Janahi, A. L. 1995. I*slamic Banking, Concept, Practice & Future,* 2nd ed. Manama: Bahrain Islamic Bank.

Khalaf, Roula. 1995. "Banking the Islamic Way." *World Press Review* Jan. 95, Vol. 42 (1, January): 35.

Khan, M. M., and M. I. Bhatti. 2008. "Development in Islamic Banking: a New Risk-Allocation Approach." *Journal of Risk Finance* 9 (1): 40–51.

Khan, Iqbal. 2005. "Revisiting the Value Proposition of Islamic Finance", Euromoney 4th Annual Islamic Finance Summit, London, 22 and 23 February.

Khan, M S. 1986. "Islamic Interest-Free Banking: A Theoretical Analysis." International Monetary Fund Staff Papers, Vol. 33 (1): 1–25.

Kuran, T. 1986. "The Economic System in Contemporary Islamic Thought: Interpretation and Assessment." *International Journal of Middle East Studies* no. 18: 135–154.

Kuran, T. 1995. "Islamic Economic and the Islamic Sub-Economy." *Journal of Economic Perspectives,* 9 (4): 155–173.

Lewis, M. K. 1996. "Universal Banking in Europe: The Old, the New, International Symposium on Universal Banking." Korean Institute of Finance, Seoul, January.

Maylasia International Islamic Finance Centre (MIFC). 2008a. Sukuk overview. http://www.mifc.com/index.php?ch=cat_int_sukuk&pg=cat_int_sukuk_over date accessed: 10/10/08.

Maylasia International Islamic Finance Centre (MIFC). 2008b. Notable Sukuk Issuances. http://www.mifc.com/index.php?ch=cat_int_sukuk&pg=cat_int_sukuk_iss# date accessed: 11/11/08.

Mannan, M. A. 1986. *Islamic Economics: Theory Practice.* Cambridge: Hodder & Stoughton.

Red Hot Curry, http://www.redhotcurry.com/money. November 2007.

Said, al-Shaikh. 2005a. *NCB: Market Review & Outlook* 15 (6, April). National Commercial Bank, Jeddah, Saudi Arabia.

Said al-Shaikh. 2005b. *NCB: Market Review & Outlook* 15 (7, May). National Commercial Bank, Jeddah, Saudi Arabia.

Said, al-Shaikh: 2005c. *NCB: Market Review & Outlook* 15 (9, June). National Commercial Bank, Jeddah, Saudi Arabia.

Salaam.co.uk, http://www.salaam.co.uk. December 2007.

Siddiqi, M. N. 1988. *Banking without Interest,* Leicester: The Islamic Foundation.

Taylor, John. 2004. Speech given at the Forum on Islamic Finance at Harvard University. May 8.

Ul-Haque, N. U., and A. Nirakhor1986. "Optimal Profit-Sharing Contracts and Investment in an Interest-Free Islamic Economy." IMF Working Paper, No. 12, Washington: International Monetary Fund.

5　RISK–BASED SUPERVISION FOR ISLAMIC BANKING & AREAS OF CONCERN

Barth, J., G. Caprio, and R. Levine. 2006. *Rethinking Bank Regulation: Till Angels Govern.* Cambridge, UK: Cambridge University Press.

Crotty, J. 2009. "Structural Causes of the Global Financial Crisis: a Critical Assessment of the 'New Financial Architecture.'" *Cambridge Journal of Economics* 33 (4): 563–580.

Cheung, K. C., and J. A. Coutts. 2001. "A Note on Weak Form Market Efficiency in Security Prices: Evidence from the Hong Kong Stock Exchange." *Applied Economics Letters* 8 (6): 407–410.

Said, F. F., and A.G. Ismail. 2008. "Monetary Policy, Capital Requirement and Lending Behaviour of Islamic Banking in Malaysia." *Journal of Economic Cooperation* 29 (3): 1–22.

Errico, L, and M. Farahbaksh. 1998. "Islamic Banking: Issues in Prudential Regulations and Supervision." International Monetary Fund Working Paper WP/98/30.

Ismail, A.G. 2010a. *Money, Islamic Banking and Real Economy.* Singapore: Cengage Learning Asia.

Ismail, A.G. 2010b. "The Theory of Islamic Banking: Look Back to Original Idea." ISRA Research Paper no. 18, http://www.isra.my

Ismail, A. G. 2010c. "Islamic Banks and Wealth Creation." ISRA Research Paper no. 10, http://www.isra.my

Tahir, S. 2007. "Islamic Banking Theory and Practices: A Survey and Bibliography of the 1995–2005 Literature." *Journal of Economic Cooperation* 28 (1): 1–72.

Tohirin, A., and Ismail, A.G. 2010. "Islamic Law and Finance," *Humanomics,* 26 (no. 3): 178–199.

Woolley, P. 2010. "Why Are Financial Markets So Inefficient and Exploitative—and a Suggested Remedy." In *The Future of Finance: The LSE Report,* edited by A. Turner, et al. London: London School of Economics and Political Science.

Zaher, T. S., and M. K. Hassan. 2001. "A Comparative Literature Survey of Islamic Finance and Banking." In *Financial Markets, Institutions and Instruments,* edited by New York University Salomon Center. Oxford: Blackwell Publishers.

6   Iran's Islamic Banking Experience & Future

Al-Rifaee, S. S. 2010. Islamic Banking Myths and Facts. [Electronic]. Available: http://www.arabinsight.org/aiarticles/190.pdf [2009–08–01]

Baizaee, S. E. 2006. *Money, Foreign Exchange & Banking.* Tehran: Nor-e-Elem Press.

Central Bank of Iran. 1984 to 2006. Annual Report, various years.

Central Bank of Iran. 2008. The Law for Usury (Interest) Free Banking.

Mirakhor, A., and Khan, S. M. 1990. "Islamic Banking: Experiences in the Islamic Republic of Iran and Pakistan." *Economic Development & Cultural Change* 38: 353–375.

Mazarei, A. 1997. "The Iranian Economy under the Islamic Republic: Institutional Change and Macro Economic Performance (1979–1990)." *Cambridge Journal of Economics* 20 (289): 289–313.

Pourian, H. 1995. " The Experience of Iran's Islamic Financial System and Its prospects for Development." In *Development of Financial Markets in the Arab Countries, Iran & Turkey,* Economic Research Forum for Arab Countries, Iran & Turkey, Cairo.

Zangeneh, Hamid. 1996. www.financeinislam.com/article/1_35/8/287. August 2009.

7   Islamic Banking Structure & Growth in the Sudanese Islamic Banking Sector

Accounting and Auditing Organization for Islamic Financial Institutions (AAOIF) website, http://www.aaoifi.com/objectives-acc.html

Akkas, A. 1996. "Relative Efficiency of the Conventional and Islamic Banking System in Financing Investment." Unpublished Ph.D. dissertation, Dhaka University, Bangladesh.

Al-Baraka Bank of Sudan website, http://www.albarakasudan.com/english/branches.htm

Al-Osaimy, M. H., and A. S. Bamkhramah. 2004. "An Early Warning System for Islamic Banks Performance." *Journal of King Abdulaziz University: Islamic Economics* 17 (1): 3–14.

Arif, M. 1989. "Islamic Banking in Malaysia: Framework, Performance and Lesson." *Journal of Islamic Economics* 2 (2): pp. 67–78.

Belkaoui, A. R. 1998. *Financial Analysis and the Predictability of Important Economic Events.* Westport, CT: Greenwood Publishing Group.

Central Bank of Sudan website, http://www.cbos.gov.sd/

Elliott, B., and J. Elliott. 2006. *Financial Accounting & Reporting.* Upper Saddle River, NJ: Pearson Education.

Elliott, B., and J. Elliott. 2006. *Financial Accounting and Reporting.* Upper Saddle River, NJ: Pearson Education.

Faisal Islamic Bank (Sudan) website, http://www.fibsudan.com/en/

Libby, R. 1975. "Accounting Ratios and the Prediction of Failure: Some Behavioral Evidence." *Journal of Accounting Research* 13(1): 150–161.

Mohammed, N. 1988. "Principles of Islamic Contract Law." *Journal of Law & Religion* 6 (1): 115–130.

Rosly, S. A., and M. A. Abu Bakar. 2003. "Performance of Islamic and Mainstream Banks in Malaysia." *International Journal of Social Economics* 30 (12): 1249–1265.

Rosly, S. A., M. Sanusi, and N. Md. Yatim. 2001. "Khiyar Al 'Aib in Al-Bai'-Bithaman Ajil Financing." *International Journal of Islamic Financial Services* 2 (1): 36–44.

Saaid, A. E., S. A. Rosly, M. H. Ibrahim, and N. Abdullah. 2003. "The X-Efficiency of Sudanese Islamic Banks." *Journal of Economics & Management* 11 (2): 123–141.

Sabi, M. 1996. "Comparative Analysis of Foreign and Domestic Bank Operation in Hungary." *Journal of Comparative Economics* 22: 179–188.

Samad, A. 2004. "Performance of Interest Free Islamic Banks *vis-à-vis* Interest Based Conventional Bank of Bahrain." *IIUM Journal of Economics & Management*, 12 (2): 115–129.

Shim, J. K., and J. G. Siegel. 2000. *Financial Management.* Hauppauge, NY: Barron's Educational Series.

Siddiqui, A. 2008. "Financial Contracts, Risk and Performance of Islamic Banking." *Managerial Finance* 34 (10): 680–694.

Tadamon Islamic Bank website, http://www.tadamonbank-sd.com/about_us.php

8   ISLAMIC MORTGAGES

Aziz, Tayyebi. 2008. "Islamic Finance: An Ethical Alternative to Conventional Finance?" ACCA Discussion Paper, London, UK. http://www.accaglobal.com/pubs/general/activities/library/financial_reporting/other/tech_tp_if6pp.pdf [Accessed: November 2009].

Al-Jarhi, M., and M. Iqbal. 2001. "Islamic Banking: Answers to Some Frequently Asked Questions." Occasional Paper No.4, Islamic Research and Training Institute, Islamic Development Bank, Jeddah, Saudi Arabia. http://www.irtipms.org/PubAllE.asp. Accessed October 2006. [Accessed: November 2009].

Buckley, R. M. 1994. "Housing Finance in Developing Countries: The Role of Credible Contracts." *Economic Development & Cultural Change* 42: 317–332.

Dar, H.A. 2004. *Demand for Islamic Financial Services in the UK: Chasing a Mirage.* Loughborough.

DiPasquale, D., and Glaeser, E. L. 1999. "Incentives and Social Capital: Are Homeowners Better Citizens?" *Journal of Urban Economics* 45: 354–384.

El-Qorchi, M. 2005. "Islamic Finance Gears Up." *Journal of Finance & Development* 42 (4): 46–50.

Englehardt, G. 1994. "House Prices and the Decision to Save for Down Payments." *Journal of Urban Economics* 36: 209–237.

Economist. 2007a. "Finance and Economics: Bleak Houses; American Mortgages." (February 17).

Fama, E. F. 1970. "Efficient Capital Markets: A Review of Theory and Empirical Work." *Journal of Finance* 25: 383–417.

Fama, E. F. 1991. "Efficient Capital Markets II." *Journal of Finance* 46: 1575–1617.

Gapper , J. 2007. "The Wrong Way to Lend to the Poor." *Financial Times* (March 18), http://blogs.ft.com/gapperblog/2007/03/ [Accessed: October 2009]

Gait, A., and A. C. Worthington. 2007. "A Primer on Islamic Finance: Definitions, Sources, Principles and Methods." University of Wollongong, School of Accounting, and Finance Working Paper Series No. 07/05.

Haurin, D. R., T. I. Parcel, and R. J. Haurin. 2002. "Does Homeownership Affect Child Outcomes?" *Real Estate Economics* 30: 635–666.

Haqiqi, A, and F. Pomeranz. 2000. "Accounting Needs of Islamic Banking: Legal and Economic Aspects of Islamic Banking." www.associatedcontent.com/…/islamic_banking_a_new_era.html [Accessed: November, 2009]

Lewis, M., and L Algaoud. 2001. *Islamic Banking.* Cheltenham, UK: Edward Elgar.

Iqbal, M., and P. Molyneux. 2005. *Thirty Years of Islamic Banking: History, Performance, and Prospects.* Houndmills, New York: Palgrave Macmillan.

Iqbal, Zubair, Mirakhor, and Abbas. 1987. "Islamic Banking." International Monetary Fund Occasional Paper 49, Washington D.C.

Iqbal, M., and D. Llewellyn, eds. 2002. *Islamic Banking and Finance: New Perspectives on Profit-Sharing & Risk.* Cheltenham, UK: Edward Elgar.

Iqbal, Zamir, and Hiroshi Tsubota. 2006. "Emerging Islamic Capital Markets, Islamic Finance Review." In *Euromoney Handbook.* London: Euromoney Institutional Investor, pp. 5–11.

Kahf, M. 1997. Instruments of Meeting Budget Deficit in Islamic Economy Research Paper No. 42, Islamic Research and Training Institute, Islamic Development Bank, Jeddah, Saudia Arabia. http://www.irtipms.org /PubAllE.asp. Accessed May 2009 [Accessed: October 2009].

Khan, Iqbal. 2005. "Revisiting the Value Proportion of Islamic Finance." Euromoney 4th Annual Islamic Finance Summit, London, February 22 and 23.

Lewis, M., and L. Algaoud. 2001. *Islamic Banking.* Cheltenham, UK: Edward Elgar.

Mason, J. R., and J. Rosner. 2007. "How Resilient are Mortgage Backed Securities to collateralized Debt Obligations Market Disruption?" Working Paper, Hudson Institute, Washington, D.C.

Malpezzi, S. 1990. "Urban Housing and Financial Markets: Some International Comparisons." *Urban Studies* 27: 971–1022.

Mirakhor, Abbas, and Zaidi Iqbal. 1988. "Stabilization and Growth in an Open Islamic Economy." IMF Working Paper No. 88/22, International Monetary Fund (IMF), Washington, D.C.

Metwally, M. 2006. "Economic Consequences of Applying Islamic Principles in Muslim Societies." *Journal of Islamic Banking & Finance* 23 (1): 11–33.

Obaidullah, M. 2005. *Islamic Financial Services.* Jeddah: Islamic Economics Research Centre.

Paletta, D. 2007. "Obama Lays Out Plan to Stem Defaults in U.S. Housing Market." *Wall Street Journal—Europe* (February), Issue 12.

Sheng, A. 1997. "Housing Finance and Asian Financial Markets." Speech by the Deputy Chief Executive of the Hong Kong Monetary Authority, delivered to the International Union for Housing Finance in Thailand on October 27.

Siddiqui, M. N. 1983. *Banking without Interest.* Leicester: The Islamic Foundation.

Siddiqi, M. N. 2004. *Riba, Interest and the Rationale of Its Prohibition.* Jeddah: Visiting Scholars, Research Series.

Syed, Assad. 2007. "Islamic Banking & Finance." Macroeconomics term report.

Wade, Alex. 2008. "Crossing Over to Islamic Banking." Times Online, available from http://business.timesonline.co.uk/tol/business/law/article5889624.ece [Accessed: November 2009]

Zaher, T., and M. Hassan. 2001. "A Comparative Literature Survey of Islamic Finance and Banking. Financial Markets." *Institutions and Instruments* 10 (4): 155–199.

9   THE ROLE OF ISLAMIC MORTGAGES IN THE UNITED KINGDOM

Abdul, Gafoor. 2004. *Interest, Usury, Riba, and the Operational Costs of Bank.* Kuala Lampur: A. S. Noordeen.

Ahmad, Ziauddin. 1994. "Islamic Banking: State of the Art." *Islamic Economic Studies* 2 (December): 1–34.

Ahmed, S. 1992. Towards Interest-Free Banking. New Delhi: International Islamic Publishers.

Ahmed, Habib, and M. Umer Chapra. 2002. *Corporate Governance in Islamic Financial Institutions* (translated into Arabic). Jeddah: Islamic Research and Training Institute, Islamic Development Bank Group.

Al-Jarhi, Mabid Ali, and Munawar Iqbal. 2000. "Islamic Banking: FAQs." Jeddah: IRTI Occasional Paper No. 4.

Al-Tamimi & Company. 2004. *The Development of Shariah Compliance Services.* 2004. Al-Tamimi & Company Islamic Banking Seminars.

Aryan, Hossein. 1990. "Iran: The Impact of Islamisation on the Financial System." In *Islamic Financial Markets*, edited by Rodney Wilson. London: Routledge, pp. 155–170.

Calhoun, C. A., and Y. Deng. 2002. "A Dynamic Analysis of Fixed and Adjustable-Rate Mortgage Terminations." *Journal of Real Estate Finance & Economics* 24 (1/2): 9–33.

Campbell, J., and J. Cocco. 2003. "Household Risk Management and Optimal Mortgage Choice." *Quarterly Journal of Economics* 118 (November): 1449–1494.

Chapra, M. 2000. "The Future of Economics: An Islamic Perspective." Leicester, UK: The Islamic Foundation.

CIA World Factbook. 2007. https://www.cia.gov/library/publications/the -world-factbook/

Council of Mortgage Lenders. 2004. Annual Mortgage Surveys, done for CML by NOP/MINTEL, February.

Dar, A. H., and J. R. Presley. "Islamic Finance: A Western Perspective." International Journal of Islamic Financial Services 1 (April–June): 1–6.

Dar, Humayon A. 2002. "Islamic House Financing in the United Kingdom: Problems, Challenges and Prospects." *Review of Islamic Economics* 12: 47–71.

Davies, Ross. 2002. "Super-Rich Ranks Growing Again." *Evening Standard* (London), 8 February, http://www.thisismoney.com/20020208 /nm44034.html

Druckers, John. 2002. *Birmingham Post*, September 21.

Financial Services Authority (FSA). United Kingdom, www.fsa.gov.uk /pages/library/communication/pr/2006/041.shtml.

Fisher, Irving. 1945. *The Theory of Interest*. New York: Macmillan.

El-Gamal, M. 1997. "Can Islamic Banking Survive a Micro-Evolutionary Prospective?" *International Journal of Islamic Financial Services*, Feb 21.

El-Qorchi, Mohammed. 2005. "Islamic Finance Gears Up." *Finance & Development* 42 (4): 46–50.

Erol, C., E. Kaynak, and R. El-Bdour. 1990. "Conventional and Islamic Banks: Patronage Behaviour of Jordanian Customers." *International Journal of Bank Marketing* 8: 25–35.

Friedman, M. 1969. *"The Monetary Theory and Policy of Henry Simons."* In *The Optimum Quantity of Money and Other Essays,* edited by M. Friedman. Chicago: Aldine, pp. 16–23.

Haqiqi, A. W., and F. Pomeranz. 2005. "Accounting Needs of Islamic Banking." IBF Net (Islamic Business & Finance Net), International Institute of Islamic Business and Finance, http://www.iiibf.org. http://islamic-finance.net/islamic-ethics/artcile12.html, retrieved on 10/16/2005.

Haron, Sudin, Norafifah Ahmad, and Sandra A. Planisek. 1994. "Bank Patronage Factors of Muslim and Non-Muslim Customers." *International Journal of Bank Marketing* 13: 74–34.

Hasan, K. 2007. "Islamic Financial Services." Presentation at KPMG Insurance Industry Leadership Conference, location?, November.

James, Mawson. 2002, February 25. ÒSurvey – FTFM: Western Funds Find Faith in Islamic Investing: Despite the September 11 Attacks, Fund Managers See Strong Growth in Muslim Countries This Year. *Financial Times.* Available at: <URL:http:www.ft.com>.

Khan, M. 1986. "Islamic Interest-Free Banking: A Theoretician Analysis." *Staff Papers of the International Monetary Fund,* 33:1–27.

Khan, M. 1999. "Financial Modernization in 21st Century and Challenge for Islamic Banking." *International Journal of Islamic Financial Services* 1 (3): October–December.

Khan, M. 2002. "Monetary Policy and Central Banking in an Islamic Context." Paper presented at the Islamic Banking Conference, London, May 7–8.

Lewis, M. K. and L. M. Algaoud. 2001. *Islamic Banking.* Cheltenham, UK: Edward Elgar.

Matthews, Robin, Issam Tlemasani, and Aftab Siddiqui. 1999. "Islamic Finance Research Paper." census report, http://datamonitor.com

McDoughall, G., and Lévesque. 1994."A Revised Review of Service Quality Dimensions: An Empirical Investigation." *Journal of Professional Service Marketing* 11 (1): 189–210.

Mortgageman. United Kingdom. www.mortgageman.co.uk

Naser, K. 1988. "Comprehensive of Discolour of Non-Financial Companies Listed on the Amman Financial Market." *International Journal of Commerce & Management* 2: 56–65.

Norwood, G. 2002. "The Housing Boom that Forgot Muslims." *The Observer,* June 16. http://money.guardian.co.uk/homebuying/mortgages /story/0,1456,739195,00.html

Robinson, Karina. 2007. "Islamic Finance Is Seeing Spectacular Growth." *International Herald Tribune,* 05 November, 2007, available at http://www.iht.com/articles/2007/11/05/business/bankcol06.php.

Simons, H. 1948. *Economic Policy for a Free Society.* Chicago: University Chicago Press.

Tan, Chin Tiong, and Christina Chua. 1986. "Intention, Attitude and Social Influence in Bank Selection: A Study of Oriental Culture." *International Journal of Bank Marketing* 4: 88–127.

Wilson, R. 1997. "Islamic Finance and Ethical Investment." *International Journal of Social Economics* 24 (11): 1325–1342.

Zarqa, M. 1983. "Stability in an Interest-Free Islamic Economy: A Note." Pakistan Journal of Applied Economics 2: 181–188.

10   THE ISLAMIC BANK OF BRITAIN: A CASE STUDY

Ahmad, A. 2002. *Development and Problems of Islamic Banks.* Jeddah: Islamic Research and Training Institute, Islamic Development Bank.

Ahmad, Ziauddin. 1994. "Islamic Banking: State of the Art." *Islamic Economic Studies,* 2 (December): 1–34.

Almossawi, Mohammed. 2001. "Bank Selection Criteria Employed by College Students in Bahrain: An Empirical Analysis", *International Journal of Bank Marketing* 19 (Iss 3): 115–125.

Al-Baraka Bank website. year? http://www.barakaonline.com/financial/annual.htm

Al-Omar, F. and Abdel-Haq, M. 1996. *Islamic Banking: Theory, Practice and Challenges* Karachi: Oxford University Press.

Alford, B. L., and D. L. Sherrel. 1996. "The Role of Affect in Consumer Satisfaction Judgements of Credence-Based Services." *Journal of Business Research* 37: 1 71–84.

Anderson, W., Cox, J. E. P., and Fulcher, D. 1976. "Bank Selection Decisions and Marketing Segmentation", *Journal of Marketing* 40 (no.1): 40–5.

Babbie, E. 2001. *The Practice of Social Research,* 8th ed. Belmont, CA: Wadsworth.

Banker, The. 2001. "Islamic Banking: Sensitive Issues." *The Banker,* December.

Bank of England website. 2001. Page can no longer be found, http://www.bankofengland.co.uk/publication/speeches/2001/index.htm

BBC News. 2004. "HSBC Offers Islamic Pension Fund." April 13. http://news.bbc.co.uk/1/hi/business/3621653.stm

Beaulieu, P. 1996. "A Note on the Role of Memory in Commercial Loan Officers, Use of Accounting and Character Information." *Accounting, Organizations & Society* 21 (6): 515–528.

Beaulieu, P. 1994. "Commercial Lenders: Use of Accounting Information in Interaction with Source Credibility." *Contemporary Accounting Research* 557–585

Briston, R., and A. El-Ashker. 2002. "Religious Audit: Could It Happen Here?" *Accountancy* October, 120–121.

Collins, L. 2002. "Stock Brokers under Pressure." *Australian Financial Review* 21.

Cunningham, Andrew. Feb 1994. "The Growth of Islamic Financing" *Project & Trade Finance.* 130–34.

Denton, L., and Chan, A. K. 1991. "Bank Selection Criteria of Multiple Bank Users in Hong Kong", *International Journal of Bank Marketing* 9 (no.5): 23–34.

Dubai Islamic Bank. 2008. Bank website, www.dibpak.com (accessed July 23, 2008).

Duncan, R. G. 2006. "Characteristics of Organizational Environments and Perceived Environmental Uncertainty." *Administrative Science Quarterly* 17: 313–327.

Erol, C. and El-Bdour, R. 1989. "Attitude, Behavior and Patronage Factors of Bank Customers towards Islamic Banking," *International Journal of Bank Marketing* 7(6): 31–37.

Erol, C., Kaynak, E. and El-Bdour, R. 1990. "Conventional and Islamic Banks: Patronage Behavior of Jordanian Customers," *International Journal of Bank Marketing* 8(4): 25–35.

288   References

Gambling, T., and R. A. A. Karim. 2004, *Business and Accounting Ethics in Islam*. London: Mansell.

Gray, David E. 2004. *Doing Research in the Real World*. London: Sage, 2004.

Haron, Sudan, Norafifah Ahmad, and Sandra Planisek.1994. "Bank Patronage Factors of Muslim and non-Muslim Customers." *International Journal of Bank Marketing* 13: 74–34.

Hegazy, I. A. 1995. "An Empirical Comparative Study between Islamic and Commercial Banks' Selection Criteria in Egypt", *International Journal of Contemporary Management* 5 (no.3): 46–61.

HSBC Bank website. 2004. "Brief History." February (no longer accessible). http://www.hsbc.com/1/PA11S5/content/assets/abouthsbc/briefhistoryfeb2004.pdf

Hussey, Jill, and Roger Hussey. 1997. *Business Research: A Practical Guide for Undergraduate and Postgraduate Students*. London: Macmillan.

Huu Phuong Ta and Kar Yin Har. 2000. "A Study of Bank Selection Decisions in Singapore using the Analytical Hierarchy Process", *International Journal of Bank Marketing* 18 (Iss 4): 170–180.

Iqbal, M., and D. T. Llewellyn. 2001. *Islamic Banking and Finance: New Perspectives on Profit-Sharing & Risk*. Cheltenham, UK: Edward Elgar, p. 3.

Islamicbank.com website. 2008. http://www.islamicbank.com/islamicbanklive/MCFAQs/1/Home/1/Home.jsp. December.

Jankowicz, A. D. 1995. *Business Research Projects*, 2nd ed. London: Chapman & Hall, 1995.

Jones, Ross, Jim Nielsen, and Rowan Trayler. 2002. "The Bank Selection Process and Market Definition in Australia", *Journal of Financial Regulation and Compliance* 10 (Iss 1): 22–30.

Karim, R. A. A. 2005. "The Independence of Religious and External Auditors: The Case of Islamic Banks." *Accounting, Auditing & Accountability Journal* 3 (3): 33–44.

Kaynak, E., O. Kucukemiroglu, and Y. Odabasi. 1991. "Commercial Bank Selection in Turkey," *International Journal of Bank Marketing* 9 (4): 30–39.

Khazeh, K. and W. H. Decker. 1992. "How Customers Choose Banks." *Journal of Retail Banking* 14 (winter): 41–44.

Kutty, Faisal. 1995. "Islamic Law Meets Western Finance", CA Magazine, September 1995, p. 10.

Laroche, M. and T. Taylor. 1988. "An Empirical Study of Major Segmentation Issues in Retail Banking." *International Journal of Bank Marketing* 6 (1): 31–48.

Laroche, Michel, Jerry A. Rosenblatt, and Terrill Manning. 1986. "Services Used and Factors Considered Important in Selecting a Bank: An Investigation across Diverse Demographic Segments", *International Journal of Bank Marketing* 4 (Iss 1): 35–55.

Lewis, Mervyn K., and Latifa M. Algaoud. 2001. *Islamic Banking*. Cheltenham, UK: Elgar Monographs, p. 14.

Llewellyn, D. T. 2006. "Capital Adequacy." In *Managing Bank Assets and Liabilities*, edited by J. S. G. Wilson. London: Euromoney Publications.

Llewellyn, D. T. 2001. "Capital Regulatory Convergence: The Basel Proposals." *Butterworths Journal of International Banking & Financial Law* (October): 441–445.

Llewellyn, D. T. 2005. "Bank Capital: The Strategic Issue of the 2005s." *Banking World* (January): 20–25.

Martenson, Rita. 1985. "Consumer Choice in Retail Bank Selection." *International Journal of Bank Marketing* 13: 74–76.

McDougall, G., and T. J. Lévesque. 1994. "A Revised Review of Service Quality Dimensions: An Empirical Investigation." *Journal of Professional Service Marketing* 11 (1): 189–210.

Metawa, S. A., and M. Almossawi. 1998. "Banking Behaviour of Islamic Bank Customers: Perspectives and Implications." *International Journal of Bank Marketing* 16 (7): 229–313.

Moyer, S. E. 2005. "Capital Adequacy Ratio Regulations and Accounting Choices in Commercial Banks." *Journal of Accounting & Economics* 13:123–154.

Naser, K., A. Jamal, and L. Al-Khatib. 1999. "Islamic Banking: A study of Customer Satisfaction in Preferences in Jordan." *International Journal of Bank Marketing* 17 (3): 135–150.

Nienhaus, V. l986. "Islamic Economics, Finance and Banking - Theory and Practice", *Journal of Islamic Banking and Finance*, 3(2):36–54.

Nienhouse, V. 2002. "Islamic Economics, Financing and Banking: Theory and Practice." In *Islamic Banking & Financing*. London: Butterworths.

Owen, D. L. 2005. "Towards a Theory of Social Investment: a Review Essay." *Accounting, Organizations & Society* 15 (3): 249–265.

Perks, R. W., D. H. Rawlinson, and L. Ingram. 2005. "An Exploration of Ethical Investment in the UK." *British Accounting Review* 24 (1): 43–65.

Rosenblatt, Jerry, Michel Laroche, Alan Hochstein, Ronald McTavish, and Maureen Sheahan. 1988. "Commercial Banking in Canada: A Study of the Selection Criteria and Service Expectations of Treasury Officers", *International Journal of Bank Marketing* 6 (Iss 4): 19–30.

Royal, C., and R. Althauser. 2002. "Working in the Turbulence of Mergers and Acquisitions: The Shape of Careers and Labour Markets in Three Divisions of an International Investment Bank." Working paper series, School of Industrial Relations and Organizational Behavior, University of New South Wales, 143.

Saleh, N.A. 2005. *Unlawful Gain and Legitimate Profit in Islamic Law*. London: Graham & Trotman.

Shepherd, W.C. 1996. Integrating Islamic and Western finance. *Global Finance*, 10 (5): 44–50.

Shirazi, H. 2005. *Islamic Banking.* Sevenoaks, UK: Butterworths, 2005.

Sinkey Jr., J. F. 2001. *Commercial Bank Financial Management in the Financial Services Industry.* New York: Simon & Schuster.

Sudin, H., Norafifah, A., and Planisek, L. 1994. "Bank Patronage Factors of Muslim and Non-Muslim Customers", *International Journal of Bank Marketing* 12 (no.1).

Tan, Chin Tiong, and Christina Chua. 1986. "Intention, Attitude and Social Influence in Bank Selection: A Study of Oriental Culture." *International Journal of Bank Marketing* 4: 88–27.

Trochim, W. 2001. *The Research Methods Knowledge Base,* 1st ed. Mason, OH: Atomic Dog Publishing, 2001.

Wilderdom.com. 2007. "Qualitative vs. Quantitative Research: Key Points in a Classic Debate." February 28. http://wilderdom.com/research /QualitativeVersusQuantitativeResearch.html

Wohlers-Scharf, T. 2003. *Arab and Islamic Banks.* Paris: Organization for Economic Cooperation and Development.

Zawya.com. 2008. "Islamic Banks Post 26.7% Growth Rate." March 25. website, http://www.zawya.com/story.cfm/sidZAWYA20080325033525

Zechmeister, E. B., J. S. Zechmeister, and J. J. Shaughnessy. 2007. *A Practical Introduction to Research Methods in Psychology,* 3rd ed. New York: McGraw-Hill.

Zineldin, Mosad. 1996. "Bank Strategic Positioning and some Determinants of Bank Selection", *International Journal of Bank Marketing* 14 (Iss 6): 12–22.

INDEX